THE ETHNIC HANDBOOK FOR THE CHICAGO AREA

A Guide To The Cultures
And Traditions of Our Region's
Diverse Communities

Second Edition

Edited by
Cynthia Linton

A publication of
Chicago Area Ethnic Resources

Printed in the United States of America
ISBN 978-0-615-69139-8
Chicago Area Ethnic Resources
PO Box 2204, Glenview, IL 60026
www.chicagoethnic.org

To inquire about quantity discounts for libraries, schools, government agencies and other institutions, please contact the publisher at admin@chicagoethnic.org.

Chicago Area Ethnic Resources is a nonprofit, 501 (c) (3) organization, founded to help the mainstream public understand and respond to diversity and changing demographics and to give voice to the ethnic communities that call our region home.

TABLE OF CONTENTS

A Word of Caution About Population Numbers

This book uses Census data, as the most reliable available. But the numbers are far from certain, especially for small ethnic populations. Much of the data come from the Census Bureau's American Community Survey, an annual look at personal and economic characteristics that is based on a sample. Because the samples are small, the margin of error is wide. We have used an average of three consecutive years to try to improve reliability – either 2008-10 when available or 2007-09.

Also problematic is the fact that the Census Bureau relies on people checking off their racial group and ancestry. Ethnic leaders tell us that some people do not participate in the Census at all, or do not bother to check off race or ancestry. Members of the newer immigrant groups are more likely to not participate, while third- and fourth-generation groups, especially European, may be erratic in checking off ancestry, especially if there are multiple ones.

As a result, most of our authors tell us the Census Bureau numbers are far lower than their own estimates, often based on religious and organizational affiliation. Yet these numbers are the best we can get with consistency across groups. Just take them with a grain of salt.

Metro area, for this book, is the greater metro MSA (metropolitan statistical area), which includes pieces of Wisconsin and Indiana. Keep in mind that metro includes the city of Chicago.

INTRODUCTION

In 1997 the Illinois Ethnic Coalition (IEC), published the first edition of The Ethnic Handbook: A Guide to the Cultures and Traditions of Chicago's Diverse Communities. As an organization whose membership comprised the many ethnic and racial communities participating in civic life, IEC focused on helping the wider public better understand diversity. We worked under IEC to produce the original Handbook and other publications that were widely distributed in our city and beyond.

In the wake of 9/11, a near economic collapse in 2007, a historic 2008 presidential election, and the introduction of controversial immigration legislation in Arizona and other states, familiar nativist winds blew in: Who was a "real" American and what right did "they" have to be here? We knew it was time to update the Handbook. We did so under a new nonprofit, Chicago Area Ethnic Resources (CAER).

Much has changed since the first edition, and the need for cross-cultural understanding is even greater. The 2010 Census revealed that the city proper lost approximately 215,000 residents, the overwhelming majority of them African American. Latino and Asian groups significantly increased their numbers both in Chicago and statewide, with Latinos surpassing blacks as Illinois' largest minority and Asians becoming the state's fastest growing minority.

By 2020, minorities will make up more than 50% of the Chicago metropolitan area's population, according to the New Metro Minority Map released by the Brookings Institution in 2011.

We are fascinated by the many ethnic, racial and cultural groups here, newcomers as well as the more established communities that once faced their own varying degrees of prejudice and discrimination. And despite decades or centuries of assimilation and acculturation, yesterday's immigrants, the indigenous populations and those who were brought here in chains have and continue to leave an indelible mark on "American" culture. Together with more recent arrivals, they define our region.

The U.S. Census ranks Illinois sixth in the nation for percentage of foreign-born (almost 14%). Unlike earlier cohorts, many immigrants now are bypassing the city altogether and transforming suburban and once-rural enclaves. The Illinois State Board of Education reports more than 136 language groups in the state's public schools; Spanish, Polish, Arabic, Urdu, Pilipino (Tagalog), Korean, Gujarati, Cantonese, Vietnamese and Russian are the top 10 spoken by English Language Learners.

We think it's important to provide a roadmap for all of us grappling with change. Much of the literature on racial and ethnic groups is the domain of academia, think tanks and advocates. For that reason, it is often inaccessible to the general public. We designed the Handbook to be a user-friendly resource for the mainstream, and to provide a counterpoint to the sound-bite portrayals that often accompany this difficult topic. While ethnic groups are indeed different, they share many commonalities, as you will see on these pages.

This second edition of the Ethnic Handbook contains many updates, all new demographic information and four new chapters on Bosniak, Iranian, Muslim and Pakistani Americans. All four chapters focus on the growing Muslim presence in the area; the Muslim chapter itself, although it crosses many ethnic and national boundaries, is included because of the level of misunderstanding and discrimination that this religious community often confronts.

A project of this magnitude would have been impossible if not for the many scholars, community leaders, CAER board members and donors who helped us pull it all together with their time, expertise and financial resources. We are especially indebted to the Walter S. Mander Foundation for its major funding. Matthew Holzman contributed hundreds of hours to the design and layout of the Handbook and website. Zach Gephardt, Ph.D. candidate in Political Science at the University of Illinois at Chicago, worked tirelessly to provide the Census data. Brandon Campbell advised on social media strategy. Finally, our friends Alexander Domanskis, Anthony Fornelli, Emile Karafiol, Jae Choi Kim, and Mark Peysakhovitch provided encouragement and support. We thank them all.

Jeryl Levin
President

Cynthia Linton
Editor

AFRICAN AMERICANS

Chicago population:
887,608 (African American alone)
960,756 (alone or in combination with other races)

Metro population:
1,645,993 (alone)
1,721,578 (alone or in combo)

Foreign-born:
About 3% in both city and metro

Demographics:

In 1990 Chicago African Americans made up about 40% of the population. By 2010, with considerable migration to the suburbs, it's closer to 33%. Most are concentrated on the South Side, from 26th Street to 131st Street and from Ashland Avenue to Lake Michigan; on the West Side from Garfield Park to the city limits, between Lake Street and Cermak Road; and in a relatively compact settlement on the near North Side, west of Halsted and south of Division Street. These three areas are contiguous and form the condition that caused population experts to call Chicago "the most racially segregated city in the United States." In these

The first Great Migration from the South to Chicago came during and just after WWI.

areas there is a considerable amount of education and affluence and a tremendous amount of poverty. There are African Americans, Africans and Afro-Caribbeans throughout the city, including the far North Side, but an estimated 90-95% live in these three areas. No other ancestry group is so segregated.

African Americans also are found in growing numbers in many south, west and southwest suburbs, such as Maywood, Oak Park, Harvey, Dolton, Country Club Hills, Flossmoor, Olympia Fields, Robbins and Ford Heights, and in north suburban Evanston and North Chicago. Early moves to the suburbs in most cases were met with stiff resistance. That is no longer true. The median household income of metro-area African Americans is $36,192, about $24,000 below average. In the city it is $30,512. Nearly 80% of those over the age of 25 in the city have a high school diploma, 83% in the metro area. Some 17% in the city have a bachelor's degree (low compared with other groups) and 20% in metro. In Chicago 6.4% have a graduate or professional degree, with a similar 7% in metro. About 27% of those in the labor force in Chicago are in professional or managerial positions, and 29% in the metro area. Nearly one-third of African Americans in Chicago live at or below the poverty line, while about one-fourth do in the metro area.

(Ed. note: Population figures are from the 2010 Census. Other demographic data, on education and economics, come from the 2007-09 Census Bureau American Community Survey.)

Historical background:

The first permanent settler in Chicago was a black man from Haiti by the name of Jean Baptiste Pointe du Sable, who was a trader here in the 1770s. He later moved, but blacks have lived in the area since that time and have formed a small but important part of the population since 1840.

The first Great Migration had its strongest momentum during and immediately after WWI, with the population growing from 44,000 in 1910 to 277,000 by 1940. Migrants came from the South for basically the same reason millions left Europe before WWI: better economic conditions. Many saw opportunities, including an adequate education, denied them in the South. They also left because of the Jim Crow system of discrimination, fleeing political and economic repression and physical terrorism.

What they found in Chicago was less than they hoped for but better than they left. They found racial prejudice, segregation, and discrimination in housing, jobs and social conditions; but they also found political freedom and economic opportunities they never dreamed of in the South, and took full advantage of both. The sudden mass arrival of African Americans created new tensions and problems for the old residents and recently arrived immigrants from Europe. The competition for jobs, housing and recreation space intensified. It was during that time that the Chicago race riot of 1919 broke out, when whites at the 35th Street Beach stoned black swimmers because they had crossed an imaginary line. The riots lasted four days, leaving 38 dead, 520 injured and thousands of homes damaged.

Blacks were confined to the "Black Belt," stretching from 26th Street to 47th Street and from the Rock Island Railroad tracks to Cottage Grove Avenue, concentrated at 81,000 per square mile compared with 19,000 for the rest

In the '70s, schools deteriorated, tension increased, and white flight accelerated.

of the city. Their work generally was in menial jobs in the Stockyards, where they could make 10 times what they had made picking cotton, and in the steel mills of South Chicago, International Harvester and small businesses inside the Black Belt. Later that area was to take on the names of "Bronzeville" and "Black Metropolis." Bronzeville was a self-supporting community, distinguished by notable accomplishments in both business and politics. Thriving businesses included Robert S. Abbott's Chicago Defender, Jesse Binga's first state-chartered African American bank in the U.S. and Anthony Overton's cosmetics business.

By the mid-1920s, Chicago was the black business capital of the country. In politics, three congressmen — Oscar DePriest, Arthur Mitchell and William Dawson — were elected before Harlem ever elected Adam Clayton Powell. There was fun, friendship and joyful noise all over the ghettos of the South and West Sides. But it was much too crowded for human health, so there was pressure to move beyond its confines and constant, sometimes violent, resistance from those on the outside who wanted to confine this population.

The second Great Migration came with the U.S. entry into WWII. Hundreds of thousands of blacks and poor whites left the cotton and tobacco fields of the South for better-paying jobs in the war industry. Chicago's black population skyrocketed to near one-half million in 1950. A Chicago Renaissance occurred on the South Side from about 1945-60 that included the South Side Community Arts Center, the writings of people like Margaret Walker, Margaret Burroughs and Gwendolyn Brooks, gospel music and urban blues, the Johnson Publishing empire, and the founding of DuSable Museum.

Starting in the 1970s, schools began to deteriorate, tension increased and white flight to the suburbs accelerated. Industry and business left the city, claiming they needed more trained, disciplined, skilled workers. The result for Chicago in the final decades of the 20th century was an erosion of both the industrial base and the middle-class population, leaving an increasingly unskilled, poor black and Hispanic population to forage for themselves. The increase in disappointment, frustration, anger, poverty, violence and crime seemed to be the natural outcome of these historical economic, social and cultural changes.

Current migration patterns:

Most of the movement is to the suburbs, because of relaxed housing restrictions, better schools, safer streets and relatively inexpensive housing. African Americans accounted for nearly 90% of the 200,000 people who left Chicago 2000-2010. Some also left more expensive suburbs with high home prices, like Evanston. During the decade, south and west suburbs such as Matteson, Lansing, Berwyn, Cicero and Plainfield saw their black populations swell, in some cases more than doubling. Other suburbs with high African American populations include Flossmoor (48%), Country Club Hills (87%), Calumet City (71%), Dolton (90%) and Maywood (75%).

The migration from the South has all but stopped. The reason is economic — the vast industrial base that once attracted migrants to Chicago no longer exists. On the contrary, many African Americans are returning to the South, mainly retirees and young people without jobs going home to live with relatives.

Religion:

Most are Christians of various denominations, such as Episcopal and Methodist or a combination of the two (African Methodist Episcopal, Christian Methodist Episcopal, A.M.E Zion), and also Baptist, Lutheran and

Nearly 90% of the 200,000 who left Chicago 2000-2010 were African Americans.

Catholic, as well as increasing numbers of Pentecostals and Jehovah's Witnesses. There also are growing numbers of traditional Muslims, in addition to those in the Nation of Islam. Churches have played a major role in African American issues, from the vigilance committees of the 1850s that protected runaway slaves to the religious groups that spearheaded the Civil Rights Movement. Many churches have provided food, housing, health care and other social services to the community.

Important traditions:

Religion and extended family are traditionally very important among African Americans. Births and deaths are celebrated, expressing a reverence for life. New babies are cherished, and at funerals friends and family celebrate the life of those who have passed on. For the substantial number in the middle class, there tend to be stable two-parent families who pass along to their children traditions of religion, education, honesty, fidelity and careful spending habits. But for many others, a lack of job opportunities and poverty have had a devastating effect on the African American community and the family. Marriage, in contrast to the past, is at a low ebb. For those who do marry, separation and divorce are frequent, and one-parent families are the norm (also a growing trend in the population at large). Teen pregnancies are high, in part because abortion is not acceptable. For large areas of the city, the infusion of drugs and guns in disproportionate amounts have created an aura of insecurity and instability to all the institutions and traditions of a formerly stable community. In the early days, the entire African American community was like a family. That community support has deteriorated. The relationship between family and economics is strong. The African American family was undermined in large part by the abandonment of the inner city and disappearance of unskilled and semi-skilled jobs since the '60s. Conditions today make it difficult for many families to pass down traditional values to their children.

Holidays and special events:

Birthdays, Easter, Thanksgiving, Mother's Day, Christmas and now Kwanzaa are important times for celebration. Kwanzaa, the festival of the harvest (of life) is the coming together of the community to celebrate life and enjoy the fruits of life. A new holiday, Kwanzaa is born out of the African tradition and occurs around the same time as Christmas and Chanukah, but is not a religious holiday. Dr. Martin Luther King Jr.'s birthday (Jan. 15) is celebrated with special programs and at City Hall. It is a state and school holiday (celebrated on the closest Monday). Black History Month (February) is also an occasion when schools, churches and other institutions plan special programming. Juneteenth (in June) marks the signing of the Emancipation Proclamation. And the traditional Bud Billiken Parade (second Saturday in August), celebrates the mythical figure who protects children. It was started by the Chicago Defender to honor its newsboys.

Foods for special occasions:

During holidays and celebrations, the preparation and eating of food is important. Aside from the usual turkey, ham, chicken, greens, roots, herbs, barbecue and drink at Thanksgiving and Christmas, many families

Turnout for the 2008 presidential election was 72% in Chicago's majority-black wards.

indulge in a dish called chitterlings (chittlins), which derives from plantation days in the South when blacks had to make do with the leavings of the master's meals. Such dishes were prepared with great care and became almost delicacies.

Dietary restrictions:

None for Christians. Muslims avoid pork and alcohol.

Names:

Formerly, most African Americans continued to use their slave names, such as John, Joe, Robert, Walter and Mary, along with nicknames like Tim, Rob, Skeeball, Arch and Slim. Since Malcolm X, many of the younger generations have turned to African and other non-Western names such as Tuisha, Aesha and Hakim. Traditional last names came from plantation owners. Some also have changed their last names to African names.

Major issues for community:

Almost without dissent, Chicago's African Americans are united on issues of racism and the denial of equal access to decent affordable housing, jobs, quality education and neighborhood safety. Crime and violence are probably the top issues, followed closely by the need for adequate employment and decent housing, the poor state of the Chicago Public Schools, and the problems of youth in general. There is inadequate transportation to get to where the jobs are. And the jobs themselves have changed, with more in the white-collar and service sector, requiring computer skills. Two other issues hotly debated in the community are the threatened elimination of affirmative action and how much assimilation is too much.

Political participation:

Since Franklin Roosevelt was president, African Americans have voted overwhelmingly for Democrats (before that they were loyal to Abraham Lincoln's Republican party). Participation in politics depends on the issues, the candidates and the section of the city involved. In some places interest is very low; the middle class tends to be more active. In the campaign and election of the late Mayor Harold Washington, almost every man, woman and child was involved in one way or another. He was elected only because this was so. After his death, candidates did not seem to reflect the needs and concerns of the community, especially the poorer and younger members. Political interest lagged. For many there is a growing distrust of government and a sentiment of "What difference does it make?" In the '90s turnout was very low, even among registered voters.

That changed when Barack Obama ran for president in 2008, though he wasn't as well-known in the community as Washington had been. Majority black wards saw a turnout of 72% of registered voters, just 2 points lower than the rest of the city. In some impoverished black wards turnout was low and pulled down the average. (Nationwide, black turnout increased almost 5 percentage points from 2004, mostly attributable to young black voters, up nearly 9 points.) Election of a black president brought new hopes and dreams to places like Bronzeville. But then came the disappointment when the black president was not able to improve the lives of the less advantaged, who were hard hit by the recession. Technology and fear of violence all but ended the practice of precinct captains and door-to-door canvassing. With the 2012 election pending, community organizations, merchants groups and unions sought to organize and inspire black voters once again.

In city elections, in 2011 Rahm Emanuel was elected mayor with nearly 60% of the black vote, helped by his identification with Obama, for whom he was chief of staff, and the support of the major black politicians. After about 180,000 African Americans left the city the first decade of the 2000s, blacks managed to keep the same number of seats in the City Council but lost influence and patronage jobs. It was clear that African Americans and the growing Hispanic population were now in competition for the same rewards.

Links to homeland:

African Americans have a relationship with the African continent through business, tourism, the arts, folklore and politics. There are strong ties to South Africa, where they long advocated an end to apartheid. Events there, as well as in other African and Caribbean nations, are of particular interest. Some have tried to trace their roots, a difficult task because their ancestors were brought here in chains many generations ago. There is a divide between American-born blacks and the elite African immigrants they rejected as "foreign."

Special health concerns:

Many blacks in Chicago suffer from a serious lack of health care. Neighborhood hospitals like Provident and St. Lukes are no longer there. National statistics confirm that African Americans as a group face higher death rates than whites for the most common life-threatening diseases. For example, the death rate for diabetes is double, cancer is 25% higher, heart disease 30% higher, and strokes 40% higher, according to the Centers for Disease Control. Health risk factors are high for blacks, as 25% of men smoke (and 18% of women), 37% of men and 51% of women are obese, and 39% of men and 44% of women have high blood pressure. They are 20% less likely to get flu shots and nearly 25% less likely to be vaccinated for pneumonia. Nearly 21% under 65 have no health insurance.

African Americans are disproportionately impacted by HIV/AIDS, with more than half the new cases diagnosed in Illinois. African Americans accounted for 60% of the new diagnoses in Chicago in 2006, and were more than half of the 15,000 people living with HIV/AIDS in the state that year, according to the AIDS Foundation of Chicago. In 2009, three-quarters of the women diagnosed with HIV in Illinois were African American.

Sickle cell disease, an inherited blood ailment that affects those of African descent, strikes one in 500 newborns. Those with the disease have inherited the mutated gene from both parents, making them prone to infections.

There is no cure, but pneumonia vaccinations have helped reduce mortality for children 0-3 by 68%. The 1 in 12 blacks who carry just one gene instead of two are said to have sickle cell trait. They have no symptoms, but pass the gene on to their offspring.

By Timuel Black, Professor Emeritus of City Colleges of Chicago

ASSYRIAN AMERICANS

Chicago population:
3,823 (first ancestry)

Metro population:
14,377 (first ancestry)

Foreign-born:
73% in the city, 66% in Cook County

Demographics:

There is very little Census breakdown on Assyrians, who come from several different countries. The most recent available breakdown of Assyrians is the 2000 Census. It showed that in Chicago, with a reported population of 7,121, about 85% spoke a language other than English at home. About 3,000 held a high school diploma while less than 1,000 had a bachelor's degree or higher. About 10% were below the poverty level.

Their homeland is in northern Iraq, southeast Turkey, northwest Iran and northeast Syria.

The largest concentration of Assyrians in Chicago is in West Rogers Park. There is a smaller group in Albany Park. Others are scattered in other North Side neighborhoods such as Edgewater, East Rogers Park, Budlong Woods, Ravenswood, Andersonville, Peterson Park and Hollywood Park. A growing number live in north and northwest suburbs like Skokie, Morton Grove, Niles, Des Plaines, Itasca, Schaumburg and Arlington Heights, and in Kane and Lake counties.

(Ed. note – While population figures for Assyrian/Chaldean/Syriac are from the 2008-10 American Community Survey, the most recent Census breakdowns for education, economics and place of birth are from 2000.)

Historical background:

Assyrians are an ethnic minority from the Middle East. They are Christian and speak their own language. Their homeland is located in what is now northern Iraq, southeastern Turkey, northwestern Iran and northeastern Syria, territories that are inhabited largely by Kurds and Azerbaijani Turks. Assyrians here claim a heritage that goes back to the ancient Assyrian Empire (in Mesopotamia). The history of Assyrians in Chicago dates from 1889, when they began to come as theology and medical students.

In the first decade of the 20th century, a significant number began to settle permanently. By 1909, there were 600 young Assyrian men living in Chicago, and 30 families. Most worked as masons, carpenters, painters, tailors or in other trades. A few were employed in factories, stores, hotels and restaurants. During WWI, Assyrians were victims of famine and genocide, which led to a new influx, causing the community to swell to about 2,327, according to a Census published in 1924. Males between the ages of 20 and 40 predominated, and they clustered in the Near North neighborhood around Clark and Huron. The later arrivals were generally less educated and worked primarily as cooks, waiters, janitors, hotel men and unskilled factory workers. The majority in these early waves came from villages in northwestern Iran. In the 1930s Assyrians tended to move northward in the city into Lincoln Park, Lake View and Uptown. Small numbers trickled in from Iran, Iraq and Syria through WWII. According to one estimate, there were 5,000 Assyrians in Chicago in 1944, more than three times as many as in any other American city.

Following a Kurdish and Azerbaijani insurrection in northwestern Iran in 1948, another wave of Assyrians entered from that country. Starting in the 1960s, a growing number began arriving from Baghdad, Kirkuk, Basrah and other cities in Iraq. In 1975-76, during the Lebanese Civil War, up to 1,000 Assyrians living on the outskirts of Beirut were accepted for resettlement in Chicago. This was the first group of Assyrian newcomers who got government benefits as a refugee-like group. Earlier arrivals were helped by Assyrian aid societies and churches, as well as through family support networks.

A significantly larger wave came to Chicago from Iraq in the 1970s and '80s, primarily to escape the Iran-Iraq War. According to the Office of Refugee Resettlement, 1,955 Iraqis came to Chicago with refugee status from 1983-94, the vast majority of them Assyrians. This does not include the many Assyrians who came to Chicago from Iraq,

During WWI, Assyrians were victims of famine and genocide, leading to a new influx.

Iran, Syria and Lebanon as students or as family-reunification immigrants. The Assyrian Universal Alliance Foundation and Assyrian National Council of Illinois helped all classifications of Assyrian immigrants, while Catholic Charities and Interchurch Refugee and Immigration Ministries assisted those classified as refugees to adjust and find jobs.

Current migration patterns:

The movement of Assyrians to the north and northwest continues in Chicago. Assyrians have moved into communities where other Assyrians already live, though they have not settled in the same blocks but scattered throughout those communities. Few Assyrians have returned permanently to their countries of origin. Conditions in Iraq, in particular, have been precarious in recent years and many Assyrians from Iraq were in refugee camps in Syria in 2012.

Language:

Most Assyrian immigrants in Chicago speak modern Assyrian, sometimes called neo-Syriac, modern Syriac, Surit or neo-Aramaic. It is a Semitic language related to Hebrew and, more distantly, to Arabic. Many dialects can be heard in Chicago, but the majority speak either a relatively standardized urban Iraqi dialect or an equally standardized Iranian one. Since governments in the Middle East generally have discouraged the teaching of modern Assyrian, relatively few can read and write in this language, which has its own unique alphabet. The vast majority of Assyrian immigrants also speak, read and write the language of their country of origin, usually Arabic or Persian.

Religion:

Almost by definition, Assyrians are Christian. Before the influence of Western missionaries, they belonged to either the Church of the East (also known by the misnomer "Nestorian") or the Syrian Orthodox Church (known by the misnomer "Jacobite"). In Chicago, Assyrians belong to various denominations. The largest single one is the Church of the East, with three sizable churches in Chicago and one in Bartlett. Some, who reject some reforms in the Church of the East, have formed a separate Ancient Church of the East, and have an active congregation in Chicago. Smaller groups of Assyrians belong to the Chaldean Uniate and Syrian Orthodox churches. Some Protestants have separate Assyrian churches, including Presbyterian, Assyrian Evangelical (United Church of Christ), Evangelical Covenant and Pentecostal.

Important traditions:

Modern Assyrian identity is more than an attachment to a Christian heritage. It is also rooted in ties to the homeland, to language and to distinctive cultural traditions. They are a close-knit community and those from one tribe, clan or village feel closely related to people from the same tribe, clan or village. Assyrians have distinctive life-cycle ceremonies, which many families celebrate, regardless of religious affiliation. These include *ma'modita* (baptism), *talibuta* or *shirinligh* (betrothal parties), and large

Almost by definition, Assyrians are Christian.

weddings. When a person dies, the funeral is followed by several days when immediate relatives accept visitors to pay their respects, literally "to cure the head" (*basamta d-risha*). On the third, seventh and 40th days of mourning, as well as after one year, there are special gatherings.

Assyrians take matters of hospitality very seriously, frequently welcoming guests into their home, and hosting special events and holiday gatherings. The demands of contemporary American life put a strain on the ability of some families to live up to traditional hospitality standards. Assyrians also place great value on extended families (or "houses") maintaining a good reputation (*shimma spay*). This includes high standards of modesty and propriety. Assyrian men and women mix more in public than many other Middle Easterners. The adaptation to American mores has varied dramatically from one family to another. In some families, as with other immigrants, this has caused a generation gap.

Holidays and special events:

Assyrians celebrate the major Christian holidays of Good Friday, Easter and Christmas. They consider Easter the "Big Holiday" (*'ida gura*) and Christmas the "Little Holiday" (*'ida s'ura*). Another major religious holiday is the *Ba'uta d-Ninwayé* or Rogation of the Ninevites (usually in February). This commemorates the prophet Jonah's mission to the people of Nineveh, the capital of Assyria, and usually includes a three-day partial fast. Assyrians continue the tradition of celebrating Saints' Days, to commemorate both the birthdays and the death anniversaries of the saints. Many are local saints, so their celebrations are hosted by Assyrian tribes or villages with whom those saints are associated. The commemorations of saints are called *shahras*, and can range from small family reunions to huge outdoor picnics.

Another important holiday is *Kha B'Nissan* (April 1), the Assyrian New Year. In recent years it has been marked by a parade down King Sargon Boulevard (Western Avenue), followed by large parties. Assyrian Martyrs' Day (Aug. 7), which was first instituted to mark the 1933 massacre of Assyrians by the Iraqi army, now commemorates the martyrdom of Assyrians throughout their long history of persecution.

Foods for special occasions:

Dukhrana, a sacrificial meal on shahras and other occasions, consists of distributing the meat of a sacrificial lamb. Another popular Assyrian dish for special occasions is *harisa* (wheat cooked with chicken, lamb or mutton, whipped and served with melted butter). It also can be baked, with ground coriander seeds. *Girdu* is rice baked in yogurt or sour milk and served hot with melted butter on the top. *Dolma* is vine leaves, zucchini, eggplant, tomatoes or bell-pepper stuffed with chopped vegetables and ground or diced meat.

Dietary restrictions:

Assyrians traditionally refrain from eating meat and/or dairy products on Wednesdays and Fridays, as well as during Advent, the 25 days before Christmas, and Lent, the 50 days preceding Easter.

Names:

A large number of Assyrians have biblical names, taken from both the Old and New Testaments. Common ones include: Oraham (Abraham), Yako (Jacob), Yosip (Joseph), Astar (Esther), Rabka (Rebecca) and Maryam (Mary). Names of ancient Assyrian gods, goddesses, kings and queens also are common. Male names include Ashor, Sargon and Sankheru. Female names include Atorina, Ninwé and Shamiram. A few have ancient Persian names such as Diryawash (Darius) and Kurosh (Cyrus) for boys and Narjis for girls. Some boys are named after Christian saints in the Syriac tradition, such as Aprim, Narsay and Zaya. Some compound names from the Syriac tradition are also used, such as Odisho (servant of Jesus) and Sorisho (hope of Jesus).

Nowadays, many Assyrians, especially girls, have non-biblical Western names, such as Linda, Diana, Janet and Louisa. In Iraq it was not unusual for Assyrians to name boys after the last names of British officers, such as Wilson and Johnson — or less commonly, girls after cities or countries their sojourning fathers visited, like Berlin and Argentina. It was usual for Assyrians to have a given name, followed by that of their father and grandfather. Clan names, usually preceded by *bet* (house of), were generally suppressed by the Iraqi government, but have been resurrected by some Assyrians in Chicago. Many go by informal nicknames.

Major issues for community:

Many Assyrians are worried about melting into American society and losing their distinctive culture. Assyrian nationalism is very strong in the Chicago community.

Political participation:

Because the majority are newcomers, relatively few Assyrians vote, though a growing number have become active in politics in both the Democratic and Republican parties. John Nimrod (Republican) was a long-time state senator from Glenview and Adam Benjamin (Democrat) a long-time U.S. congressman from Gary, IN. Many Assyrians, whether they vote or not, follow international affairs closely.

Links to homeland:

The majority of Assyrians, who left their homeland under duress, have not maintained their original citizenship. Many, however, have said they want to return if political and economic conditions improve. As time goes on, the desire to return usually dims. Many have sent money to relatives taking refuge in Jordan, Turkey, Russia, Greece and other countries of temporary asylum. Organized charities, such as the Assyrian Aid Society of America, have raised money to help support refugees. Such charities have helped pay for educational materials in refugee camps. Assyrians maintain close contacts with Assyrians dispersed all over the world, through magazines newspapers, faxes, videotapes, cable television and the Internet.

Original by Daniel Wolk, then a Doctoral Candidate in anthropology at the University of Chicago; also contributing: Homer Ashurian, Executive Director of Assyrian Universal Alliance Foundation. Updated with help from Ashurian.

BOSNIAK AMERICANS

Chicago population:

NA

Metro population:

NA

Foreign-born:

NA

Editor's note: The vast majority of Bosnians in America, and in Chicago, are Muslim and call themselves Bosniaks. This chapter deals largely with that population, as the two other groups from Bosnia, Serbs and Croats, are described in the Serbian and Croatian chapters in this book.

Demographics:

While no Census numbers are available, Chicago is believed to have one of the largest Bosnian communities in the U.S., with estimates as high as 50,000. The new Bosnian community has settled in the northern part of the city between Lawrence and Howard, Kedzie and Lake Michigan. Many Bosnians have relocated

Chicago is believed to have one of the largest Bosnian communities in the U.S.

to the suburbs, especially to the north and northwest in Lincolnwood, Evanston, Skokie, Des Plaines, Mt. Prospect, Arlington Heights, Niles and Northbrook. There are numerous Bosnian businesses between Lawrence, Lincoln and Western – doctor's offices, law offices, travel agencies, video rental stores, bakeries, restaurants, and markets with supplies from Bosnia-Herzegovina.

Historical background:

There were four waves of immigration from Bosnia to the Chicago area. The first started at the end of the 19th century and lasted until 1945; the second began at the end of World War II and lasted to mid-1960, the third started at the end of 1960 and lasted until the dissolution of Yugoslavia, and the fourth began during the Bosnian War in 1992-1995 and is still going on today. Most in the first wave came in search of a better life and financial success, while the later waves were a result of political and ethnical/religious persecution. The first immigrants were poor and illiterate. They worked in factories, in mines and on railroad construction.

The second wave was a consequence of WWII and the new communist reality. These new immigrants were educated and many were professionals, such as professors and engineers. At the end of the 1960s, the third wave came as a result of Yugoslav President Marshal Tito's effort to loosen travel restrictions in an effort to increase the influx of money into his country. Bosniaks (those who are Muslim) from these last two waves joined forces and founded their mosques, clubs, newspapers and, in 1964, a local radio station *"Glas Bosnjaka"* (Voice of Bosniaks), which still operates today. The last and largest wave of immigration into the U.S. occurred after the aggression on the Bosnia-Herzegovinia Republic, ethnic cleansing and cultural annihilation in the Bosnian War in the 1990s.

Current migration patterns:

Since the early 1990s, people from all walks of life emigrated from Bosnia, and the number of young and educated people was notably larger than in previous immigrations. In 1994, Bozniaks in Chicago formed the

About 70% of Bosnians in the U.S. are Muslims, and call themselves Bosniaks.

Bosnian and Herzegovinian American Community Center to serve wounded and traumatized Bosnian War refugees arriving in Chicago. It offers assistance to all immigrants from the former Yugoslavia without regard to ethnicity or religion. Bosniaks are still coming here today.

Religion:

About 70 percent of Bosnians in the United States are Muslim, and are called Bosniaks. Bosnian Croats are Catholic and Bosnian Serbs are Eastern Orthodox Christians.

Important traditions:

Family values are an essential component of life. All holidays are celebrated with family, and family ties are very tight. Marriage is considered extremely important, and divorce is a last-resort measure. Bosniaks are taught to respect the elderly and strangers, and to care for their parents when they are no longer able to care for themselves.

Holidays and special events:

Bosniak Americans celebrate all Muslim holidays, including Ramadan (*Ramazan*), *Eid-ul Fitr* (*Ramazanski Bajram*), *Eid-al Adha* (*Kurban Bajram*), and the Islamic New Year (*Hidžretska Nova Godina*). These religious holidays follow the lunar calendar, and fall 10 days earlier each year. The Gregorian New Year is celebrated on Jan. 1 when Bosniak Americans usually put up a New Year's tree. Bosnians in Chicago, regardless of religion or ethnicity, celebrate the Bosnian Republic Day Nov. 25 to observe when Bosnia was recognized as a country within the Yugoslavian federation in 1943. And Bosnian Independence Day has been celebrated March 1 since 1992, honoring Bosnia's independence from Yugoslavia. Other non-religious holidays include March 8, International Women's Day, and May 1, Labor Day. The first Women's Day was Feb. 28, 1909, in the United States, and Labor Day commemorates the laborers' demonstrations May 1, 1886, in Chicago.

Foods for special occasions:

Traditional Bosniak American foods include *sogan dolma* (stuffed onions), *punjene paprike* (stuffed peppers), *sarma* (stuffed sour cabbage), *pita* (phyllo dough filled with anything from meat to cheese, onions, potatoes, etc.), *ćevapi u somunu* (miniature skinless sausage links made from beef and/or lamb, on a soft bread). Traditional sweets include *baklava* (phyllo dough filled with chopped walnuts covered with a sugar solution), *halva* (flour sautéed, then glazed with a sugar solution), *hurmašice* (baked sweets) and cakes for special occasions. Traditional meals on religious holidays usually include *burek* (meat pita), roasted lamb, baklava and halva.

Dietary restrictions:

Bosniaks do not consume pork or its byproducts. Also, during the month of Ramadan, they fast from sunrise to sunset, abstaining from food, drink (even water), smoking and sexual intercourse.

Language:

The Bosnian language uses the Latin alphabet, although many elderly Bosnians are able to read and write the Cyrillic alphabet, since both were required in the educational curriculum when Bosnia was part of Socialist Federal Republic of Yugoslavia.

Names:

Bosniak last names generally end with -ić or -ović. This plays the same role as "son" in English surnames such as Johnson or Wilson. There are also some last names that do not end in -ić. These last names are derived from

Many suffer post-traumatic stress disorder, from the Bosnian War and losing family members.

place of origin, occupations or other factors in the family's history (e.g. Zlatar, meaning Goldsmith). Some Bosniak last names also have Hungarian, Vlach or Turkish origins (i.e. Vlasić and Arapović). First names have mostly Arabic, Turkish or Persian roots, such as Osman, Mehmed, Ismet and Kemal. South Slavic names like Zlatan are also used, primarily among non-religious Bosniaks. Female names generally end with –a, while male names end with –al, -im, -ir, -er, -id, -ed.

Major issues for community:

Problems encountered by Bosniaks in Chicago include: preserving family relationships and Bosniak identity (religion, language, traditions and culture); increasing participation in political, social, economic and religious matters in the U.S.; and decreasing the gap between generations and cultures. A major concern for the community is bringing to justice the war criminals responsible for genocide and ethnic cleansing in their homeland from 1992 to 1995.

Political participation:

Most Bosniak immigrants do not participate in politics beyond voting. However, some still show their pride as successful American Bosniaks by becoming active in political parties, as well as supporting candidates in local and congressional elections. One prominent Bozniak, Džafer Kulenović, was named advisor on Islamic matters to Illinois Gov. Pat Quinn.

Links to homeland:

Bosniaks maintain strong ties to their homeland. They give financial help to family members still living there, and they visit their homes there often. Many also financially assist students in their home country. There is a Bosnian Investment Group and "Buy Bosnian" efforts.

Special health concerns:

Common health problems include post-traumatic stress disorder, depression, hypertension, diabetes, and hyperlipidemia (high cholesterol). The PTSD and depression resulted mostly from the experiences during the Bosnian War, including loss of family members and friends. Hypertension, diabetes and hyperlipidemia are thought to be hereditary in most cases.

By Bedrija Nikocevic and Azra Terzic-Nezirevic, board members of the Bosnian and Herzegovenian American Community Center.

CAMBODIAN AMERICANS

Chicago population:
1,204 (Cambodians alone)
1,404 (alone and in combination)
Cook County population:
1,772 (alone and in combo)
Foreign-born:
97% in Chicago, 90% in Cook County

Demographics:

In the 2000 Census, about one-third had a high school diploma and just 13% in both the city and Cook County as a whole had a college degree or more, very low compared with other ethnic groups. Median household income in Chicago was $52,500, while Cook County reported a median of $55,233. This may be because of large households, because individual income was $11,594 for the city and $12,332 for the county. A reported 26% were living in poverty in the city, with the exact same number for Cook. While many Cambodian children have grown up, graduated from college and found good jobs, others have dropped out of school.

They began coming to Chicago in 1975 as refugees from war-torn Cambodia.

(Ed. note: Census numbers for Cambodians are scarce and extremely unreliable because of the small size of the community here. The latest Chicago population numbers are from the 2010 Census. Beyond that, the most recent data available are from 2000, including foreign-born and all Cook County data. Even then, numbers were not available for the other metro counties, probably because the number of Cambodians is miniscule. It is widely believed many Cambodians did not fill out the Census, which adds to the unreliability of the data.)

Historical background:

Cambodians began coming to Chicago in 1975 as refugees from war-torn Cambodia. The communist Khmer Rouge ruled Cambodia from April 1975 to January 1979. During this period, as many as 3 million (out of 7.5 million) Cambodians were killed and many others were forced into work camps in the countryside. Border conflicts resulted in the invasion of Cambodia by the Vietnamese communist government, which then helped install a Cambodian regime trained in Hanoi. The indiscriminate killings of innocent people during the Khmer Rouge era and subsequent armed conflicts between the Khmer Rouge and new regime forced many Cambodians to flee to Thailand and seek asylum in third countries. Continued fighting and burning of rice reserves led to famine and starvation in 1979-80.

Although Cambodian refugees were resettled to the United States for two decades, the largest numbers came from 1980-85. Most settled in California. Only 4% came to Illinois, with about half of those settling in Chicago in neighborhoods like Uptown and Albany Park, where housing was inexpensive and agencies were available to help them. Uptown, especially, seemed an ideal port of entry for these reasons. Agencies helping to resettle the refugees included Travelers & Immigrants Aid, Lutheran Child & Family Services, Catholic Charities, World Relief and Jewish Family & Community Service. The Cambodian Association, a community self-help effort in Uptown, was founded in 1976 to provide translation services and help the refugees carry on their traditions. In 1980 it got funding to provide social services such as employment and counseling, to help newly arrived Cambodians become self-sufficient.

The first wave of Cambodians resettled in Chicago were better educated than the later immigrants, who tended to come from rural areas. Most of the refugees came here in late 1979 and early 1980. Immigration of Cambodians slowed in 1985. Coming from rural areas, many of the refugees were not literate and had difficulty adjusting to life in urban America.

Cambodian immigrants are mostly from a rural background, with little or no education.

Current migration patterns:

Only a few Cambodians are now arriving in Chicago, mostly through family-reunification. Some city dwellers, who have gotten good jobs and could afford it, have moved northwest to such suburbs as Skokie and Niles for better schools. A few have moved to Lowell, Mass., where there is a substantial Cambodian population.

Language:

They speak Cambodian, also known as Khmer. People speak various dialects, which differ from one another mostly in pronunciation.

Religion:

Theravada Buddhism. More than 80% are Buddhists. The rest include Muslims, Christians and Hindus.

Important traditions:

Cambodians teach their children to value traditional clothes, dance, food and weddings, as well as ways of talking, acting and respecting one another. They believe the young should listen to older people, such as older brothers and sisters, grandparents, aunts and uncles. Young people should not look at an older person's eyes when talking to them. Likewise, older people should take care of the younger ones. Cambodian parents expect their children to listen to them and respect them. Talking back to parents and other older people is bad. Students should listen to the teacher. Parents depend completely on teachers to teach their children everything. Parents listen to the teacher more than their children do.

Cambodian parents don't allow their children to have boyfriends or girlfriends at a young age. Males and females aren't allowed to touch unless they are married. Marriage is arranged by parents. Children must be good in order to maintain the family's reputation. When Cambodians resettled in America, the youth adopted the new culture, which caused conflicts at home. Their parents still wanted them to behave with traditional Cambodian values, but the children no longer accepted these values as relevant to their lives. Parents, themselves, are having problems adjusting to the new culture, which makes them want to hold on to their traditional culture even more.

Holidays and special events:

Cambodian New Year is celebrated in April, for three days. *Maha Sangkran* Day (April 14) is the last day of the old year. *Vana Bat* Day (April 15) divides the old year from the new. And *Loeung Sak* Day (April 16) is when the New Year begins. In Cambodian villages, some celebrated for as long as a month. Before the New Year, Cambodians clean and decorate the house and set the table with flowers, fruit, incense and candles to wait for the new guardian angel. The next day, they cook, meet with family, bring food and gifts to their parents and food to the temple. At the temple, monks pray to the dead and bless everyone for the year. People offer food to the monks. Then they eat together and bathe their parents. After that everyone washes the Buddha statue and asks for blessings for the year to come. Finally, friends and family throw water at one another for best wishes, and build sand or rice dunes to symbolize prosperity in the coming year.

Bon Phchum Bend (the Ancestor Festival) comes in September, for 15 days. Cambodians believe when people die they are reincarnated, and that those who committed bad deeds in their last life became ghosts. These spirits wait for food and blessings from friends and relatives, offered to them through monks. The first 14 days of this festival, *Kaun Bend,* people divide into 14 groups and each brings food to the temple one day. The 15th day, *Phchum Bend,* is when everyone comes to the temple and eats together. The monks pray for

The community suffers greatly from the loss of family members, viciously killed in Cambodia.

forgiveness for the sins of the departed and offer good will and food to the wandering spirits who might come to receive them. *Visakh Boja* celebrates the birth, enlightenment and death of Buddha. It is celebrated in May because all these events occurred on the full moon in *Visakh* (May). Buddhists offer food to the monks in the morning and incense and flowers in the afternoon. At night they go to the temple to hear sermons and the chanting of *Buddhappawatti.*

Food for special occasions:

On Bon Phchum Bend families prepare food to offer to ancestors. *Num ansom* (cylinder cake), *non kaom* (sweet, coconut, sticky rice cake), *samlaw misuor* (noodle soup) and sticky rice balls are put in banana leaves so the spirits will be able to carry them on their journey to places they will have new lives.

Names:

Cambodians give their children names that rhyme with the names of family members. Surnames come first in Cambodia, but most Cambodian Americans have switched the order of first and last names, to follow the custom here. Most of the names have meanings, like Bopha (flower).

Major issues for community:

Because they are mostly from a rural background, with little or no education, Cambodian immigrants in Chicago have found it difficult to get well-paying jobs. The language barrier is difficult to overcome because many adults were illiterate when they arrived, unable to read and write in even their own language. This community suffers greatly from the loss of family members, caused by the vicious killing in their home country. Many families are headed by widows, and often there is little adult supervision. Adults who themselves are struggling to survive, often are unable to give their children direction. The result has been a severe generation gap, causing some youths to join gangs as a support system. Because of its small size, the community has difficulty getting funding and attention to help solve its problems.

Political participation:

Few Cambodian Americans vote and there is no political clout. Cambodians Americans report few crimes because they don't trust police, who they think don't understand their culture and way of life. Only a few community leaders are involved in government activities.

Links to homeland:

About 30-40% of adult Cambodian Americans have become U.S. citizens. Only about 2% maintain Cambodian citizenship. Many have returned to Cambodia to visit relatives or friends or the country itself. A few have returned there to live and work. Many send money home to help families and friends.

Special health concerns:

Cambodian immigrants suffer from mental illness because they have gone through such traumatic experiences, having worked in slave-like conditions under communism, often without enough to eat, being physically abused and witnessing the killing of family members. These experiences were followed by life in refugee camps, where they were confined to a small space with limited food. On top of that, adjustment to America has been difficult because the language and culture are so completely different. Their silent fear and anger impact their ability to be fully productive. They have feelings of hopelessness and self-hatred, and lack self-confidence and self-esteem. In 2004, the Killing Fields Memorial on Lawrence Avenue was built not only to honor those who died in Cambodia but also to heal survivors and help them become productive members of society.

Original by Borita Khim, a teacher at Stockton Elementary School and Kompha Seth, Executive Director of the Cambodian Association of Illinois. Revised in 2012 by Seth.

CHINESE AMERICANS

Chicago population:
42,060 (Chinese alone)
46,446 (alone or in combination)

Metro area population:
80,522 (alone)
92,712 (alone or in combo)

Foreign-born:
69% in Chicago, 70% in metro

Demographics:

In the metro area, the distribution of Chinese Americans is almost evenly split between Chicago and the suburbs. Chinese Americans are geographically dispersed throughout the city with one exception. About one-fourth of the Chinese American population in the city resides around Chinatown, unofficially bounded by the south branch of the Chicago River and 18th Street on the north, the Dan Ryan on the east, 35th Avenue on the south,

Chinese immigrants were excluded from the U. S. by law from 1882-1943.

and Halsted Street on the west. Also ethnic Chinese, largely from Southeast Asian countries, are concentrated on the North Side of Chicago, with business districts around Argyle Street and Broadway. In northern Cook County, suburbs like Skokie, Lincolnwood and Morton Grove have the highest percentages of Chinese. In DuPage County, Oak Brook, Glendale Heights and Naperville have large numbers.

More than 80% of Chinese in Chicago and the metro area speak a language other than English at home. Just over half (51%) in Chicago say they speak English "less than very well" and 45% in metro do. In the city, 74% of Chinese have finished high school, compared with 83% in metro. In the greater metro area 56% have a bachelor's degree and 32% a graduate or professional degree, very high compared with others. The median household income in Chicago is $49,454. For the whole metro area it is $68,914. While 44% in the city have management or professional jobs, about 55% in metro do. In Chicago 17% of the Chinese live in poverty, reflecting both recent immigrant and elderly populations. That number is 11% for metro.

(Ed. note: Population figures for Chicago are from the 2010 Census. Population for the metro area is from the 2010 Census [Chinese alone] and 2007-09 American Community Survey [Chinese alone and in combination]. The 2010 numbers exclude Taiwanese, who number about 1,000 in the city. All breakdowns for education and economics are from 2007-09.)

Historical background:

There were four distinct periods of Chinese immigration to the U.S. mainland: free immigration from 1849-82; exclusion from 1882-1943; limited entry from 1943-65; and revived entry from 1965 to the present. Chinese immigrants came to California in the late 1840s to work in the large gold-mining operations. For the next two decades, Chinese laborers arrived on the West Coast by the tens of thousands. They were recruited to fill labor needs in agriculture, small industries and railroads, but by the late 1870s conditions had changed. With a major recession in California, an anti-Chinese movement erupted. By 1882, the first exclusion law targeting a specific group was enacted. The Exclusion Act prohibited Chinese laborers from entering the U.S., and those already here were denied citizenship and civil liberties. Given this chilly climate on the West Coast, cities like Chicago beckoned.

The first Chinatown was established here in the 1880s, near Clark and Van Buren. In 1872, as the city recovered from the Great Chicago Fire, the first Chinese laundry opened at 167 W. Madison. Two years later there were 18 such laundries. While several other occupations were open to Chinese, including restaurant ownership and railroad jobs, the rise of the Chicago Chinese laundry reflected the growth of the Chinese immigrant community and its limited occupation opportunities. During the 1870s, most of the laundries were concentrated on South Clark Street. By 1884, they totaled more than 200 and could be found in almost every neighborhood. Downtown Chinatown fulfilled business and social needs. Unlike other American Chinatowns, it was not a residential enclave.

At first, few women were allowed to enter. In 1910 there were 65 women and 1,713 men.

This lack of traditional community and family life was fueled by two factors. First, few Chinese women were allowed to enter the U.S. (In Chicago, in 1910, there were 65 women and 1,713 men. This severe imbalance would not change until after WWII.) Second, with hard lessons learned from their West Coast experience, most Chinese chose not to live in Chinatown, preferring to "dilute" themselves, scattering around town and living behind their storefront businesses. Chinatown instead hosted several grocery stores, two Tong organizations, family associations, and a Chinese Baptist Mission. The majority of the early Chicago Chinese pioneers were Toishan-speaking men, from an impoverished area in Canton province. Most of them were sojourners — intending not to settle here, but to work a few years, accumulate wealth and retire well in China. They were willing to work long hours, in any menial labor, as long as they could save and send money back to China to support their families.

By about 1910, higher rents and internal factionalism in the original Chinatown led the leaders to expand to a second Chinatown, around Wentworth and Cermak, which provided low-rent storefronts and apartments. The Loop Chinatown remained until 1975, when it was razed to prepare for the Metropolitan Correctional Center. During the 1920s and '30s, Chicago's Chinese Americans continued to participate mainly in laundry or restaurant-related businesses. Again, this was due not to a natural proclivity (Chinese are not engaged in such occupations in China), but because of economic and structural barriers. Even for the second generation, who had requisite language skills for employment outside the ethnic enclave, job opportunities outside of Chinatown or the ethnic economy were severely restricted.

With the end of WWII and the 1949 establishment of the People's Republic of China, many Chinese immigrants and students no longer thought of returning to China. The exclusion laws against Chinese had been repealed in 1943, reunifying many Chinese American families. An influx of new immigrants arrived in the 1950s, mainly Mandarin-speaking professionals displaced by the 1949 Revolution in China. Many of them settled outside of the central city and in the suburbs. New Cantonese-speaking immigrants and refugees from China and Hong Kong tended to live around Chinatown, joining the growing second-generation community in renovating and expanding the South Side Chinatown.

By the mid-1970s, another major immigration occurred, as China and America renewed relations and the 1965 Immigration Act allowed annual quotas of 20,000 per country.

Immigrants arrived from mainland China, adding to the majority of Chinese from Taiwan, Hong Kong and Southeast Asia. Accompanying this growth spurt, a second Chinatown developed on the North Side, around

Argyle and Broadway, with the arrival of ethnic Chinese refugees and immigrants from Southeast Asia. While this new Chinatown is also known as Little Saigon or Asian Village, Chinese dialects are easily heard and Chinese Americans are well-represented among shoppers, business owners, residents, nonprofit groups and other community participants.

Current migration patterns:

Nearly 10,000 immigrants came to the Chicago area from China, Taiwan and Hong Kong from 1990-94. In the last decade, since 2000, the Chinese American population has risen nearly 15%. With current immigration policies favoring professionals, the self-supporting or those reuniting with family members, it is expected many of them will bypass inner-city enclaves and settle on the North and Northwest Sides and suburban areas. The most likely candidates for out-migration or the reverse "brain drain" are highly skilled professionals facing blocked mobility or the "glass ceiling" in corporate America, who may see better opportunities back in the newly industrialized Asian countries, including Taiwan and the People's Republic of China.

In the past decade, the Chinese American population has risen 15%.

Access to the Internet and high tech telecommunications allows more Chinese American business professionals to maintain their trans-national ties and businesses without relocating back to Asia. From their Chicago-area base, they can direct their business enterprises across the globe and maintain their family households in Illinois. Entrepreneurial parents who need to travel regularly back to Asia have the resources to drop off their "parachute kids" (referring usually to minor children who may maintain their own household or be with relatives or friends), allowing them to reap the benefits of an American education for secondary or higher education degrees.

Languages:

Cantonese, Toishanese, Mandarin, Teochiu, Fukienese, Taiwanese and others.

Religion:

Buddhism, Christianity, Ancestral Worship, Taoism, Confucianism (a philosophy). These are not necessarily mutually exclusive. Many in South Side Chinatown are Christians. The largest church there, the Chinese Union Christian Church, has services in three languages or dialects and has expanded to 5 satellite locations.

Important traditions:

Family harmony and filial piety emphasize the interdependence of family members and respect for authority accorded the older generation. The younger generation should yield to the guidelines and preferences of their parents. Those traditions are problematic for some Chinese American families, where second-generation members adhere to the American value of placing the individual first and to the American need to assert oneself and demand one's rights, particularly after they reach 18. Marriage traditions vary with religious practices and levels of acculturation.

When babies are born, there is a one-month-old celebration, a family and community event heralding a healthy future for the child. When people die, the preference is for full-body burial in a local cemetery. Older Chinese still would like to be buried in their ancestral family home or, if they die before returning to China, have their bones sent back to the native village for burial. Many Chinese Americans maintain practices related to ancestral worship in the home or at public occasions by burning incense, paper money and candles, and providing food or other necessities for the afterlife on alter tables at home or at gravesites.

Holidays and special events:

Lunar New Year (varies with the lunar calendar, usually late January to mid-February) is the most important holiday. It is celebrated by parades in both Chinatowns, family banquets, eating special foods, and dissemination of "red" envelopes filled with cash or "lucky money" from the older generation to children or unmarried adults. For all ages, occupations and regional groups, the New Year ranks as the premier celebration. By New Year's Day, debtors are supposed to settle their accounts. Everyone, especially children, tries to wear new clothes especially in the good luck color, red. Households are not supposed to cook on New Year's Day because it can bring bad luck. Traditional households begin New Year's preparation about a month earlier. On New Year's Day, traditional beliefs include how people should be ready to receive guests and celebrate the day; one must not engage in any housekeeping (if you sweep, you might sweep out the good fortune) like cleaning house, lighting fires or pouring water. Fragrant candles are lit

Parents who travel a lot to Asia, leave 'parachute kids' here with friends and relatives.

and, in their newest finery, people entertain guests. Mahjong is a popular pastime among the women, while the more devout go to temples. Children and their fathers might go out to a public celebration or movie. Businesses shut down for several days.

August Moon Festival celebrates the harvest and full moon of the eighth lunar month. It is celebrated by sharing moon cakes with friends and families. On special birthdays, at age 70 or 80, children honor their parents by hosting banquets to acknowledge their family lineage. Chingming/Ghost Festival (usually April) marks the coming of spring and honors those who have passed away. People visit gravesites, bringing special foods, and gravesites are swept, pruned, and maintained.

Foods for special occasions:

At New Year's Chinese traditionally eat *jaozi* (meat and vegetable dumplings); whole chickens, ducks and pigs in soy sauce; glutinous rice flour dumplings; *niangao* (steamed cake made from glutinous rice flour and brown sugar); fresh whole fish; special vegetarian dishes with symbolic foods, pig's knuckles; and finally, tangerines and oranges, which symbolize good luck and may be given as gifts. At the month-old baby anniversary, hard-boiled eggs, dyed red, are given away. On special birthdays fresh noodles are served long and uncut (the longer the noodles, the longer the life), as are pastry peaches symbolizing longevity. For August Moon, relatives and friends exchange moon cakes filled with black bean paste, fruits with meats and nuts, yellow bean paste or crushed lotus seeds and nuts, surrounding a center of salted cooked duck's egg. For Chingming/Ghost Festival, cold dumplings, cooked red lotus root, whole chickens, barbecued pork, rice wine and other special foods are arranged at gravesites, then sometimes eaten by relatives.

Dietary restrictions:

Devout Buddhists are vegetarians. Some Chinese, like other Asian Americans, have a lactose intolerance.

Names:

Most Chinese Americans who were born here have Western first names, though they may also be given a Chinese name to be used by family and close friends. That name may be revealed at the one-month anniversary. Studies show the most popular practice for Chinese Americans is for infants to have two Western given names. There are only 100 Chinese surnames. Common ones are Chan, Moy, Liu, Ong and Wong. Early immigrants often joined name societies, which were very powerful. After the 1960s, when many more Chinese began arriving, people tended to join societies based on region or dialect instead.

Major issues for community:

Issues of common concern include: future policies of the People's Republic of China and how they will affect Hong Kong and Taiwan in particular, and impact on reunification of families; how to build community, including in enclaves like Chinatown, to serve a wide range of residents and business interests; how to forge unity and

In recent citywide elections, estimated turnout in Chinatown was less than 10%.

a "Chinese American identity" among Asia-born and American-born Chinese in the U.S.; reunification of families; and U.S. immigration policies. Beyond that, issues vary by circumstance and class.

For recent inner-city immigrants, the primary issues are economic survival and maintaining their families. Common concerns for those immigrants, refugees, or residents from lower socioeconomic backgrounds and the "working poor" include: affordable housing, unemployment, underemployment, linguistic isolation, lack of English proficiency. They also worry about access to basic services like health care, quality education for their children, child care, elderly care, and maintaining intergenerational households. Those in impoverished neighborhoods face daily survival, street crime and security for their families.

For ethnic Chinese from privileged or professional backgrounds, issues include the glass ceiling; finding jobs commensurate with their education and experience; attaining certification in their profession; retention of ethnic pride and heritage, especially among the second generation in white-dominated neighborhoods; developing schools for heritage, language and cultural training; intergenerational conflicts; upward mobility; political empowerment; and civil rights. Overall, given the rapidly changing demographics of the Chinese American population and widening diversity, a dominant issue focuses on how to promote Chinese American unity or coalitions. Is building "community" or solidarity a realistic goal when Chinese Americans are so dispersed by residence, socioeconomic status, dialect, generation, education, occupation, nativity, homeland and local politics, and lifestyle preferences?

Political participation:

Local politicians and the politically connected say there is limited active participation among first-generation Chinese immigrants. In a recent citywide election, estimates for the Chinatown voter turnout was less than 10%. The overwhelming perception is that they are focused on survival and acculturation. If anything, they are more involved in homeland issues. Research shows Asian Americans in general have the highest naturalization rates, but extremely low voter-registration rates. That seems to change over time as they become more acculturated. The lack of political clout in the Chinese American community was particularly evident during the 1992 congressional remap. Both Democrats and Republicans were eager to maintain three strong African American districts and to create the strongest possible Latino district. Chinatown was used to help form the Latino district. In the recent decade however, more nonprofits have formed to advocate for community empowerment particularly in Chicago Chinatown.

The Coalition for a Better Chinese American Community (CBCAC) was launched specifically to allow immigrant & other minority communities to have a fuller voice in government, increase voter registration and to make elected officials accountable to communities like Chinatown. CBCAC played a critical role in lobbying for the passage of the Illinois Voting Rights Act of 2011 which kept communities of interest from being divided. Leaders of the Chinatown-based CBCAC wanted to keep their voting power from being diluted when Chinatown has been divided into four state rep districts, three state senate and three congressional districts. Questions remain whether the new legislation will help empower communities like Chinatown to elect their own officials or continue their reliance on mainstream officials to lobby for Chinatown's progress. With Chinese widely dispersed in the suburbs, only Chinese American candidates with broad appeal to mainstream voters would be viable political candidates winning local elections.

Links to homeland:

If they have immediate family there, Chinese Americans probably visit China as often as possible, and some parents here send their children back to Asia for the summer, especially for language training and retention. Financial support, especially for parents and the elderly, is common and part of the tradition of filial piety. Business with the homeland and Asia-based enterprises has been evident.

Special health concerns:

Chinese Americans, like other Asian Americans, face both health problems and disparities in treatment. For Asian Americans and Pacific Islanders, the leading cause of death is cancer, followed by heart disease and stroke. Although data by ethnicity is not available, with Chinese Americans being the largest AAPI group, generalizations can be made about the group. Chinese Americans represent a higher proportion of chronic Hepatitis B and tuberculosis cases. Chinese American women have almost double the rate of non-compliance with screening guidelines for cervical, breast and colorectal cancer compared with the average. A recent study showed that Asian Americans were more likely than whites to die in hospitals after having a heart attack.

Access to health care remains a major issue. Health disparities could be the result of language barriers and other forms of institutionalized discrimination. Such access is highly correlated with the availability of a linguistically and culturally proficient health-care workforce. Many new immigrants speak dialects other than the official Mandarin language. Since most of the newly arrived immigrants and refugees are linguistically dependent on enclaves like Chinatown, if providers are not available in such areas, these patients will not receive the preventive and emergency care needed. Moreover, racial discrimination has been proven to be a key risk factor for stress. Chinese Americans are among the top three Asian groups reporting perceived discrimination. Another factor influencing health is neighborhood safety, stability and cohesion. Among all Asian groups, Chinese have the lowest rates of strongly agreeing that people in their neighborhood know each other, reflecting lower social interaction.

Finally, mental health disparities are of growing concern. Chinese Americans, like other Asian Americans, tend not to access mental health treatment given the strong stigma related to mental illness. Popularly stereotyped as "model minorities," Chinese Americans may be misdiagnosed as problem-free because of their success image. Access to the mental health care system is further limited by the shortage of mental-health providers with appropriate linguistic and cultural competencies. Chinese like other Asian Americans are reluctant to divulge problems to outsiders. Chinese culture traditionally views physical and psychological problems to be highly interconnected, which also deters seeking counseling or therapy.

Asian American women, particularly the elderly, have higher rates of suicide than other groups. While suicide may be in conflict with some Chinese religions, it is condoned by traditional thinking if it protects the family from shame and disgrace. A growing area of concern is the number of Asian American students attempting suicide. Recent studies point to the disproportionate numbers of Chinese and Asian American students attending "elite" institutions who report having lower levels of "self-efficacy and self-esteem." Stereotyped as the "whiz kids" or "model students," many Asian American students experience significant pressure to be high academic achievers and may be at higher risk for depression and suicide.

By Dr. Yvonne Lau, Director of Program Development and Outreach & the Chinese Language Academy, DePaul University, Department of Modern Languages.

CROATIAN AMERICANS

Chicago population:
*4,661 (first ancestry)

Metro area population:
*27,823 (first ancestry)
34,904 (first, multiple ancestry)

Foreign-born:
12% in metro

Another 5,590 in Chicago and 14,802 in metro checked off Yugoslavian. A significant but undetermined number of these would be Croatians.

Demographics:

In the greater metro area 91% have a high school diploma and 36% a college degree or higher. Median household income is $67,848 and 40% are in a management or professional job. Some 82% speak English only, while 18% speak another language at home. Individuals living in poverty are 4.5%. Traditional Croatian

Between 1880 and 1914 up to 600,000 Croatians immigrated to America.

neighborhoods on Chicago's South Side essentially no longer exist. Many Croatians have relocated to the suburbs, especially to the north and northwest, where they like to construct their own homes with ample space for growing fruit and vegetable gardens.

(Ed. note: Population figures for only or first ancestry named are from the Census Bureau's American Community Survey 2008-10. Other data come from the 2007-09 ACS. Croatian leaders here say the number is much higher, based on accounts from churches and institutions in the community.)

Historical background:

Starting in the 1600s, Croatian ships traveled with some regularity from Dubrovnik and other Croatian ports to trading centers in North and Spanish America. Those traveling on these ships were not just sailors but also missionaries, merchants, craftsmen and adventurers.

The first well-known Croat in the Chicago area arrived in the late 1830s. This was Fr. Josip Kundek, the first Vicar General of the Vincennes Diocese, which at that time comprised the entire state of Indiana and most of Illinois. Fr. Kundek was instrumental in establishing several cities and the St. Meinrad Abbey in Indiana (1854). His missionary work took him as far as the Chicago area, then a wild and trackless land with only a small settlement around Fort Dearborn. Some Croatian settlers were in Chicago by 1860, but the great surge of Croatian immigrants came to Lake Michigan's shores in the 1880s. The first Croatian-language newspaper (Croatian Dawn), was published on Aug. 4, 1892, by Janko Kovacevic, who came to America in 1890. Only two months later, on Oct. 21, Nikola Polic began a second Croatian newspaper, entitled Chicago.

Between 1880 and 1914 up to 600,000 Croatians immigrated to America. Finding themselves without any socioeconomic security here, they started organizing their own fraternal associations in Chicago in 1892. At the beginning of the 20th century, there were about 20,000 Croats in Chicago, according to the city's Croatian newspapers. The massive immigration continued, so the number of Croatians in metropolitan Chicago could have been as great as 70,000 by the late 1920s.

The Quota Law of 1921 greatly restricted further immigration. When WWI and the forced inclusion of Croatia, Bosnia and Herzegovina into the dictatorial Yugoslav Kingdom had extinguished all hopes of Croatian immigrants returning to their homeland, they started bringing wives and children here and permanently establishing

Beginning in 1900, Croatians established Catholic parishes where they lived in large numbers.

their families in America. Many children were born here as well. A case study of the Croatian Ethnic Institute indicates that between 1914 and 1925 a total of 1,644 children were baptized in Sacred Heart Croatian Parish in South Chicago and 1,860 at St. Jerome's Church.

Beginning in 1900, Croatians established Croatian Catholic parishes in areas where they already lived in large numbers; and new immigrants were most likely to settle where the parishes were. Thus were established: the "Western Colony" around Holy Trinity Church, 1850 S. Throop St., the "Dalmatian Colony" around St. Jerome's Church (2823 S. Princeton Ave.), the "Southern Colony" around Sacred Heart Church (2846 E. 96th St.), "Sixtieth Street" settlement near Assumption of B.V.M. Croatian Church (6001 S. Marshfield Ave.) and the "Zumberak Colony" around the Croatian Byzantine Catholic Church (3048 S. Central Park). The Croatian-language parishes not only addressed the faith, language and solidarity among Croats, but also were catalysts for adapting to the new homeland, spreading American patriotism through the parish schools and many parish societies. This was particularly expressed when America needed it most — during the two World Wars. From one parish alone, for example (Sacred Heart in South Chicago), 707 men and women served in WWII, 21 of whom gave their lives for America.

WWII and the subsequent occupation of Croatia, Bosnia and Herzegovina by communist Yugoslavia was a terrible shock to American Croats. Practically everyone lost family members or friends in the war. During and immediately after the war, some 250,000 Croatians succeeded in escaping to other Western countries. Those who escaped often waited years in refugee camps until they were accepted overseas. Another 405,000 Croatians left or were driven out during the 45-year reign of Yugoslav communism from 1945-90. An estimated 20,000 came to the greater Chicago area. Among them were a considerable number with university degrees and training in medicine, electrical engineering, toolmaking, architecture, manufacturing, and all fields of the humanities. The Croatian parishes, and especially the Croatian Franciscan Monastery in Chicago (4851 S. Drexel Blvd.), invested enormous efforts caring for the new immigrants, obtaining employment for them and introducing them to the American way of life.

Current migration patterns:

The outbreak of the war against Croatia and Bosnia and Herzegovina in 1991-92 created millions of refugees and displaced persons. In December 1992, Croatia was caring for 663,000 displaced persons and refugees, mostly Muslims and Croats. Hundreds of thousands of others were accepted by Germany, Austria, Switzerland, Hungary and other European countries, and relatively few by the U.S. Newcomers from Croatia and Bosnia and Herzegovina during the 1990s, thus far probably total about 1,000 in Chicago, mostly displaced families and young individuals.

Language:

The Croatian language is written with the Latin alphabet. For the most part, third and later generations of Croatian Americans do not speak Croatian, though in recent years adults in these groups have shown a growing interest in learning the language.

Religion:

More than 95% of Croatians came to the United States as Roman Catholics.

Important traditions:

Family values and religious education are strong traditions among Croatians. Baptism, confirmation, first communion and marriage are the central family celebrations, often attended by many relatives and friends.

Croatians here celebrate their freedom from communism and from Yugoslavia on May 30.

Namesdays or the feast days of the personal patron saints also are celebrated. American Croats gather in large numbers in their churches for prayers and Masses for the deceased. Few Croatians enter marriage outside the Church and divorce is relatively uncommon.

Holidays and special events:

Christmas, Easter, the Assumption of Mary and New Year's Day are celebrated as major religious, family and community feasts. In addition to American national holidays, American Croatians celebrate their freedom from communism and from Yugoslavia in 1990 on Croatian Independence Day (May 30). Each year on Assumption Day (Aug. 15), Chicago Croatians enjoy a large traditional celebration and procession through the streets at St. Jerome's Church, 2823 S. Princeton Ave.

Foods for special occasions:

Coming from a country that is at once Central European, Adriatic-Mediterranean, and Pannonian, American Croatians brought with them to America a very diverse and rich culinary tradition. The Croatian diet is built around fresh fruits and vegetables; thick, rich soups; ragouts and stews; sausage and sour cabbage; a variety of meat- and rice-stuffed vegetables; and a selection of grilled meats and fish. No Christmas celebration would be complete without *pecenka* (a whole roast piglet) and no Easter without *peceno janje* (a young lamb roasted over live coals and served with green onions and homemade whole wheat brown bread). The blessing of food at Easter is a tradition Croatian Americans value highly. On Holy Saturday they prepare and bring to church baskets containing homemade bread, *pisanice* (decorated eggs), onions, ham and various pastries. The women compete to make the nicest cloths, with embroidery and needlepoint, to cover the baskets. Before the *Paschal* (Easter) meal, people must first taste some of the blessed food.

Croatian culinary creativity is best expressed in pastries and sweets, as they have been enamored with breads and pastries for centuries. Among the most distinctive pastries are *savijaca* (various fillings in layers of flaky pastry), *torta* (baked in layers, filled with creams and glazes), puff pastries, *pita* (a crumbly shortcake filled with fruits, almonds, walnuts, meat, cheese, potatoes or vegetables), *pokladnice* (light round yeast cakes filled with jam, fried and served warm), *orehnmjaca* and *makovnjaca*. The latter two are the famous Croatian coffee-cake rolls filled with walnuts or poppy seeds, favorites for dessert or with coffee.

Dietary restrictions:

Except for days of religious fasting, there are no dietary restrictions.

Names:

First names are most often saints' names from the Church calendar, or are taken from original national documents of the Croatian Kingdom from the seventh through the 10th centuries. Common Croatian national names are Tomislav, Jelena, Branimir, Ljubomir and Zvonimir, while the saints' names commonly given include Ivan, Ante, Marija, Ana and Josip. Family names often are derived from the name of a paternal or maternal ancestor, formed by adding a suffix to the first name: Tomislavic, Ivanic, Marijic, Josipovic. (The suffix "ic" is only one of some 430 possible variants and "c" is pronounced like the "t" in "future").

Major issues for community:

The Census Bureau method of presenting the Croatian language as Serbo-Croatian, and Croatian ancestry as Yugoslavian, are experienced by the American Croats as injustice and injury, especially after Yugoslavia waged war in 1991-95 against Croatia and Bosnia and Herzegovina and millions of people experienced the horrors of "ethnic cleansing."

Political participation:

Politics among Croatian Americans has always been a two-way street: Croatians have strong feelings about their homeland, yet this has neither prevented them from becoming U.S. citizens nor kept them from voting or serving in the U.S. armed forces. Tens of thousands served in both World Wars, and hundreds were killed in action. A long list of American Croatians have been awarded Presidential citations, victory medals and ribbons with multiple battle stars; and at least four have won the Congressional Medal of Honor. Croatian Americans, whether they are Democrats or Republicans, are most likely to support the American government that has a good relationship with Croatia. Public opinion about America in Croatia seems to be directly influenced by the American Croats. A survey in Croatia conducted in 1994 by the U.S. Information Agency showed opinion of the U.S. in Croatia is exceedingly positive, more so than anywhere else in the region, including Western Europe.

Links to homeland:

American Croatians, along with those in their native homeland, welcomed the renewal of Croatia's independence and democracy in 1990 with great enthusiasm. Yugoslavia — both the royal and the communist — was for Croatians a state in which their human and civil rights were suppressed: freedom of thought, speech and the press, the right to their language and national identity. Croatians generally didn't feel Yugoslavia was their country. For these reasons, receiving U.S. citizenship and a passport, especially for Croatians who fled from Yugoslavia, was a great experience because by their own choice they were able to be citizens of an independent and free nation for the first time.

Following the re-establishment of a free and independent Croatia, many American Croats wanted to have Croatian citizenship as well, so that they could feel comfortable in both homelands. During the war against Croatia and Bosnia and Herzegovina (1991-95), all the Croatian parishes, fraternal organizations and societies in the U.S. collected and sent humanitarian and financial aid in abundance. American Croatians fully supported the initiative and leading role of the U.S. in the peace process in Croatia and Bosnia and Herzegovina, especially the Washington and Dayton agreements, and they anticipated even stronger involvement by the U.S. in rebuilding those countries and enabling the people driven out to return to their homes.

By Ljubo Krasic, Director of the Croatian Ethnic Institute in Chicago.

CUBAN AMERICANS

Chicago population:
8,331 (Cubans alone)

Metro population:
20,663 (Cubans alone)

Foreign-born:
40% in metro

Demographics:

Cubans are among the most assimilated Hispanics and live all over the metropolitan area. They do not form clusters or Latino neighborhoods as is the case with some other ethnic groups. Median household income in the greater metro area is $63,616, higher than for other Hispanic groups. They are well educated, with 82% in the metro

Cubans are among the most assimilated Hispanics and live all over the metro area.

area having a high school diploma, 40% a bachelor's degree and 17% a graduate or professional degree.

Nearly 40% work in managerial or professional jobs. In the metro area, 21% say they speak English "less than well" and 13% live in poverty. It is believed that Cubans (especially second-generation and those living outside the Miami metropolitan area) tend to out-marry at a higher rate than other Hispanics.

(Ed. note: While total population figures are from the 2010 Census, other demographic data come from the 2007-09 Census Bureau American Community Survey.)

Historical background:

Most Cubans came to Chicago after 1959, in the aftermath of Fidel Castro's successful revolution. In 1960 there were fewer than 2,500 Cubans in Chicago. From 1959-73 an estimated 20,000 came to the area. Fleeing as political refugees, they came to Chicago lured by job opportunities, financial aid and resettlement programs provided by the U.S. government, local churches and other private agencies.

The first wave (1960-62) included many professionals, such as doctors, dentists, lawyers, accountants and teachers. The first Cubans tended to live together in the same neighborhoods, mostly in Edgewater, Uptown and Logan Square. The second wave (1966-73) coincided with the "freedom flights," that let Cubans reunite with their families in the United States. Because of stiffer exit regulations in Cuba, another hiatus in direct immigration occurred from 1973-80. But during this period, many Cubans came here from third countries, especially Spain.

In 1980 a third wave was composed mostly of those who came in the Mariel boatlift. Some had relatives in Chicago, some did not. Many in this and the next wave were single men in their 20s.

The fourth wave comprised those coming from Guantanamo, often with help from Catholic Charities. Since 1980, Cubans who have come to Chicago tended to be less educated and younger than those who arrived earlier. As a whole, they have not adapted as well or as quickly as those who came in the '60s or '70s. But still there are many success stories among these late-comers. The new arrivals tend to live on the North Side, especially in Logan Square. As they became more assimilated, Cubans moved to the suburbs. The fifth and last wave are those, mostly young, who came and settled in Chicago for professional reasons. Some came as students to the local universities. Many others moved to the north and northwest suburbs. Most are fluent in English, and many are second-generation Cubans who find Chicago more attractive than the Miami area, where they came from.

Current migration patterns:

From 1990-94, about 350 Cubans arrived legally in the Chicago area. Some were *balseros* (boat people) who were picked by the U.S. Coast Guard and later transferred to Guantanamo or Panama. Lately, because of stiffer immigration guidelines (in both Cuba and the United States), some undocumented Cubans are coming to Chicago from Mexico, Central America and other Spanish-speaking countries, but as with any illegal flow,

Most Cuban Americans are now U.S. citizens and less than 20% would return there.

numbers are difficult to obtain. There also is some outmigration. Many Cubans, including retirees, have left Chicago for the Miami area, where they owned real estate before they left Chicago. Since 1994 U.S. laws have not considered Cubans political refugees, so the last wave gets fewer benefits.

During the Obama administration, travel restrictions to and from Cuba were eased. More Cuban Americans in Chicago travel to Cuba directly and take more money and gifts to their relatives than ever before. Cubans living in the Island visit Chicago more often and for longer periods of time than in years past. Also Chicago is a must stop for Cuban artists, musicians and intellectuals who are allowed to visit the U.S. with more frequency.

Language:

Cubans speak Spanish with a marked Caribbean accent. Many second-generation Cubans speak Spanglish (a mixture of English and Spanish). Many older Cubans incorporate Anglicisms into their everyday language as well.

Religion:

Cuban Americans in Chicago are predominantly Roman Catholic, but some are Baptist, Methodist, Assembly of God or Pentecostal. A sizable number of Cubans are Jehovah's Witnesses, and many others practice *Santeria*, a mix of African religion and Roman Catholicism.

Important traditions:

Many older Cubans in Chicago celebrate their saint names, act as chaperones for their daughters, and encourage unmarried children of both sexes to live at home. They celebrate girls coming of age at 15, not as elaborately as Mexican Americans but with close family and friends. Older Cuban men like to play dominoes and women play Bingo and Lotto.

Holidays and special events:

Many Cubans in Chicago celebrate the birth of José Marti on Jan. 28 by attending civic events. Marti was a patriot in the Spanish Civil War and leader in exile who was killed when he returned to Cuba. They also observe the Feast of Our Lady of Charity, patroness of Cuba, Sept. 8 by attending a Mass at St. Ita's Church, where the main celebrant is usually a Cuban priest from Miami. The Birth of the Cuban Republic is observed May 20. Most Cubans celebrate Catholic religious holidays such as Christmas and New Year. In Chicago, Cuban American children generally receive their Christmas toys Dec. 25. The tradition back in Cuba is to get gifts Jan. 6, the Feast of Epiphany. Most Cuban Americans in Chicago also celebrate American traditions and holidays such as Thanksgiving and July 4. Cubans who practice Santeria celebrate the feasts of St. Barbara (Dec. 4) and St. Lazarus (Dec. 17), two Catholic saints who are worshipped as *orishas* (African deities).

Foods for special occasions:

On *Nochebuena* (Christmas Eve) and on special occasions such as marriages, baptisms, celebrations for 15-year-old girls and national holidays, many Cuban Americans celebrate with native dishes. These may

A majority of Cuban Americans now favor lifting the U.S.-imposed embargo.

include, but are not limited to, *lechon asado* (pork roast), *moros y cirstianos* (rice mixed with beans), *ropa vieja* (shredded beef), *boliche* (pot roast) or *pollo asado* (roast chicken). Popular staples are *platanos fritos* (fried plantains), and the native roots *malanga* and *yucca*. For dessert they serve *flan* (custard), *arroz con leche* (rice pudding), or *natilla* (egg pudding), and Espresso coffee.

Names:

Cubans, like most Hispanics, have two surnames and many have hyphenated last names. Married women keep their maiden name and add to it their husband's last name. Common first names for males are José, Juan, Luis, Carlos, Manuel, Alberto and Julio. Popular women's names are María, Carmen, Lourdes, Josefa, Caridad, Mercedes, Barbara and Teresa. It is common for men to have two first names, like Juan Carlos, and women also, as in Ana María.

Major issues for community:

Cuban Americans rally around the issues of human rights, the U.S. embargo of Cuba and the Island political system. Many Chicago Cubans pay attention to other issues, such as unemployment, discrimination, housing, political empowerment, education and health care.

Political participation:

Cuban American activists have lobbied Illinois politicians to help enact embargo laws and other regulations that would shorten the Castro regime. Most popular political and civic organizations have been — and in many cases still are — local chapters of national Cuban American organizations such as the Cuban American National Foundation, La Junta Patriótica Cubana and Cuba Independiente y Democratica. Most Cuban Americans vote in local elections and some prominent residents have been appointed to governmental commissions and boards. Professionals with the most political influence in the city include doctors, lawyers, teachers and those in media and marketing. Many Cuban Americans are leery of government programs because they failed to serve their needs back home.

In the 2000s Cuban Americans have softened their stand on the U.S.-imposed Cuban embargo. Now, a majority favor the lifting of the embargo. During the Clinton presidency Cuban Americans became very vocal in favor of retaining a boy (Elián) in the United States, against the wishes of his father, who is a Cuban resident. In the last presidential election, most Miami-area Cubans voted for Barack Obama.

Links to homeland:

Most Cubans have become American citizens and relatively few — no more than 20% —would return to Cuba should the political climate change there. Many have gone back to visit family, however. They also send them money, medicine and clothes regularly. Cuban Americans in Chicago communicate with their families in Cuba by telephone rather than by mail, as there is no direct mail service between Cuba and the United States.

Special health concerns:

Cuban Americans do not enjoy as good health as non-Hispanic whites, but in general they fare better than other Latinos in the USA. For example, they are less likely to die in an accident than Mexican Americans. Facing illness, some Cuban Americans will turn to Santeria (a form of voodoo) and medicinal herbs. The leading cause of death among Cuban Americans is coronary heart disease, at a comparable rate to non-Hispanic whites. Many Cubans are overweight, smoke cigarettes and suffer from Type 2 diabetes. Frequent intake of eggs, pork and beef contribute to an increase in cholesterol levels among Cuban Americans.

By Dr. Jorge Rodriguez-Florido, Professor of Spanish at Chicago State University, author of "El lenguaje en la obra literaria" and two books of Spanish poetry.

CZECH AMERICANS

Chicago population:
*6,610 (first ancestry)

Metro population:
*60,129 (first ancestry)
112,429 (first, multiple ancestries)

Foreign-born:
2.7% in metro

In addition to those who reported Czech ancestry, 1,196 in Chicago and 10,322 in the whole metro area gave Czechoslovakian as their first ancestry. It is impossible to tell how many of these are Czechs and how many Slovaks, a distinction that became more important with the breakup of the country into the Czech and Slovak republics.

Demographics:

The overwhelming majority of Czech Americans now live in the suburbs. Though people of Czech ancestry are quite spread out, some favorite suburbs include North Riverside, Stickney, Brookfield, Riverside and Hinsdale. In the city, many live on the Southwest Side in places like Garfield Ridge, West Elsdon, West Lawn, Gage

Early settlers lived by Pulaski and Foster, site of the 1877 Bohemian National Cemetery.

Park, Ashburn and South Lawndale, and most recently on the North and Northwest Sides. In the greater metro area, 95% have high school diplomas, 40% a bachelor's degree or higher and 16% a graduate or professional degree. Only about 1% say they do not speak English very well. Nearly 45% have management or professional jobs. Median household income is $70,754, about $10,000 above average. Less than 4% live in poverty.

(Ed. note: Overall population numbers for Czech first ancestry are from the 2008-10 Census Bureau American Community Survey, as are numbers of those who listed Czechoslovakian. Other Czech data come from the 2007-09 ACS.)

Historical background:

Immigration of the Czech people to the U.S. dates back to 1640. The 1730s brought the Moravian brethren, a religious community. Hundreds of thousands of Czechs came to America in the later decades of the 19th century and the early 20th century. Both of these large migrations brought Czech people to Illinois. Manufacturing and other jobs attracted them to the Chicago area. Mass immigration occurred because of political persecution in the Austrian Empire and the revolutionary events of 1848. Settlers were concentrated in the manufacturing belt of the East and Midwest states. Mines, steel mills, factories, business, railroads, farming and construction were large draws for the immigrant population. Many who came at that time were farmers or laborers. The early settlers in Chicago lived around Pulaski and Foster, site of the Bohemian National Cemetery, founded in 1877. A significant number entered the banking and savings-and-loan field, which for this very thrift-oriented people proved a successful venture.

Other major immigration waves followed, because of political persecution and events in 1938 (Nazi invasion), 1948 (communist government) and 1968 (Soviet invasion). These political refugees often were highly educated professionals, though many had to take work other than their education dictated. Many Czechs were entrepreneurial and opened businesses such as mortuaries, retail shops, contracting firms and restaurants. Although various other immigrant groups tended to associate only with their own counterparts, many also did business with those of Czech heritage. Fraternal, religious, social and cultural organizations were formed over the years, some splitting onto multiple groups, others merging to form larger, stronger groups.

By the 1930s and '40s, the Czech settlements were more concentrated in Pilsen and what is now known as Little Village. The 1950s and '60s moved the Czech concentration farther out into areas such as Cicero, Berwyn, Riverside and North Riverside. LaGrange Park, Westchester, Downers Grove and Hinsdale soon followed. There has been a definite westward pattern, generally staying between Roosevelt and 39th Street. In the mid-

Moravians, from the eastern half of the Czech lands, are predominantly Catholic.

1990s, the Bohemian Home for the Aged, now known as Tabor Hills, moved from the city to the west end of Naperville, an area increasingly central to the Czech population.

Current migration patterns:

The Velvet Revolution that ended communism in 1989 brought some limited immigration. In many cases this represented the migration of family members who had been left behind. Current immigration is more sparse, mostly because Czechs now have the freedom to come and go. In recent years, those who have come to America tended to settle on the Northwest Side of the city, where they mixed and worked more in the Polish community than mixing with earlier Czech groups. Some who came as visitors or students and overstayed their visas have more recently either sought legal status or, if they could not survive the economic downturn, returned to the homeland.

Religion:

Moravians, from the eastern half of the Czech lands, are predominantly Catholic. Czechs also may be Protestant (Hussites) or rationalists, who often use the term "Freethinkers." In the case of the latter group, fraternal organizations such as CSA Fraternal Life or Masonic orders often filled the sociological role of a church community.

Language:

Czech. Some Saturday language schools for children still function in the area; one is Catholic. Several organizations offer adult language education. The recent emigres have utilized space in a former "Freethinker Czech School" to start preschools and alternative children's Czech language schools specifically designed to keep their children fluent in their native tongue in anticipation of either a return to the homeland, or for extended stays when families visit and enroll their children in schools in the Czech Republic.

Important traditions:

In addition to retaining language, important traditions include music, physical fitness, dance and folklore. The Sokol gymnastics organizations operate several local units in the Chicago area, with the national organization headquartered in Brookfield. They provide gymnastic and calisthenic training and other athletic programs for members, from toddlers to senior citizens. In addition, several folk dance groups meet regularly and perform for many events throughout the year. A Czechoslovak Heritage Museum in Oak Brook features hundreds of artifacts, folk costumes both life-size and on dolls, a library, and archives of thousands of volumes.

Holidays and special events:

St. Joseph Day (March 19) is a celebration for all people named Joseph (a fairly common name among Czechs) that is similar to a birthday. The celebration of such days is a widespread custom, and because certain names often recur in a family, it can become a significant family event. Lidice (June 10) commemorates the annihilation of a small Czech town in 1942 by the Nazis, seeking revenge for the murder of Reinhard Heydrich, Hitler's top operative in Czechoslovakia. All the men were shot, and women and children were sent to concentration camps where most of them died. The town itself was leveled and Hitler tried to wipe the name Lidice from the face of the earth. Instead towns all over the world changed their names to Lidice. Commemorative ceremonies are conducted at a monument in Crest Hill (near Joliet), where a service is held each year on the Sunday closest to June 10.

They are private about politics because historically it was dangerous to be on the wrong side.

St. Wenceslaus (*Svaty Vaclav*), on Sept. 28, is the feast of the patron saint of the Czech people. He is the same one heralded in the Christmas Carol. Czechoslovak Independence Day (Oct. 28) celebrates the founding of the Czechoslovak Republic in 1918. In addition, festivals held annually include Czechoslovak Day Festival (the last Sunday in July); Moravian Day (the fourth weekend in September); the Houby (Mushroom) Festival (the weekend preceding Columbus Day); and Moravian Folk Fest (the first Saturday in November).

Foods for special occasions:

Vanocka (a sweet-egg bread twist with raisins and almonds slivers) is traditionally prepared for Christmas, but also is popular in local bakeries year 'round. *Bochanek* is a round Easter version of the same. The top is usually cut in a cross to symbolize the crucifixion. *Svickova* (a marinated beef dish, with a heavy sour-cream gravy made from the vegetables and marinade used in cooking) is a festival meal, and served with dumplings. Carp is the traditional fish served on Christmas Eve. It was acquired live and allowed to swim in a tub at home to "clean it out." *Kuba* (a mushroom-garlic-barley casserole) also is prepared for Christmas Eve. Roast goose or duck is the traditional Christmas Day dinner, served with sauerkraut or cabbage and dumplings. Lentils are the good luck food for New Year's Day. The round shape resembles coins and therefore they are expected to bring prosperity.

Names:

Given names are often passed from generation to generation. Common male names include Anthony, Frank, George, John, Joseph, Petr (Peter), Vaclav (James), Vladimir and Zdenek. Common female names include Anna, Emily, Jarmila (Geraldine or Jerri), Jirina (Georgina), Marie, Mildred, Vera, Vlasta (Patricia) and Zdenka. Surnames often end in "in," "ak," "ek" "ik," "a," or "ky," but not exclusively.

Major issues for community:

This is a proud community, seldom resorting to any welfare or even unemployment benefits. They are savers and take pride in ownership. Any perceived denial of ownership rights, such as not having power over whom to sell to, is very serious.

Political participation:

The culture is private about its politics because history has shown it can be dangerous to be on the wrong side. Czechs are civic-minded in that they become citizens at the earliest opportunity; and they vote, but do not like to be polled or asked about their politics. There is no strong voting bloc because of the privacy of their beliefs. The people are not stereotypically either Democrats or Republicans, although both parties could count a large following among Czechs. The date and reason for their immigration plays a large part in their individual politics. Refugees from communism tend to be more conservative and Republican. The offspring of turn-of-the-century immigrants who came here for jobs are more likely to be Democrats. Few run for public office unless they are several generations removed from immigration. Famous Czechs who have held public office include: Mayor Anton J. Cermak, Gov. Otto Kerner and State Treasurer and then Comptroller Judy Baar Topinka. Former U.S. Secretary of State Madeleine Albright was born in Czechoslovakia.

Refugees from communism tend to be more conservative and Republican.

Links to homeland:

Only those whose immediate families remain in the old country tend to retain original citizenship for the convenience of travel. Until recently, a visa was required from the Czech government and some feared it would be denied if they gave up Czech citizenship. Some have chosen to retire to the Czech Republic because their U.S. pension dollar goes further. This phenomenon is more common now that the communists are not in power. Visits to the homeland are more common since the "Velvet Revolution" of 1989; previously, many who had fled communism feared returning under that government. Immigrants who came earlier and second- and third-generation Czechs traveled there frequently even during communism. Money was sent home more when the oppressive government allowed no free enterprise. The Czech government now has a Consulate General in Chicago, and offers grants to organizations for cultural and language preservation and promotion.

The Czech Republic is now part of NATO, thanks in part to support of the U.S. and lobbying efforts of Czech Americans. It is also a member of the European Union, but maintains its own currency. Czech American organizations have supported charitable causes in the homeland, Czech/American relations and commerce, and the reconstruction of the Wilson Monument in Prague, as well as other symbols of Czech/ American cooperation.

By Vera A. Wilt, Second Vice President of the Czechoslovak American Congress.

ETHIOPIAN AMERICANS

Chicago population:
2,079

Metro population:
3,280

Foreign-born:
79% in Chicago

Demographics:

Census data on Ethiopians are sparse and unreliable. Community leaders say few filled out the forms, and the sampling for a population so small has a wide margin of error. Estimates based on information from the Department of Health and Human Services, Ethiopian Community Development Council and other sources suggest about 90% of Ethiopians in the metropolitan area live in Chicago, with the biggest concentration in Uptown,

Some Ethiopians migrate out of Chicago to Wheaton, where they still live as a community.

Edgewater and East Rogers Park. The rest live all over the suburbs, with the largest clusters in Elgin and Wheaton. The 2000 Census indicated that 78% had a high school diploma and 32% a college degree. Median household income at that time was $23,958, about $15,000 below the city average. The average household was two people. In the city, 39% were below the poverty line, a very high number compared with other groups. Many Ethiopian Americans work and go to school at the same time. Some 83% spoke another language at home in 2000, but community sources say most Ethiopians speak English well.

(Ed. note: Total population numbers are from the 2008-10 American Community Survey. Other demographic data come from the 2000 Census.)

Historical background:

The Ethiopian population in Chicago before 1980 consisted mainly of students. Because of civil war raging at that time in Ethiopia, 70-80 refugees arrived in Chicago in 1980, mainly from the Sudan and Djibouti refugee camps. Nationally, about 8-10% of these refugees had a college education and most (75-85%) had a high school education; almost all (95%) were young adults in their 20s. Those who came to Chicago lived in Uptown and Edgewater when they first arrived. Many Ethiopians who were here earlier accepted the refugees with open arms and helped make their adjustment easier. Most refugees were young people who lacked transferable skills. And, because of language and cultural barriers, most had menial jobs with no future: washing dishes, keeping house, busing tables.

The 1980 Refugee Act set the ground rules for resettlement of refugees, providing financial, material and educational assistance, including job training. Resettlement agencies helped with cultural adjustment, English as a Second Language, and job training and placement. Refugees also got cash and medical assistance from the federal government through the state. From 1980-92 an estimated 2,000 Ethiopian refugees came to Chicago. From 1985-92 the demographic characteristic of the refugees coming changed from urban to rural and from highly educated to less educated.

Current migration patterns:

Since 1992, resettlement of Ethiopian refugees has declined significantly because of the end of the civil war. The number of people coming to Chicago as legal immigrants (through family reunification, the diversity visa lottery, or as visitors and students changing their status to political asylees) has dramatically increased. About half of the Ethiopian population here probably came after 1990 through these immigration venues. Some came legally but overstayed, and some might not have been granted political asylum so they have undetermined status. The outmigration is balanced by immigration from other cities and states. The number returning home is very insignificant (maybe 25-40 people have returned to Ethiopia since 1991. Those coming since 1991, either as refugees or immigrants, tend to be from urban areas, with at least a high school education. Some Ethiopians migrate out of Chicago to Wheaton, where Ethiopians still live as a community.

It was only about 30 years ago that Ethiopian refugees started to arrive.

Language:

More than 70 languages are spoken in Ethiopia. Most of the refugees, however, speak one or more of the three major languages: Amharic, Tigrigna or Afa Oromo.

Religion:

Earlier refugees were predominantly Christians. Since 1991, the Muslim population has increased moderately. Although Muslims constitute about 35% in Ethiopia, the Muslim immigrant population in Chicago area is only about 15%.

Important traditions:

Extended family relationships, parental control of children, and younger members of the family accepting the authority of elders are traditions dearly held. It is important for children to help their parents in the home without being asked. Children have problems accepting these traditions because of peer influence and the different social values and expectations of the mainstream society. There is intergenerational conflict, with children on one side and parents on the other. Parents want to discipline their children but their way of disciplining may conflict with the law. There is tension in many families, particularly those with teenagers. Parents seem to be nervous and totally unprepared to handle the situation.

Holidays and special events:

The Adwa Victory (March 2) is celebrated each year with a strong sense of patriotism and nationalism. The battle of Adwa was fought between Ethiopia and Italy on March 2, 1896, at Adwa in Tigray, in Northern Ethiopia. At this battle the modern colonial army of Italy was decisively defeated by the Ethiopian peasant army lead by Emperor Minilik II. The outcome of the battle of Adwa shocked the world and gave birth to black and other oppressed peoples' movements around the world against colonialism. The Adwa Centennial was celebrated by Ethiopians, other Africans, and people of African descent around the world, including in Chicago. In Ethiopia it was celebrated with memorial prayers, rallies and patriotic songs that reinforced the need to maintain independence. The Ethiopian New Year falls on Sept. 11 of the Western calendar, except following Ethiopian leap year, when it is Sept. 12. The New Year celebration starts with lighting or burning of *chibo* (candlewood) on New Year's Eve, which continues into an overnight party. On New Year's Day people stay home and prepare food.

In the afternoon, they start the festivities with homemade foods and homemade drinks. It is an eating and partying holiday.

The Ethiopian Christmas is celebrated Jan. 7 of the Western calendar, as in other Eastern Orthodox churches. Christmas is celebrated by playing a mass hockey-like game, baking breads, and drinking homemade beer called *tella*. The game is the major aspect of the celebration. *Gena* is an all-men's game, played by children and adults of all ages. Epiphany is one of the most colorful and highly spirited holidays. It is a celebration in commemoration of the baptism of Christ, observed Jan. 19 in the Western calendar. On the eve of Epiphany, all churches take the arc (a wooden tablet) to a fountain or riverside, accompanied by a huge crowd singing and dancing. The priest and clergy put on their colorful church dresses and slowly accompany the chief priest, who carries the arc on his head. They spend the night near the fountain or riverside. Then, about noon, after prayers and rituals, they proceed back to each church. On Epiphany, women put on their best dresses and the saying goes, "If people do not wear their best dresses on Epiphany, having a dress is of no value."

In the Ethiopian Orthodox, Muslim and Jewish religions, pork is not edible.

Eid-ul-Fittir is celebrated by Muslims at the end of the fasting month of Ramadan. All family members put on newly purchased or clean clothes and go to the mosque for morning holiday prayer. Then they go back home and have lunch with the family. Later in the day, mainly children go around the neighborhood to visit family members and relatives, who give them cash to spend as they wish.

Foods for special occasions:

These include spicy chicken stew with *doro wat* (boiled eggs), *kitfo* (tartar with spices and hot pepper), *injera* (pancake-like bread made of a tiny grain called teff), *dulet* (a kind of steak tartar consisting of liver, stomach and lung as well as brisket that is hot and spicy, sometimes with a small drop of bile for taste), *tella* (home-brewed beer), *tej* (honey wine brewed at home), *katicala* (a home-distilled 80-proof alcoholic beverage), and *kurt* (raw meat, mainly brisket, served with hot spicy pepper).

Dietary restrictions:

In the Ethiopian Orthodox, Muslim and Jewish religions, pork is not edible. Shellfish also is restricted by the three major religions practiced in Ethiopia. During Lent or any fasting season, Ethiopian Christians do not eat meat, dairy products and poultry; they eat cereals and vegetables.

Names:

Most Ethiopian names have a meaning that reflects the circumstances around the time of birth. If someone is born immediately after a close family member dies they call her/him Masresha, which means "compensation." Names usually express the environment and family mood and wishes during the birth of a child. People also are named after a grandfather or mother or friend who has passed away. Other names are simply biblical and koranic. In Christian tradition religious names like Gebre Michael, Gebre Yohannes and Gebre Mariam are common. "Gebre" means servant; Gebre Michael is servant of St. Michael. Except in very few cases, male and female names are made distinct by adding a suffix to the root word of the name. For example "worq" is a root word that means "gold." Adding "neh" makes it male and adding "nesh" makes it female.

Major issues for community:

Access to economic development opportunity, health services, cultural maintenance, and opportunities for cultural expression are the major issues of concern in the community.

Political participation:

The Ethiopian community in Chicago is relatively new and small. It was only about 30 years ago that Ethiopian refugees started to arrive. Participation in political and civic life of the mainstream society is very limited. In recent years the need to participate is acutely felt. In fact, there was a candidate from the Ethiopian community for the last aldermanic election in Chicago. With a feeling of belongingness, political and civic participation follow. There is an increased interest in participation and pursuing the American Dream.

Links to homeland:

Even though the trend is to become naturalized citizens, many maintain their Ethiopian citizenship. Since 1991 no less than 60-70% of Ethiopians have gone back to Ethiopia for visits but almost all have returned here. Nearly all Ethiopians here maintain contact with relatives there. Some family members in Ethiopia absolutely depend on money they receive from relatives in the United States. The majority of Ethiopians here oppose the current Ethiopian government's policies of politicizing ethnicity. Many opposition groups lobby the U.S. government to withdraw its support for the Ethiopian regime. The U.S. is one of the strongest supporters of the current Ethiopian government, which was installed in 1991 with all-around support from the U.S. and other Western powers. The Chicago Ethiopian community has been active with the famine situation in Ethiopia for the past 28 years, raising money to support relief efforts of agencies like UNICEF, World Vision, Oxfam, Save the Children and the Ethiopian Red Cross. Some Ethiopians here do business with Ethiopia and some have small investments there. The community stays informed about developments in Ethiopia through popular websites and online journals, mostly operated in the United States.

Recent arrivals often have significant changes in diet and exercise, harming their health.

Special health concerns:

Access to health services, particularly to health education, is a critical issue facing the community. Generally, new refugee and immigrant families do not have insurance and face great challenges in accessing health care. Financial, language and cultural barriers make them reluctant to ask health-related questions, seek out mainstream services and access benefits or government programs that are available for them. Furthermore, newcomers often have limited access to preventative and early intervention services, and consequently, become vulnerable to disease, including diabetes. According to a 2002 survey by the National Diabetes Education and Prevention Project, 16.7% of the 1,641 African immigrants surveyed were diabetic; Chicago results exceeded this rate at 30.9%. Moreover, complications from diabetes are more prevalent among racial minorities and may include heart disease, stroke, high blood pressure, kidney disease and blindness.

Recent arrivals to the United States often have significant changes in their diet and exercise routines, perhaps doubling their caloric intake and engaging in far less physical work; these lifestyle changes negatively impact their health, and without knowledge of what health-related services are available to them, or assistance in accessing those services, individuals can face life-threatening consequences.

By Erku Yimer, Executive Director of the Ethiopian Community Association.

FILIPINO AMERICANS

Chicago population:
29,664 (Filipino alone)
35,188 (alone or in combination)

Metro population:
109,423 (Filipino alone)

Foreign-born:
69% in metro

Demographics:

In Chicago, Filipinos tend to live on the North and Northwest Sides with concentrations in Albany Park and North Park, though in general they are scattered throughout the metropolitan area. Suburbs with large concentrations are Skokie, Morton Grove, Glendale Heights, Bolingbrook and Darien. Most Filipinos live in Cook County but there are significant numbers in DuPage and Lake counties. In the greater metropolitan area, 95%

After U.S. acquisition of the Philippines, young males began coming here as students.

have a high school diploma, while a relatively high 62% have a bachelor's degree or higher and 9% a graduate or professional degree. About half (51%) are in professional or managerial jobs. Median household income is higher than for most other groups, at $81,981. About 7% in the metro area fall below the poverty line.

(Ed note: Total population numbers are from the 2010 Census. All other statistics come from the Census Bureau's American Community Survey 2007-09.)

Historical background:

Following American acquisition of the Philippines in 1898, young male Filipinos began coming to the Chicago area, first as government-scholarship students designated as *pensionados* or family-supported students and later as self-supporting students who expected to combine attending classes with employment. Brothers, cousins and townmates followed, creating enclaves on the Near West and Near North Sides.
In 1920, the U.S. Census counted 154 Filipinos in Chicago; and in 1940, 1,740. Unofficial estimates put Filipino numbers at approximately 5,000 during the 1930s. Prior to WWII, the typical Filipino in Chicago was a high school graduate with some college who continued studies upon arrival in Chicago. Employment was sought in the service sector. Several hundred worked with the Pullman Company or with the U.S. Post Office. In 1940, among those over the age of 20, Filipinos (men) outnumbered Filipinas (women) 21:1. Ninety percent of marriages were interracial, with most wives American-born daughters of European immigrants.

Until the mid-1930s, Filipinos were classified as "nationals" and permitted unrestricted entry into the United States, but were not eligible for citizenship. The Tydings-McDuffie Act of 1934 promised the Philippines independence after 10 years and limited Filipino immigration to 50 per year. After independence, Filipinos were to be totally barred from entering the United States. In 1946, largely in recognition of their valor during WWII, Filipinos in the U.S. became eligible for naturalized citizenship and the annual quota was raised symbolically from 50 to 100. Between 1952-65, however, most Filipinos came as non-quota immigrants under the family-reunification provisions of the McCarran-Walter Act of 1952.

After passage of the Immigration Act of 1965, Filipino immigration surged. Occupational-preference provisions enabled many professionals, especially nurses, doctors and accountants, to qualify for entry. Over time, however, family reunification became a more significant factor, permitting the chain immigration of extended family units. By 1970, the Filipino population in the Chicago area was 9,497, with more women than men. In 1980, it was 41,283 for the metro area.

Current migration patterns:

Filipinos are the fourth largest group immigrating to the Chicago area (after Mexicans, Poles and Indians). From 1990-94, about 2,500 came each year, totaling 12,370, according to the INS. The 2000 Census estimated 27,874

Until the mid-1930s, Filipinos were permitted unrestricted entry into the U.S.

Filipinos live in the city of Chicago, 54,595 in Cook County, 14,111 in DuPage, and 6,988 in Lake County. Nearly all Filipinos in Illinois are concentrated in the Chicago region.

Language:

Coming from an archipelago of more than 7,000 islands, eight major languages and up to an estimated 121 dialects, Filipino immigrants are commonly multilingual. Depending on their level of education, they typically learn Tagalog — the language of Manila and nearby provinces, which has been designated the Philippine national language and renamed Pilipino — as well as English, which was used in school above the second grade for many years. They also speak the dialect of the locale where they were raised. The eight major languages are Tagalog, Cebuano, Hiligaynon, Ilocano, Bicol, Samareño, Pampango and Pangasinan.

Religion:

Catholics make up about 80% of the Filipino American population. There also are some Protestants and Muslims.

Important traditions:

In their immediate and extended families, Filipinos in the U.S. continue to prize the close family ties, strong family values and religious strength characteristic of Filipino culture. The traditional practice of choosing multiple godparents (*compadrazo* or ritual co-parenthood) for a baby's baptism binds real and fictive kin to the baby's family and is typically expected to provide on-going sustenance. Wedding celebrations, debutante balls and anniversary parties bring together family and friends and further serve to demonstrate a family's social status.

Holidays and special events:

For many years, Rizal Day (Dec. 30) in Chicago was celebrated dedicated to the memory of Dr. Jose P. Rizal (1861-96), a surgeon, novelist, sculptor, poet and linguist who focused national and international attention on Spanish misrule and became the Philippines' national hero. He was executed in Manila by a Spanish firing squad Dec. 30, 1896, at the onset of the movement for Philippine independence. In Chicago,

Rizal Day was commemorated as early as 1905 at the University of Chicago. By the 1930s, festivities were typically co-sponsored by provincial and work-related clubs and included a banquet, "queen" contest and dance at a downtown hotel. Organizational rivalry has produced multiple celebrations in a single year. Today, in the Filipino American communities in the city and suburbs, Rizal's birth on June 19 is celebrated as a public event rather than his death.

Philippine Week events are celebrated before, on and after June 12, to commemorate that date, in 1898, when the Philippines won their independence from Spain. The Philippines became a U.S. colony following the Spanish-American War, and independence from the U.S. was granted July 4, 1946. During Philippine Week and throughout the year, activities include theater, film festivals, talent shows, a parade, a picnic, sports, art exhibits, receptions and grand dinner galas. Filipino Americans are also engaged in multicultural civic programs.

Religious celebrations are prominent in the annual calendar of festivities. In the Philippine tradition, the Christmas season begins on Dec. 16 with a series of pre-dawn Masses (*Misa de Gallo* or *Simbang Gabi*). After the final Mass at midnight Christmas Eve (*Misa de Aquinaldo*), families gather for a joyous midnight supper (*noche buena*), the year's most important dinner. In Chicago, the Simbang Gabi is an evening mass which takes place in many churches.

Filipino food reflects Malay, Islamic, Chinese, Spanish, Mexican and American influences.

The Lenten ceremony (*Salubong*) is followed by Easter Sunday, when statues of the Blessed Virgin, wearing a black shroud of mourning, and of the Risen Christ are carried in a procession. *Flores de Mayo* is a month-long celebration in May dedicated to the Blessed Virgin, whose crowning has been an annual event in Chicago since the 1940s. *Santacruzan*, the rite commemorating the discovery of the true cross, is re-enacted as a religious procession in May with beauty queens dressed as biblical characters. In addition, new immigrants typically celebrate the feast of the patron saint of their town of origin.

Foods for special occasions:

Filipino dishes reflect the historical presence of Malay, Islamic, Chinese, Spanish, Mexican and American influences. One of the oldest is *kinilaw* (fish cooked lightly in vinegar). Traditional main courses include *lechon* (a whole pig roasted over charcoal and hot stones and served with a tangy liver sauce), which was prepared in the pre-Spanish era after the harvest or hunt; *adobo* (a pork, chicken and/or seafood stew cooked in vinegar), which is popularly regarded as the Filipino national dish; *pancit* (noodles cooked with meat and vegetables); *pinakbet* (boiled vegetables and pork seasoned with *bagoong*, a fermented shrimp or fish paste); *kare-kare* (oxtails stewed in peanut sauce); and *kalderetta* (goat stew). Most dishes are served with rice. *Lumpia* resembles the Chinese egg roll; "fresh" lumpia, the Chinese spring roll. *Paella Valenciana* (a melange of meats and seafood), served on special occasions, and *leche flan*, (an egg-custard dessert made in a caramel-lined pan) are Spanish in origin. *Bibingka* (a sweet, sticky rice cake made with coconut milk) and *halo-halo* (a sundae made with sweet beans and strips of sweetened coconut in syrup) are also popular desserts. *Lambanog*, (a coconut wine) and *basi* (a fermented rice wine) are now served as after-dinner liqueurs.

Names:

While some Filipino family names can be considered indigenous — for example, Bacdayan and Macapagel — others derive from the Chinese, such as Cojuangco, Soliongco and Sylianco, or from the Spanish, as in Gonzales,

Alamar and Lopez. The mother's family name usually becomes the child's middle name. A Filipino first name is often the name of the saint celebrated on that person's birthday. Sometimes the firstborn son is given his father's first name. Less typically, all sons are named after their father and distinguished by their order of birth, such as Florentino, Florentino II and Florentino III. Or, all children in a family are given first names starting with the same letter or syllable — as in Arturo, Arlinda and Arleen. Nicknames can shorten a name (Pedro becomes "Pido" and Guillermo, "Mo"); or end in "ing" for a daughter or "oy" for a son (e.g. Benigno becomes "Ninoy"). Or, a nickname might represent an element of character or a physical attribute.

Major issues for community:

Like many other Americans, Filipino Americans struggle to cope with the problems caused by separation and divorce, teenage pregnancy, gang affiliation, disinterest in education and multiple wage-earning. Those who hope to be joined in the U.S. by family members still in the Philippines are concerned about proposed legislation that might restrict immigration. Some Filipino Americans have mobilized to win full pay and veterans benefits for the almost 175,000

Filipinos are the 4th largest group immigrating to the Chicago area.

Philippine Scouts and Philippine Army soldiers who served in the U.S. armed forces in the Pacific during WWII and became eligible for U.S. citizenship in 1990. Locally, Filipino Americans often lament the absence of unity in the community. It is common for new organizations to form quite frequently.

Political participation:

Socioeconomic position, occupational affiliation, and family tradition typically determine the political party affinity of U.S.-born and naturalized Filipino Americans. Most now realize that political power can be achieved only through active civic engagement and have become pro-active in the political process. Two Filipino Americans in Chicago have been elected to serve as judges.

Links to homeland:

Family ties are reinforced through letters and frequent telephone calls, and by money sent to relatives in the Philippines. When returning home to visit relatives, the *balikbayan* fills large boxes with popular name-brand American goods. Many social clubs are named after the Philippine province or town of origin. The latest news from the Philippines is an important feature of local Filipino American newspapers.

Special health concerns:

While Filipino Americans have been shown to have high rates of hypertension, diabetes, TB, breast cancer mortality, lung disease and asthma, compared with other some other ethnic groups, perhaps the largest problem for the community is lack of health awareness and access. Language difficulties, cultural beliefs that rely heavily on traditional medicine and self-healing, and costs all play a role. Lack of insurance is a problem, especially for elderly immigrants not eligible for Medicare. The Filipino American Health Initiative of Chicago was started to increase awareness of the health disparities, intervene and educate the community. It holds free health screenings and classes such as heart-healthy eating.

Original chapter by Dr. Barbara Posadas, then Associate Professor and now CLAS Distinguished Professor of History at Northern Illinois University, and Estrella Alamar, President of the Filipino American Historical Society of Chicago, as well as Justo Alamar, Willi Buhay and Romeo Munoz. Update by Estrella Alamar.

GERMAN AMERICANS

Chicago population:
118,713 (first ancestry)
223,049 (first, multiple ancestries)

Metro population:
991,982 (first ancestry)
1,625,703 (first, multiple ancestries)

Foreign-born:
2.6% in Chicago, 1.5% in metro

Demographics:

Recent Census data show German Americans remain the Chicago area's largest European ethnic group. German Americans are highly educated, with 95% holding high school diplomas, 60% in the city and 42% in the metro area having a college degree, and 24% in the city and 15% in metro with a graduate or professional degree.

German Americans are the Chicago area's largest European ethnic group.

More than half in the city (55%) work in a management or professional job, while 44% in metro do. Median household income is $69,385 in Chicago and $73,843 in metro. About 8% live in poverty in Chicago; 5% do in the greater metro area. In Chicago, seven neighborhoods traditionally have had large concentrations of people of German descent: Beverly, Edison Park, Forest Glen, Jefferson Park, McKinley Park, Montclare and North Center. The German American community is especially strong in the suburbs. German Americans have assimilated readily with Italians, Scandinavians, Poles, French and many other European groups.

(Ed. note: First-ancestry population figures are from the 2008-10 American Community Survey. All other data, including multiple ancestry, come from the 2007-09 ACS.)

Historical background:

German immigration to Chicago started in the 1830s, with some relocating from Pennsylvania. By 1860, there were more than 22,000 Germans in Chicago. Large numbers came in 1849 because of political and economic upheaval at home. They worked in the meatpacking plants, helped build the Michigan-Illinois canal, and entered manufacturing and the building trades. Numerous churches were founded in 1846-80, starting with St. Paul's Evangelical Lutheran and St. Peter's Catholic Church in 1846.

The German population tripled from 1870-1900. There were more than 400,000 by the end of the century, about one-fourth Chicago's population. There was a large community east of the river between Diversey and Devon, much of it clustered around Lincoln Avenue; and smaller settlements were in Hyde Park, South Shore, Humboldt Park and Albany Park. The Orchestral Association, founded in 1891, had a German conductor, Theodore Thomas, and most of its members were German immigrants. Orchestra Hall was built to house that orchestra in 1905. After 1865, German was taught in the public schools. The coming of WWI, however, ended that. After a period of vocal nationalism during the years of American neutrality, German American activities and institutions were dealt a sharp blow when the U.S. entered the war.

Most organizations active today were founded after the last large-scale immigration, in the 1950s. Prior to WWII the immigration pattern mirrored the political, religious and economic struggles in their homeland. After WWII, in the late '40s and particularly the '50s and early '60s, a large percentage of immigrants were the so-called "displaced persons" who fled from the communists or were expelled from their ancestral homes in Hungary, Romania, the former Yugoslavia and Czechoslovakia, Poland and Russia, where they were a large minority. Immigration often was sponsored by American religious organizations, state agencies and commercial enterprises. In most cases initial jobs and lodgings had to be guaranteed by American sponsors. There was virtually no "illegal" immigration.

Current migration patterns:

Current immigration is relatively small, with maybe a couple hundred coming each year. During the Korean and Vietnam War years immigration of young male Germans to the U.S. declined substantially. Also, rapidly improving economic conditions in Germany contributed to a slowdown in emigration. In the '90s the opportunities in Europe, as well as generous fringe and social benefits, kept most young Germans at home. For those already here, a greater degree of affluence has led many German Americans to move to the suburbs, and the traditionally German area in Chicago is now mainly confined to Lincoln Square.

After 1865, German was taught in the public schools. WWI ended that.

Language:

German and, depending on the displaced person's country, they also may speak Hungarian, Romanian, Croatian, Czech or Polish. The German language is spoken mainly by first-generation immigrant families, less by second and later generations.

Religion:

Predominantly Catholic and Lutheran. Also, many American Jews came from Germany.

Important traditions:

Many German customs have become American customs over the generations — such as kindergarten and the Christmas tree. Music is important, with waltzes, operettas and classical music coming from composers that include Mozart, Bach and Hayden. Saengers (singers) societies continue today, with one of the largest having more than 4,000 members across America. There are many Germanic fraternal organizations, some centering on music, others on sports (such as soccer), karnevals and other cultural interests. The word "fest" is one of many German words adopted by Americans as their own.

Holidays and special events:

The Steuben Parade (a Saturday in September) takes place in downtown Chicago, followed by a weekend Germanfest in the old German neighborhood at Lincoln/Leland/Western, with food, music and entertainment. The parade commemorates Gen. Friedrich von Steuben's achievements during the American Revolution. German-American Day (Oct. 6) commemorates the first organized immigration of Germans and is celebrated nationally. Thirteen Mennonite families from Krefeld, Germany, landed on that day in 1683 in Philadelphia and founded Germantown, a few miles away. Karneval (Nov. 11), Oktoberfest and wine festivals are cultural and social events Germans brought with them to America, which have become popular American festivals as well. Main religious holidays for Christians are Easter and Christmas.

Foods for special occasions:

German cuisine is diversified, depending on region, and often is hearty, because so many worked in the fields and needed a substantial diet. Many dishes have become American favorites, including hamburgers, wieners, bratwurst and cutlets. For festive events like Christmas, goose is traditional. On Christmas Eve or Christmas Day, families traditionally enjoy roast goose served with red cabbage and potatoes. Christmas Day is a time to invite friends for traditional German sweets, such as *stollen* (fruit cake), *lebkuchen* (honey cakes) and *pfeffernusse* (spice cookies). *Wienerschnitzel* (veal pounded, seasoned, breaded and deep-fried) and *sauerbraten* (beef marinated in vinegar and spices) are popular dishes, as well as pork shanks with sauerkraut and dumplings.

The word 'fest' is one of many German words adopted by Americans.

Major issues for community:

Nurturing German American heritage, culture and language; and taking a stand against ethnic bigotry and anti-Germanism.

Political participation:

German Americans take their citizenship seriously. Even though they tend to be politically reticent, they are active voters. Involvement in civic and governmental activities are mainly cultural and educational.

Links to homeland:

German American societies, sister-city arrangements and exchange programs all contribute to maintaining links to the ancestral land. There is considerable travel back to Europe, and the German American National Congress facilitates contacts between German and American businesses.

By Ernst Ott, Honorary National President of the German American National Congress.

GREEK AMERICANS

Chicago population:
13,883 (first ancestry)
20,714 (first, multiple ancestries)

Metro area population:
83,822 (first ancestry)
90,461 (first, multiple ancestries)

Foreign-born:
20% in Chicago, 19% in metro

Demographics:

More than six times as many Greeks live in the suburbs as in the city of Chicago. The most popular suburbs for Greeks are: Lincolnwood, South Barrington Hills, Palos Hills, Palos Park, Oak Brook, Niles, Morton Grove, Skokie, Hickory Hills, Mount Prospect, Glenview and Orland Park. The area around the suburbs of Niles, Morton Grove and Glenview has, in recent years, been referred to as "The Greek Triangle," because of a large

The Niles-Morton Grove-Glenview suburban area is referred to as 'The Greek Triangle.'

concentration of Greeks living in the area. Typically, Greek Americans will flock to towns or neighborhoods near a Greek Orthodox Church. Traditionally, Greeks had concentrations in city neighborhoods such as Lincoln Square, Rogers Park and West Ridge on the North Side; Woodlawn, Englewood, South Chicago, Hegewisch, Ashburn and Beverly Hills on the South Side; and Austin on the West Side. Today, the largest numbers are found in Lincoln Square and the surrounding area, plus Norwood Park (Northwest Side), with a growing number in areas like the South Loop. In recent years, with condo and high-rise development in and around Greektown on Halsted Street, plus its great accessibility to downtown and transportation, some Greeks are moving to the Greektown area.

Since 1960, the U.S. Census has reported Greeks as having high educational and income levels, compared with many other immigrant groups. Some 88% of Greek Americans in the greater metro area have a high school diploma; 41% have earned a bachelor's degree, and 16% have a graduate or professional degree. City dwellers hold more advance degrees – 49% graduated from college and 19% hold a graduate or professional degree. Just over 50% of Chicago Greeks are in a management or professional job, while 46% in the wider metro area hold these positions. Median household income for Greeks is $66,117 in the city and $71,098 in the metro area – both figures are significantly higher than the general population. Just 6% in both areas are living in poverty, less than half of those in the general population. In the city of Chicago, 13% of Greeks indicated that they did not speak English "very well." This holds true for 11% of those living in the greater metro area. By 2011, 67% of marriages were between couples of different faiths, according to the Greek Orthodox Archdiocese of America's website on interfaith marriage. When the number of weddings performed outside the Greek Orthodox Church are considered, the rate could be as high as 75%.

(Ed. note: Total first-ancestry population numbers are from the Census Bureau's 2008-10 American Community Survey. Other data are from the 2007-09 ACS.)

Historical background:

Greek immigration to Chicago did not begin in earnest until after the Great Chicago Fire of 1871. Realizing that job opportunities were available in rebuilding the city, young Greek men came to Chicago. Prior to this, only occasional Greek seamen arrived by the way of the Mississippi and Illinois rivers, settling in Chicago and intermarrying with Irish and Italian women. The numbers increased rapidly during the first decade of the 20th century. In 1890 there were only 245 people of Greek birth in Chicago; by 1920 the number had risen to

The Greek Delta (Harrison, Halsted, Blue Island) was displaced by the U of I Chicago campus.

11,546. Greek immigration was primarily a male phenomenon; young boys and men coming to America to escape the extreme poverty in Greece, in the hope of returning with enough money to pay off family debt and provide marriage dowries for their daughters or sisters. It was not until after 1900 that Greek women began to emigrate. Most immigrants to Chicago came from the provinces of Laconia and Arcadia, giving the Greek population of Chicago its Peloponnesian character. The initial illiteracy rate for Greek immigrants was 27%. But because of their strong belief in education, they encouraged schooling for their children, resulting in many of the second and third generations becoming highly educated and entering the professions.

At the turn of the century, Greeks concentrated on the Near West Side, known as the Greek Delta (Halsted, Harrison and Blue Island streets), which emerged as the most prominent and largest Greektown. There also were settlements on the Near North Side at Clark and Kinzie streets and on the South Side in Woodlawn and Pullman. Initially, most Greek immigrants lived in the central city in order to be close to their place of work, especially to the wholesale market area (Fulton and South Water markets), where they had to procure produce for their food-peddling businesses. For more than a half-century the Delta was the site of the main Greek community of Chicago, attaining a Greek population of more than 30,000, until it was displaced by the University of Illinois Chicago campus in the 1960s.

By the late 1920s the Greeks were among the foremost restaurant owners, ice cream manufacturers, and florists, plus fruit, confectionery and vegetable merchants in Chicago. According to the old Chicago Herald and Examiner, they operated more than 10,000 stores — 500 of them in the Loop doing business of over $2 million a day in the 1920s. One-third of the wholesale commission business in Chicago's markets on South Water and Randolph streets, estimated at $250 million annually, was done with Greek-American merchants. With passage of the National Quota Act in the 1920s, Greek immigration to the United States came to virtual standstill.

After WWII a new wave of immigration to the United States took place, with many coming to Chicago under the Displaced Persons Act. This immigration surge was accelerated with the 1965 repeal of the National Quota Act. As a result, the Chicago area received many new Greek immigrants, making it the largest urban Greek population in the world outside of Greece. (Today New York City has the largest Greek-American population.) Greek immigrants never intended to stay. Once enough funds were saved, many returned home. About 40 percent of Greeks who came to America returned to Greece. The devotion to the homeland is reflected by the financial help they sent their families, which between 1919-28 averaged $52 million annually. Those who remained formed a stable and well-organized community, participating in the life of the city. Immigrants continued to arrive through the late 1960s, then began to decrease sharply. By the 1980s, few were arriving here.

Current migration patterns:

Greek immigration to America has virtually stopped. However, this is expected to change now due to the economic crisis in Greece. Greeks in Greece are already seeking jobs and new lives abroad.

Language:

Greek. While most Greek Americans speak English as their native tongue, many second- and third-generation offspring still have a spoken knowledge of Greek. Nevertheless, as future generations of Greek Americans become further removed from the immigrant, the number decreases dramatically. A fair number of Greek Americans from two generations do not speak Greek at all. Immigrants who came to this country in the first half of the 20th century experienced discrimination. Therefore, some wanted their children to assimilate quickly — to focus on learning English (and without an accent) and to be just like everyone else. This resulted in a portion of a generation that did not learn to speak Greek, thus giving birth to another generation that also didn't speak Greek. Some of the children from that latter generation have begun to study Greek as adults. There are seven Greek-American day schools in the Chicago metro area, and most of the area's 20+ Greek churches have an after-school or Saturday program to teach Greek language. Adult programs are growing in popularity — filled by those who didn't learn the language growing up, as well as non-Greeks who are dating or married to a Greek. Thus, the Greek language is still actively taught and widely spoken.

About 40 percent of Greeks who came to America returned to Greece.

Religion:

Greek Americans are overwhelmingly Greek Orthodox. There is a growing number of Greek Americans – due to interethnic and interfaith marriage – who are of other Christian religions, and a very small minority who are Jewish. There are more than 20 Greek Orthodox Churches in the Chicago area. The Greek Orthodox Metropolis of Chicago includes parishes from six states, and the presiding hierarch has the title of Metropolitan.

Important traditions:

For Greek Americans, family is always top priority. It is not unusual to still see multiple generations living in the same household. Families help each other though financial, health and other crises. For older Greek Americans, the community came together in 2002 to build the Greek American Rehabilitation and Care Centre. Residents there continue to enjoy aspects of the Greek culture. Family traditions of observing namesdays (children must have a saint's name at baptism, and the day that saint is celebrated is the namesday) as well as birthdays, and the baptismal custom of naming children after grandparents, continue to be an important part of Greek heritage. Many Greek Americans continue the tradition of having an "open house" on their namesday, when their house is open to all visitors, or invited guests. Don't be surprised if you go out with a Greek on his namesday, and he pays the bill or buys a round of drinks, as this is customary — it is his celebration.

Baptism celebrations are typically as large as weddings; it's not unusual to see several hundred people gathered in a banquet hall, a band or DJ, and dancing into the wee hours. Music and dance are integral to Greek culture and are part of all celebrations. There are several Greek folk dance troupes in Chicago, and many Greek bands and musicians, who work diligently to keep this aspect of the culture alive. At Greek Orthodox weddings, the bride and groom do not recite vows — in fact they do not speak at all. There are many beautiful traditions associated with Greek weddings; the ceremony is quite different from weddings many have experienced. The celebrations are bigger. It's not unusual for Greek Americans to wear their wedding bands on their rights hands — as they are placed in church, and as they are worn in Greece.

Many Greek Americans still celebrate rituals characteristic of the region of Greece from which they descend. For example, on a wedding day, some Greeks in the Peloponnese write the names of unmarried females in attendance on the bottom of the bride's shoe. When she takes her first steps as a married woman, when the names are rubbed out, it is said to indicate that a marriage is certain.

Holidays and special events:

Greek Americans observe ethnic and religious holidays like Greek Independence Day (March 25), celebrating independence from the Ottoman Empire in 1821; "Greek" (Eastern Orthodox) Easter (day changes each year and always follows the Passover); Dormition of the Virgin Mary (Aug. 15); OXI Day (Oct. 28), commemorating Greek Prime Minister Ioannis Metaxas' immortal 'no' to Mussolini's ultimatum, thus bringing Greece into the Greco-Italian War, and ultimately WWII; and summertime church festivals. Most churches host a summer

It is common for Greek Americans to wear their wedding band on their right hand.

festival, and many now are hosting fall and winter festivals as well. Among the largest Greek Church festivals are St. Haralambos (Niles), St. Demetrios (Elmhurst), St. Nectarios (Palatine) and SS. Constantine & Helen (Palos Hills). The season begins Memorial Day weekend, with St. Athanasios (Aurora) always kicking off the festivities. Festivals run through September. Greektown also hosts a very large and well-attended festival in late August. Halsted Street is lined with people from open to close, coming to sample a taste of Greece in the popular ethnic enclave.

Easter is the most important holiday to Greeks. Easter is often celebrated on a different day than Western Christians, and always follows the Passover. In Greece, holiday gifts are given on New Year's Day, the day commemorating St. Basil, who is like a Santa Claus to the Greeks. Some Greek Americans still uphold this tradition, though the majority exchanges gifts on Christmas. These are large family celebrations, with foods typically served on that day.

Foods for special occasions:

For Easter, lamb is roasted on a rotisserie and served with potatoes baked Greek-style (lemon, olive oil and oregano), a special soup of lamb innards, and red eggs symbolizing the blood of Christ. On occasions such as Easter, *tsoureki* (sweet bread) is served with the main course. Popular foods include feta cheese and *baklava* (pastry with filo dough saturated with honey and nuts). Two special dishes are *pastistio* (a casserole of ground beef and macaroni topped with bechamel sauce) and *moussaka* (casserole of layered eggplant, ground beef and potatoes, with cheese). For Christmas, many Greek Americans still eat the traditional turkey, and serve *Christopsomo* (Christmas bread), as well as other Greek and American foods, including roast pork, and don't forget the *Vasilopita*. This cake (or bread, depending on region of Greece and family tradition) is baked in honor of St. Basil. A coin is baked inside, and it is said that whoever gets the piece with the coin will have good luck throughout the New Year.

It's important to note that all Greek cuisine is not the same. Greek cooking is regional, based on what is available locally. This is why the same dish from one part of Greece will be different — in preparation and taste — from another. Greeks also enjoy wine. Some have brought the ancient tradition of winemaking to the States, while others love to sample and support the growing number of boutique wineries in Greece. More than 500 varieties of grapes are indigenous to Greece. A growing number of good wines are being produced, and they are increasingly available in Chicago. Greeks like to purchase Greek products; it gives the feeling of being there.

Dietary restrictions:

Fast days for the church are meatless and dairyless. Easter Lent is 40 days, and employs a strict fast. Many will observe this type of fast in anticipation of the Dormition of the Virgin Mary, though this fast is just two weeks. Younger Greeks, if they fast at all, abstain from meat on Wednesdays (in honor of the Last Supper) and on Fridays (in honor of the Crucifixion). Strict fasting includes no wine or oil. In the Greek Orthodox Church, fasting is more than just abstaining from certain foods. It's about fasting from other things, like idle gossip and many social events, while engaging in prayer and doing good works.

All Greek cooking is not the same. It is regional, based on what is available locally.

Major issues for community:

One big issue for Greek Americans is the assumption of the name Macedonia by the former Yugoslav Republic in Skopje. Greeks want to reserve the use of the name because the area of northern Greece known as Macedonia has been a Greek province since ancient times. Greeks feel that the people of the Former Yugoslav Republic of Macedonia (FYROM) have usurped their history and some feel it is in anticipation of a future land grab. There has been no resolution of this issue to date. A second issue is the continuing illegal occupation of Cyprus by Turkey, since 1974. Greek Americans object to U.S. aid to Turkey. They feel it is against the interest of the U.S. and NATO because, they say, Turkey uses the aid to buy weapons to use against neighboring countries. Finally, they are concerned about Turkish human rights abuses against Armenians, Kurds and the Ecumenical Patriarchate (in modern-day Turkey), world center of the Greek Orthodox Church.

Two more ongoing issues of current concern are sovereignty over the Aegean Sea and Islands, where Turkey has for years been violating air and water space, and the human rights of people of Greek ancestry in northern Epirus, an area now in Albania. More recently, the economic crisis in Greece has been of great concern to Greek Americans. Many are seeking ways to help and lending their support to Greeks in Greece. There have been movements to bring aid to the growing number of homeless and needy in Greece, as well as the "Buy Greek" initiative, encouraging Greeks abroad to buy Greek products and "Hire a Greek," promoting the hiring of professional workers from Greece.

Political participation:

Greeks are political in nature. They see politics as an honorable tradition. The 39th vice president of the U.S., Spiro Agnew, was of Greek descent, and Greek Americans have run for many offices, including U. S. president, members of Congress, and governor of Illinois. In Chicago, Greek Americans have served in a variety of elected and appointed positions at both the city and state levels. These include state treasurer, state senators and representatives, state director of revenue, CEO of Chicago Public Schools, Cook County commissioner, and more. Among current elected officials are state Rep. Sandra M. Pihos, (R-42nd), Cook County Treasurer Maria Pappas, and DuPage County Circuit Court Clerk Chris Kachiroubas.

Greeks in the U.S. initially were Republican, but after Franklin Roosevelt became president most became Democrat because they liked the New Deal. Now they are split between the two parties, with the preponderance in Chicago probably Democrat and suburbanites leaning more Republican. Greeks thrive on political discourse. It is not uncommon for a debate to become heated, though once the conversation has passed, so has the dispute. There are no grudges or animosity.

Links to homeland:

Links to the homeland are many. Greek Americans enjoy dual citizenship because Greek law recognizes the children of Greek immigrants born abroad as Greek citizens, though they must apply for this privilege. Financial

Greeks are political and see politics as an honorable tradition.

remittances to the homeland continue, especially in light of the current economic crisis in Greece. Greek political issues such as Cyprus and Macedonia receive much support from Greek Americans, as does the ongoing conflict with the Ecumenical Patriarchate, world center of the Greek Orthodox Faith in Istanbul. Several Greek-American lobbies coordinate these efforts in the nation's capital. Greek Americans enjoy Greek music. Each year, singers come from Greece to perform concerts in the U.S. Many perform in Chicago. These concerts are well attended, especially by 20-something Greek Americans. In 2011, Greek Film Fest Chicago! made its debut, showcasing films of Greeks here and abroad.

Names:

Many are Christian. Others come from the Bible or Ancient Greece. Common names are George, Constantine (Gus), John (Yiannis), Jim (Dimitrios), Helen (Eleni), Maria, Sophia and Katherine. In Greece, women's names are changed slightly, and if the family name ends in "s," theirs will end in "ou." This practice is rarely upheld in Greek America. Many names end in "poulos" which means "son of." Endings of last names generally follow a pattern, to indicate the origin of the family. For example, people with last names that end in "-akis" are typically from the island of Crete. Last names ending in "poulos" are typically from the Peloponnese. Also, women in Greece rarely take their husband's name when they marry, but most Greek-American women take their husband's name.

Special health concerns:

Thalassemia remains a great concern to Greek Americans. The gene is passed down through the generations, and can be fatal. People can now be tested to see if they carry the gene. Many have heard the terms Sickle Cell anemia or even Cooley's anemia, all of which fall under this designation. This disease is prevalent among the Mediterranean peoples, hence the name —"*thalassa*" is Greek for sea. Thalassemia is the name of a group of genetic blood disorders in which red blood cells do not form properly, and therefore cannot carry sufficient oxygen, resulting in anemia. It begins in childhood. Some people with this disease die young, while others live longer, though they are ill quite often. Current treatments include recurring blood transfusions. The American Hellenic Educational Progressive Association, perhaps the largest Greek-American organization, has led the fight for education, awareness and screenings, and raised funds for research through its AHEPA Cooley's Anemia Foundation.

People of Mediterranean descent have an especially difficult time finding bone marrow matches. The best match is an immediate family member; second is from a relative, but if neither of those is a match, the third is from the ethnic group. In 2006, the AHEPA Bone Marrow Registry was established. According to its website, the chances of finding an unrelated match are 20,000 to 1.

Original written in 1996 by the late Dr. Andrew T. Kopan, Professor Emeritus in the School of Education, DePaul University, and author of "The Greeks in Chicago." Updated in 2012 by Maria A. Karamitsos, Associate Editor of The Greek Star newspaper, and contributor to other Greek publications.

GUATEMALAN AMERICANS

Chicago population:
17,973

Metro population:
33,573

Foreign-born:
64% in metro

Demographics:

Guatemalans are the third-largest Latino group in Chicago. In the city, many live in and around Uptown, where housing is inexpensive and there are agencies to provide services. There also are concentrations in Edgewater, Albany Park and Lincoln Square. Some live in Mexican communities like Pilsen and Little Village. In the greater metro area, 65% have a high school diploma, with just 12% holding a bachelors degree and 3% a masters or professional degree. Some 16% have a management or professional job. About half say they do not speak English very well. Medium household income is $46,301 and 15% live below the poverty line. Many are undocumented, making Census data very unreliable.

The U.S. sided with the Guatemalan government, so those who fled did not get refugee status.

(Ed. note: Chicago population is from the 2010 Census. All other data are from the 2007-09 American Community Survey.)

Historical background:

The immigration to Chicago of tens of thousands of Guatemalans over the last few decades of the 20th century came as a direct result of U.S. policies in Guatemala, which caused massive emigration to escape government tyranny, torture and death. During a period of rampant anti-communism in the U.S., a coup d'état supported by the CIA overthrew the democratically elected government of President Jacobo Árbenz Guzman. A central issue was land reform, which was opposed by the American corporation, United Fruit Company (UFCO), Guatemala's largest landowner. UFCO, which stood to lose some of its uncultivated property, asked help from then Secretary of State John Foster Dulles and his bother Allen, director of the CIA. When President Arbenz resigned in 1954, he told the Guatemalan people the country was under attack by agents of the U.S. and UFCO. After that, a series of military dictators and presidents elected under military control repeatedly tortured and intimidated Guatemalans and maintained a system of exploitation. Conditions that led hundreds of thousands of Guatemalans to flee to the U.S., Mexico and Europe included: more than 150,000 Guatemalans who "disappeared," a genocide policy against the Mayans, the destruction of about 450 villages, and the torture of 100,000 by security forces. Because the U.S. government sided with the Guatemalan government, those who fled were not given refugee status.

Most came here in the 1970s and '80s clandestinely, many with the help of religious organizations under what is known as the "Sanctuary" movement. Because almost all Guatemalans who sought asylum here were rejected, most choose to remain hidden and undocumented rather than risk being sent back to Guatemala. A large number who came through Mexico claim to be Mexicans so that if they are deported they will be sent there. Some live among Mexicans here in Chicago. Most are working at jobs below their occupational status in their home country. Some who were school teachers or secretaries are cleaning toilets; some who were accountants are now doing menial jobs. In addition to the middle-class people who came, there are many who were laborers and peasants in Guatemala.

Current migration patterns:

After the Peace Accords in 1996, new dynamics emerged in Guatemala. The socioeconomic structures remained the same, with a small oligarchy and a new group of rich that came largely from the army. The presence of gangs that nurtured themselves on ex-soldiers and ex-paramilitaries devastated the country. A third of the country cannot read or write and most children suffer from malnutrition. Drug trafficking organizations took advantage of the inequality and made Guatemala an important base for trafficking drugs to the U.S. The Zetas gang recruited ex-Kaibiles, the very cruel special forces that were responsible for most of the massacres during the war. Impunity, corruption and lack of accountability are the norm and drug cartels have infiltrated parts of the government. The situation of extreme poverty combined with massive violence from the drug cartel led to the election of governments with an agenda of *"mano dura,"* repression and further violation of civil rights. In such an environment Guatemalans continue to try to flee the country. For those already here, a change in U.S. law in 1997 allowed the undocumented from Central America to re-apply for legal permanent residency. In the Chicago metro area the Census count for Guatemalans doubled in the past two decades, from 15,771 in 1990 to 33,573 in 2010, though community estimates continue to be much higher. Some were new arrivals, some already here.

Almost all who sought asylum here were rejected, so most remained hidden and undocumented.

Language:

A total of 23 languages are spoken in Guatemala, the most of any Latin American country. Here, the principal languages are Spanish, Quiche, Cakchiquel, Tzutuhil, Mam, Ixil, Kanjobal, Pocoman, Pochonchi, Achi, Kekchi, Jacalteco and Chuj. This reality has implications for services. For example, Guatemalan children whose principal language is not Spanish are being placed in Spanish-English bilingual tracks.

Religion:

Guatemalans here include Catholics, traditional Protestants and fundamentalist Christians. More important, the old religion based in the Mayan philosophy of life is very much alive and thriving. Mayans believe everything on earth is sacred and that they have to ask permission and give thanks for everything they take from the earth. They believe they don't act just in the present, but that the present, past and future are happening in the same time, but in different dimensions.

Important traditions:

Mayan people, who make up most of the immigrants, have strong traditions and are trying to maintain some of them here. The most important are those that promote group solidarity and strength. Weaving is an important and sacred tradition, by which Mayans told history and religious stories after the Spanish destroyed their religious books. Mayans here are teaching traditional dance and musical instruments to their youth. They celebrate special events with "sweatlodges," which are traditional ceremonies that give thanks for anything from a birthday to a cured illness. Mestizos (mixed-race people), who made up the majority of the earlier immigrants, do not recognize the Indian heritage and have done little to maintain Guatemalan traditions. For the most part, they have adopted the American way of life.

Holidays and special events:

Labor Day is celebrated May 1 instead of in September. Guatemalans try not to work that day and join together to celebrate the labor laws that created the 8-hour day, much different from the longer shifts many of the earlier immigrants had to work. Mother's Day (May 10) and Father's Day (June 17) are big events for the family, celebrated on the same date every year, not on the nearest Sunday as is the American practice. The Day of the Revolution (Oct. 26) commemorates the 10 years of democracy that ended in 1954 and is a time to remember what democracy means. Guatemalans also have an Independence Day Parade (Sept.15). Christmas and New Year are also important times, with some observing eight days of prayer before Christmas.

Many were traumatized by torture, war and the disappearance or death of loved ones.

Foods for special occasions:

A series of nutritious and delicious *tamales* and *cuchitos* are very popular. Corn is a staple and sacred to the Mayans. The tamales are made from corn meal, stuffed with meat and sauces and wrapped in corn or banana leaves. Fruits are important, especially tropical fruits like mangoes, papayas and *zapotes*. There also are many regional foods.

Major issues for community:

Immigration reform is the main issue, specifically regularizing the status of the undocumented. Access to health care, education and jobs are also issues; as are justice and punishment for the individuals and institutions that committed human rights abuses at home. An important issue for those who achieved legal status here is to maintain a sense of cultural continuity with their place of origin and to strengthen social networks in the midst of a culture of distrust and suspicion.

Political participation:

Guatemalans in Chicago tend to distrust government, because they had a succession of military dictators or military governments, all supported by the USA. Another source of distrust is the anti-immigrant campaign launched in this country by important sectors of the political parties.

Links to homeland:

The majority of Guatemalans maintain their original citizenship and are proud of their nationality. Some returned after the peace accords. The principal demands of the democratic sectors both in Guatemala and in Chicago were reflected in the demands presented by the Guatamalan National Revolutionary Unity (URNG) to the government of Guatemala. These demands produced important accords, dealing with such topics as human rights, resettlement of uprooted populations, acts of violence that caused suffering in the Guatemalan population, and the rights of the Mayan people. Terror and intimidation remained although were directed at certain sectors of the population. Now, the principal mechanism of control is lack of hope, insecurity and the lack of a just system of order and law.

Special health concerns:

Many were traumatized by torture and war and the disappearance or death of loved ones. It affects them both physically and mentally and has a strong impact on entire families. They are prone to Post Traumatic Stress Disorder (PTSD), anxiety and depression. Nearly half of Guatemalan immigrants nationwide do not have health insurance, according to the Pew Hispanic Center.

By Dr. Antonio Martinez, Co-founder and Former Director of the Marjorie Kovler Center for the Treatment of Survivors of Torture.

HAITIAN AMERICANS

Chicago population:
3,253

Metro area population:
7,386

Foreign-born:
55% in city, 58% in Cook County

Demographics:

Census information about Haitian Americans is sketchy. Except for total population figures from 2010, the latest breakdowns are from the 2000 Census. At that time 74% in Chicago spoke a language other than English at home. Some 74% had a high school diploma while 31% had a college degree. The poverty rate was 11%. Most Haitians live on the South and far Southwest Sides of the city. Many also live on the North Side, especially Rogers Park, and in various suburbs, particularly Evanston, where there is a long-time population, and in Skokie.

Historical background:

Jean Baptiste Point du Sable, regarded as the first permanent resident in Chicago and its "founder," was a native of Saint Marc, Saint Domingue, present-day Haiti. He was first recorded as living here in 1790. The place where he settled, at the mouth of the Chicago River, is a National Historic Landmark. In 2009 the city unveiled a statue of du Sable, donated by Haitian entrepreneur Lesly Benodin, near the Michigan Avenue Bridge.

Before the Immigration Reform Act of 1965, the Haitian population of Chicago was sparse, although some came to Evanston following WWII. Since 1965, in part because of the family-reunification provision of the new

Most came seeking refuge from the government of Dr. François Duvalier.

law, the Haitian population has increased. Most Haitian immigrants came after the mid-'60s, seeking refuge from the repressive government of Dr. François Duvalier, who held power from 1957 until his death in 1971. Some came as permanent residents, others sought political asylum. Most of the first wave were professionals who came by plane. Haitians also left the island in droves during the presidency of Dr. Duvalier's son, Jean-Claude, who succeeded him as president for life until he was forced to relinquish power in 1986.

Passage of the Simpson-Mazzoli Act (1986), which extended amnesty to illegal aliens living continuously in the United States since Jan. 1, 1982, and cracked down on employers who knowingly hired illegals, did not deter Haitians from entering the U.S. (and Chicago) illegally. Most of those in the second surge of refugees were peasants and laborers, and included those known as "boat people." A new wave of immigrants left Haiti after the coup d'état that toppled the government of the popularly elected president, Jean-Bertrand Aristide, in 1991. These Haitians came from all rungs of the occupational ladder. Close to 10% were professionals, adding credence to the claim of Haitians that their decision to leave Haiti represents more than an economic exodus.

To help ease the adjustment of Haitian immigrants in Chicago, a Haitian Community Center in Rogers Park offers instruction in English, legal advice and a job-placement service. Other organizations have been established to help Haitians adjust to life in Chicago. The Haitian Catholic Mission provides services in Kreyòl and honors religious and Haitian state holidays. A Haitian Catholic priest is available to give assistance to Haitians living on the South Side of the city.

Current migration patterns:

According to the INS, 635 Haitians arrived legally from 1990-94, with the Chicago area as their destination. Immediately after the devastating earthquake of January 12, 2010, a number of Haitians were processed in Chicago before joining their families elsewhere, while some came to Chicago to be reunited with their family and stay. Statistics on newly settled Haitians are unavailable.

Important traditions:

Religious traditions such as baptism and marriage are celebrated here. Haitian Americans maintain their diverse cultural traditions through a number of institutions, including churches, a Masonic Lodge, numerous professional organizations such as the Association of Haitian Medical Doctors, artistic groups, small jazz bands, and athletic clubs like Louverture Soccer Club. The island tradition of both families being involved in a courtship is not reproduced here.

The Afro-Caribbean religion commonly known as Vodou is integral to Haitian life.

Language:

Most Haitians are fluent in Kreyòl only. French is spoken by a minority, mostly those with a formal education. Kreyòl is not a patois or a dialect as is commonly assumed. It is a bona fide language, derived from West African grammatical and syntactical sources, using French-derived lexicon with important contributions from English, Spanish and other languages, just as English is a Germanic language with much of its vocabulary from Norman French, Latin and Greek sources.

Religion:

Most Haitians are nominally Christians. A large percentage claim Roman Catholicism, but some belong to the Anglican Church and various Protestant denominations. The Afro-Caribbean religion commonly known as Vodou has always been an integral part of Haitian life. There are no known Vodou temples in Chicago.

Holidays and special events:

Major holidays observed by Haitian Americans in Chicago are Independence Day (Jan. 1), which celebrates independence from France in 1804; Flag Day (May 18); and major Catholic religious holidays such as Ash Wednesday, Good Friday and Easter Sunday. Haitian Americans tend to stay home or visit family members for elaborate dinners and conversation. The Haitian Consulate of Chicago organizes a public Flag Day celebration, usually on the grounds of the DuSable Museum.

Foods for special occasions:

The most popular Haitian dishes are made of rice mixed with kidney beans, rice with a special kind of black mushroom, and plain white rice. Haitian Americans also eat corn, millet, fried green plantains, and *griots* (fried marinated pork served with a very spicy sauce). *Lambi* (conch meat found inside shells) is served grilled or boiled. During special holidays such as Independence Day, Haitians consume an elaborate squash soup. They also tend to eat fish during religious weeks, particularly the week leading to Easter.

Names:

Haitians tend to give at least one "Christian name" to their children. This practice accounts in part for the commonly hyphenated first names of Haitian males and females alike, such as Jean-Baptiste, Jean-Bertrand, Jean-Jacques (Jean, French for John, is the name of one of Christ's Apostles) or Marie-Rose, Marie-Claire, Marie-Michelle (Marie being the name of Christ's mother). This practice, however, is slowly dying. Some Haitian Americans also take the last name of both parents, as in Price-Mars, Pierre-Louis, Bellegarde-Smith and Jean-Joseph.

Most Haitian Americans retain their Haitian citizenship, a badge of pride.

Many Haitians, particularly but not exclusively from the peasantry, have names that are more meaningful, poetic and intrinsically religious, such as Dieseul (God), Dieula (God is here), Dieuri (God laughs) and Jezula (Jesus is here).

Major issues for community:

Haitians in Chicago are very much concerned about the social, political and economic issues of Haiti. Although many plan to stay in the United States and an increasing number have become naturalized citizens, they keep abreast of the many facets of life in Haiti through Haitian newspapers circulated in the U.S. and radio programming, as well as frequent trips to Haiti and contact with family and friends who remain there. After the devastating January 2010 earthquake, a number of Haitian Americans became concerned about rebuilding efforts of the country. A chapter of an organization in Canada, Groupe de Réflection et d'Action pour une Haiti Nouvelle (GRAHN), was established in Chicago.

Political participation:

Haitian political organizations in Chicago focus mainly on Haiti. After the fall of Jean-Claude Duvalier in 1986, Chicago became one of the major bases for Haitian politics. In addition to a proliferation of political organizations, nearly all the prominent political parties of Haiti are represented in Chicago. In 1992, the Oganizasyon Lavalas was formed to support the ousted government of Jean Bertrand Aristide. A radio program run by Aristide supporters began to broadcast in French and Kreyòl.

While émigré politicians have agitated for the home country, other Haitian Americans have become eager participants in U.S. politics. Many Haitian Americans vote regularly, and they tend to vote Democratic. Others continue to express deep mistrust of government, as they did in Haiti. Americans of Haitian descent are active in Chicago politics. State Sen. Kwame Raoul (D-13) of Chicago and Circuit Court Judge Lionel Jean-Baptiste, also a former alderman in Evanston, are Haitian Americans with strong ties to the Haitian community.

Links to homeland:

Most Haitians in Chicago maintain strong ties to their homeland. For this reason they tend to retain their citizenship, which for many is a badge of pride. Despite political turmoil and economic hardship in Haiti, many Haitians here express the desire to repatriate. Those who have families in Haiti visit periodically, as their employment condition allows. Most Haitian Americans send money to family members and friends living in Haiti. Some send appliances, clothing, medicine and other practical items through Haitian charitable organizations.

When the earthquake that registered 7.0 on the Richter scale struck Haiti in 2010, Haitians in Chicago were quick to respond to the catastrophe by organizing activities to keep people informed about the situation in Haiti. Under the auspices of the Haitian Congress to Fortify Haiti, a non-profit organization formed by Haitians living in Evanston, they raised money, medicine, clothing and other goods for earthquake relief.

Special health concerns:

Haitians in Chicago and its environs do not face special health concerns. As the elderly population grows, a number of senior citizens struggle with high blood pressure, diabetes and other illnesses that plague the North American population at large.

By William Leslie Balan-Gaubert, Independent Scholar and Researcher affiliated with the University of Chicago.

HUNGARIAN AMERICANS

Chicago population:
4,980 (only ancestry)

Metro area population:
28,960 (only ancestry)
38,693 (multiple ancestries)

Foreign-born:
8.7% in metro

Demographics:

The Hungarian diaspora in Chicago consists of first-generation immigrants as well as Americans of Hungarian ancestry. The number of Hungarians with "only one ancestry" has been showing a decreasing trend. The number of families with one Hungarian parent, the other parent being American or some other nationality is increasing. Geographically, Hungarians live dispersed in the larger metropolitan area, the

Some Hungarians fought in the American Civil War in Lincoln's Riflemen Corps.

main concentration being to the north and northwest. Hungarian Americans, though diverse, are on average highly educated and well-off financially. In the metro area 46% have bachelor's degrees and 20% graduate or professional degrees. Just over half (51%) are in management or professional jobs. Median household income is high, at $78,322 and just 5.4% are living below the poverty line.

(Ed. note: Population figures for Hungarians alone are from the 2008-10 Census Bureau's American Community Survey. All other data are from the 2007-09 ACS.)

Historical background:

Chicago did not become a primary destination for Hungarians until the end of the 19th century. In 1870 the city had only 159 Hungarian residents, but after the turn of the century a dramatic increase was seen. The U.S. Census showed the Hungarian population in the Chicago area increasing from 1,841 in 1890 to 7,463 in 1900, 37,990 in 1910, and 70,209 in 1920. These figures, however, do not always reflect the actual numbers of the ethnic Hungarians (Magyars). Before WWI they sometimes included non-ethnic Hungarians (Germans, Slovaks, Croats, etc.) of the multinational Austro-Hungarian monarchy, and after WWI they often excluded ethnic Hungarians who came from the newly created Yugoslavia, Czechoslovakia, the enlarged Romania and eastern Austria.

The first Hungarians reached Chicago in the 1850s as part of broader westward migration within the United States. They were mainly tradesmen, shopkeepers and artisans, who with their families moved to the rapidly developing Chicago from the impoverished industrial areas of the East, seeking new opportunities. They also included emigrants who fled Hungary to escape retribution in the aftermath of the failed 1848-49 Hungarian Revolution against the Hapsburg Empire. These Kossuth émigrés were heading to New Buda in Iowa but stopped in Chicago and decided to settle here. Many of them were from the gentry, with formal education and therefore able to move into positions of civic leadership. Julian Kuné, a member of the Board of Trade, established Chicago's first private foreign-language school. Some fought in the American Civil

War in Lincoln's Riflemen Corps, organized by Géza Mihalótzy. The early immigrants were mainly men.

Hungarian immigration grew significantly between 1889 and 1913. Like migration flows of other ethnic groups of the region, the majority of Hungarian immigrants arrived from the more disadvantaged rural areas of the Austro-Hungarian monarchy. Migratory traditions of villages and familial chain migration played a major role. Although these new immigrants came from agricultural areas, most settled in industrial cities and mining areas. In Chicago many worked in the railroad yards and steel mills, and they settled in great numbers in the industrial areas of the South and West Sides of Chicago where they could find a steady supply of jobs. The largest Hungarian settlement was concentrated in South Chicago, around 95th Street and Cottage Grove, and in the Burnside ("Triangle"), West Pullman and Roseland neighborhoods. The first Hungarian Reformed Church was built in South Chicago in 1898. In the larger metro area, East Chicago and Calumet

Many worked in railroad yards and steel mills and settled on the South and West Sides.

City also had large Hungarian populations. Hungarians lived alongside people from other Central/East European countries, as well as Italy and Sweden.

The outbreak of WWI in 1914 halted mass migration, while the exclusionary U.S. immigration laws of 1921-24 introduced the quota system, permitting only 1,000 immigrants from Hungary a year. Regardless, Hungarian immigration did not cease. After the Trianon Treaty had deprived Hungary of three thirds of its territory, and 3.5 million Hungarians were forced to live outside the new borders of Hungary as an ethnic minority, many felt they could not accommodate themselves to the new circumstances and decided to leave their new country of residence. Years of chaos, revolution, counter-revolution, extreme nationalism, and anti-Semitism followed in what remained of Hungary and created many political refugees.

Immigrants coming from Hungary between the two wars were predominantly intellectuals and of urban background. They had little in common with the older working-class immigrants and tended to settle around Logan Square and in Humboldt Park, the northwest area of Chicago. St. Stephen King of Hungary Church was built at 2015 W. Augusta. On the Near North Side, Hungarians formed scattered enclaves around the edge of the old German community from North Avenue and Wells into Lake View and up Lincoln Avenue. They intermingled with the more prosperous Hungarian-speaking Germans and Jews who ran stores, restaurants, trade companies, law offices, and banks in the region.

In the aftermath of WWII, the pattern of Hungarian immigration to the U.S. changed again. About 20,000 Hungarians were accepted into the United States under the Displaced Persons Acts of 1948 and 1950. Of these, 1,000 Hungarian refugees reported Chicago as their residence in 1950. Once more the local Hungarian American communities worked tirelessly to increase the Hungarian quota. In 1956, the communist suppression of the Hungarian Revolution made another group of political immigrants seek refuge in the United States. Thousands of the 56ers eventually settled in the Chicago area. Not even the arrival of the new immigrants, however, could stop the breakdown of the Hungarian neighborhoods and their institutions. By the 1950s children and grandchildren of immigrants married and moved out from the Hungarian neighborhoods into Hegewisch on the South Side and to the south suburbs, especially Lansing, Calumet City and Burnham. On the North Side, the last vestiges remained around Belmont and Clark and on Lincoln Avenue up to the 1970s.

Current migration patterns:

As opposed to earlier major migration trends when Hungarians arrived in clusters, in the late 20th and early

21st centuries the characteristic mobility is individual and family-based migration. A large proportion of the latest immigrants are ethnic minorities from Hungary's neighboring states of Transylvania, Slovakia and the Autonomous Province of Vojvodina. Recent immigrants tend to be highly qualified professionals such as computer scientists and scholars in the health sciences and some academic fields. They receive temporary immigrant status, often followed by permanent residency as a result of their achievements as outstanding scholars. Some Hungarians also obtain legal status via the visa lottery. Those professionals who do not manage to secure legal status, due to strict immigration laws, often move to one of the Western European countries, mainly the UK. Since the political regime change in 1989, reverse migration has increased. After retiring, Hungarian Americans often move back to Hungary or spend extended periods of time there. An increasing number of second-generation young adults study and/or start their early career in Hungary. Some stay and some move back after a handful of years.

> *Since the political regime change in 1989, reverse migration has increased.*

Language:

Hungarian.

Religion:

The immigrants, mirroring the population of the homeland, were about 60% Roman Catholic; 30% Protestant, either Calvinist or Lutheran; and 10% other affiliations, such as Jewish, Eastern Orthodox Catholic, Baptist and Adventist.

Important traditions:

As part of the general phenomenon of the revival in ethnic consciousness (in response to the homogenizing effect of globalization) there is a renewed interest in Hungarian heritage and traditions in Chicago's Hungarian community. Although Hungarians here do not live in closely settled ethnic neighborhoods, Hungarian-affiliated churches, a number of organizations, especially the local Hungarian Scout Troop, and a group of literary figures have kept Hungarian language and cultural traditions alive. The oldest and most popular traditions are connected with religious and folk festivals. The tradition of St. Miklós day on Dec. 6 is popular among kids. Children receive small bags filled with goodies with a message from the accompanying Krampus, the "bogy man," that if they do not behave they don't get goodies. At Christmas the folk tradition of Bethlehem's play is performed, followed by Christmas songs by children who meet at a church and then make their rounds visiting shut-in elderly and Scout families. The Easter tradition of the girls painting eggs, and the boys sprinkling the girls with cologne, is also popular among children. The local practice for the past few years has been that many girls come together so boys can go there to sprinkle *locsolni*.

Nourishing the unique language and rich literary traditions of the old country has been paramount for the Chicago diaspora. Some of the key leaders were poets or writers themselves and/or sponsors of Hungarian culture. The Zoltán Kodály Society founded by Adam Makkai, linguistics professor at UIC, later joined by Kálmán Fiedler, Ferenc Mózsi, Lajos Szathmáry and others, operated for 10 years. During the Cold War well-known and lesser-known poets, writers and musicians from abroad were invited to perform. They were sponsored by individuals and organizations such as the Hungarian Communion of Friends (*Magyar Baráti Közösség*). A current event, which is tied to a well-established tradition in the home country, is

Day of Poetry (*Költészet napja*). It is held annually and is organized by the Hungarian Free Reformed Church. During this well-attended event, people from the general community, belonging to a variety of organizations, come and recite a favorite poem.

Language is also perpetuated by the Hungarian churches. The Catholic Church of St. Stephen King of Hungary Church and the Protestant Church of Westside (Norridge United Church of Christ) offer Sunday services in both English and Hungarian. Norridge has also started Hungarian language classes for adults. Additional active churches that contribute to community-building are the Hungarian Baptist Church of Chicago, a close-knit community celebrating its 25-year anniversary and the Hungarian Free Reformed Church. A Hungarian School and Nursery *(Csík Hágo Iskola és Óvoda)* has been in operation for the past three years and has grown to 60 students, with the potential to double in size.

The Hungarian scouting movement (*cserkészet*) in the U. S. reaches back to a long-time tradition in Hungary, which started in pre-WWI years. It was banned in Hungary, but revived in Displaced Persons camps in Austria. The Matthias Hunyadi Scout Troop is the local chapter of Chicago, founded in the 1960s. It has been the main vehicle for passing on Hungarian traditions and culture to the younger generation through songs,

Scouting was banned in Hungary but revived in Displaced Persons camps.

dances, and observation of traditions. The Scout Troop also maintains traditions for the broader community, with events such as the annual Harvest Ball, which celebrates the grape harvest in late September and early October in Hungary, and an annual Traditional Hungarian Wedding Feast, featuring a different Hungarian ethnic region each year.

While there is a revival of interest in the folkdance tradition in many diasporic communities, folkdance has never ceased to flourish in the Chicago community. From the mid-1970s to the later 1980s the community had the Dance Folk Ensemble of Rába, with many performances for both the Hungarian and American communities. About three generations of dancers grew up with the group. In the past three or four years an adult folkdance group based at the Norridge Church and a children's folkdance group called "Bóbita" have been performing for the community.

The new millennium has seen a great variety of new festivities and activities in the community. These festivities reflect modern times by opening up to embrace several generations of Hungarian Americans, including those who do not speak Hungarian but have sustained interest and curiosity about Hungarian traditions. Workshops such as Let's Bake (*Süssünk, süssünk*) began to be organized for the cultural preservation and passing on culinary traditions to the younger generations. The Hungarian Goulash Festival and Taste of Hungary festival are great community-building events, when people gather and prepare traditional meals and food. These include the hearty *gulyas* soup cooked in the traditional Hungarian cauldron over a long time and over open fires. There are samplings of regional specialties such as homemade sausages, *mititei* (a specialty from the Transylvania region), *palacsinta* (crêpes), (*kürtőskalács* (rolled sweet dough), and *lángos* (a fried bread-like dough also called 'elephant ear').

Holidays and special events:

Besides the traditional holidays of Christmas, New Year's Eve and Easter, Hungarian Americans generally celebrate three major national holidays: the Revolution of 1848 (on or around March 15), St. Stephen's Day or Constitution Day (Aug. 20), and the Revolution of 1956 (Oct. 23). In Hungary, St. Stephen's Day is celebrated with fireworks and flower carnivals. In Chicago it is celebrated with a community gathering and cultural events. Some special events are organized by Hungarian (Magyar) Club of Chicago, founded in 1922. Increased numbers of events are coordinated by the Hungarian Cultural Advisory Council of Chicago (*Csikágói Magyar Kulturtanács*), an umbrella organization comprising leaders of all the local organizations. With the advent of Facebook, special events see more and more participation from Hungarians living in Indiana, Wisconsin and Iowa.

Foods for special occasions:

Foods for the special holidays are very traditional. On Christmas Eve both Catholics and Protestants tend to abstain from meat and prefer fish. On Christmas Day stuffed cabbage is quite frequently prepared and at Easter, Hungarian ham is the main course. A pastry called *beigli* (poppy seed- or walnut-filled yeast dough) and *torta* (coffee cake) are eaten for dessert. Although not closely related with any special occasion, Hungarian *goulash* (a thin, spicy stew-like mixture of meats and vegetables eaten as a soup) is the most popular

Special events draw Hungarians from Indiana, Wisconsin and Iowa.

dish. Chicken *paprikash* is a traditional meal. It is a slow-cooked chicken stew made with lots of onions, green pepper and tomato, which can be served with sour cream. It is also traditional to smoke sausage and ham in December.

Names:

The common Hungarian names are slowly changing. Among the traditional given names the most common were Erzsébet, Margit and Magda for women, and István (Stephen), László (Leslie), József, Péter, Imre and Zoltán for men. Newly immigrated families seem more likely to give "foreign" names to their children than those who have lived here a while. Ancient Hungarian names, usually from Hungarian mythologies such as Hunor, Botond, Attila for men, Emese, Villő for women also have had their renaissance. Some Hungarian surnames represent jobs, as in Szabó (tailor), Kovács (smith) or Molnár (miller). Others are named for the region they came from, like Szathmáry.

Major issues for community:

The overarching issue for the community is to preserve language and heritage, to pass it on to the next generation, and to share it with "Americans." As in other communities of the Hungarian diaspora in the U.S. there is a fear of losing ethnic heritage. Leading members of the community say they struggle with the transition of the leadership from the generation that emigrated after 1956 to those born at the end of communism or and/or born in the U.S. Another main issue is how to bring Hungarian ethnic traditions to the attention and interest of the wider American community, similarly to other ethnic groups such as the Greeks, who have been successful with festivals and other public events. Strong focus is placed on youth to keep them connected and interested. To this end 10 years ago, the Hungarian Club of Chicago instituted a college scholarship program.

Political participation:

The community is diverse and cannot be characterized as linked to one political party. Hungarians who live in America traditionally have been members of one of the two main political parties. Some have had very strong Democratic ties. The Republican ties also have been strong since Lincoln, who had several

Hungarian generals and high-ranking officials during his presidency. The Hungarian population of Chicago does not exercise any political clout.

Links to homeland:

The Hungarian diaspora in Chicago participates in charity efforts and has links with cultural organizations in Hungary. They contribute both money and time. Newer projects include the organization of a garage sale, with the aim of donating proceeds to disaster relief. There are also opportunities for working together with Hungarian organizations that run programs specifically geared toward Hungarians living abroad.

Original in 1997 by Eva Becsei, then a Doctoral Student in History at the University of Illinois at Chicago. Update in 2012 by Dr. Eva Becsei-Kilburn, now an Honorary Postdoctoral Fellow at the University of Edinburgh's Scottish Centre for Diaspora Studies, with help from Dr. Erika Bokor and Andrea Stetz.

INDIAN AMERICANS

Chicago population:
29,948 (Indian alone)
33,528 (alone or in combination)

Metro population:
171,901 (Indian alone)
180,198 (alone or in combination)

Foreign-born:
66% in Chicago, 70% in Cook and DuPage counties

Demographics:

The Chicago-area Indian American population, mostly foreign-born, has more than doubled since 1990. In the city 55% of foreign-born are still non-citizens, while 45% have been naturalized. In the metro area more than half (54%) have become citizens. An overwhelming majority of Asian Indians in the six-county area (84%) live outside the city, with the suburban Indian population concentrated in Cook and DuPage counties.

The 1965 Immigration Reform Act paved the way for Indian professionals to come here.

In Chicago, Indians are concentrated on the North Side in West Ridge and Rogers Park, as well as other neighborhoods including the Loop, the Near North Side, and more recently Wicker Park and Bucktown.

Northwest and west suburbs such as Skokie, Niles, Schaumburg, Hoffman Estates, Mount Prospect, Naperville, Glendale Heights and Hanover Park have high concentrations of Indians. Indian Americans tend to have high incomes. In DuPage, where many are physicians and other professionals, their household median income is $97,803. Their median income in Chicago is $67,833, about $20,000 above the city average. Those living below poverty level range from 11% in the city to 5% in the metro area. Among those living in Chicago, 44% have graduate or professional degrees and 29% have bachelor's degrees. Indians in the metro area are overwhelmingly (65%) in professional or managerial occupations.

(Ed. note: The population numbers are from the 2010 Census. Other data are from the last two American Community Surveys, 2007-09 and 2008-10.)

Historical background:

Sizable Indian immigration to Chicago began with the 1965 Immigration Reform Act, which paved the way for professionals to enter the United States. Professionals came from every region of India, as well as from other countries such as England, Canada, South Africa, Tanzania, Fiji, Guyana and Trinidad. At first, Indian immigrants settled on the far North Side of Chicago, along Broadway and Sheridan Road and west along Lawrence and Devon avenues, where they found a cosmopolitan mix of diverse ethnic groups. Like other immigrant groups before them, many moved to the suburbs. Wide dispersal in the suburbs is one of the most striking characteristics of Indian settlement patterns in Chicago.

The H-1B visa program has been a major factor in the rapid growth and recent migration patterns among Indians in the United States. Since 1992, this program has permitted foreigners with special skills to come to the United States on a six-year work visa and apply for a green card with an employer's sponsorship. Indians have accounted for 40% of all H-1B visas granted since 1992 and, because most of these visas went to computer-related professionals, there was an increased migration of people from India in the high-tech industry. However, due to the decline in the "dotcoms" and the tightening of visa restrictions after the

India is a top country from which family-based immigrants now arrive.

Sept. 11, 2001, terrorist attacks, Indian immigration to the U.S. declined. Yet India remains one of the top countries from which family-based immigrants continue to arrive. For example, in 2006, Indians ranked at the top in terms of the number of visas granted to siblings of U.S. citizens.

Devon Avenue in Chicago, also known as "Indiatown," has long been a strong draw for the large Indian American population across the Midwest, who go there to shop for Indian goods and eat Indian food. The growth of the Indian ethnic neighborhood on Devon Avenue is tied to the second wave of immigration in the 1980s, which marked the arrival of the families of the earlier immigrants. These relatives frequently were less skilled, faced a local economy plagued by unemployment, and took up occupations in retail trade or other small businesses. This led to greater economic stratification between city and suburban Indians.

Language:

Many Indian Americans speak English fluently, having learned it in school as the legacy of previous British rule in India. They also often speak their native language. India has 22 constitutionally recognized languages and most are represented in the Chicago area, namely Gujarati, Hindi, Punjabi, Telugu, Malayalam, Tamil, Kannada, Sindhi, Urdu and Bengali. Limited English proficiency has increased in the Indian American community in recent years, as many of the later-arriving Indian immigrants lacked English language skills. More than 26,000 Indians in Cook County have limited English proficiency. In October 2011, the U.S. Census Bureau determined that the number of Indians in Cook County who are United States citizens but who have limited English proficiency is so high that local election boards are now legally required to provide language assistance to Indians during elections.

Religion:

As in India, most Indian Americans in the Chicago area are Hindus, but there are also Muslims, Sikhs, Jains, Christians, Zoroastrians, Buddhists and Jews. Because religion and language are seen as vital to cultural preservation, the community has built temples, mosques, gurudwaras (Sikh houses of worship), and other religious institutions, which serve as venues for ceremonies, religious education, social and cultural activities, community events and language classes.

Important traditions:

Caste considerations are usually ignored in the United States, but caste and regional origin have become more important to Indian Americans when it comes to marriage. In the early days of Indian immigration in the 1960s and '70s, when Indian Americans were fewer in number, they were reconciled to assimilation and intermarriage, if not with other Americans, at least with other Indians, regardless of caste or region. Increased immigration since the '80s has caused many to observe caste considerations more carefully. Some Indians arrange marriages within their own caste because they believe marriage needs family support to be successful. Second-generation marriages are more diverse, with some marrying within the same caste, regional and religious group and others marrying outside the Indian American community altogether.

Holidays and special events:

Indian Independence Day is celebrated Aug. 15, and many religious holidays are celebrated by Indian Americans. The Hindu population observes *Janmashtami* (in August); *Navratri* and *Dussera*, as well as *Durga Puja* (a 10-day festival in October or November); and *Diwali* (October or November). Muslims celebrate *Eidul-Fitr* and, 70 days later, *Eidul-Adha*. Jains observe *Mahavir Jayanti* (March) and Sikhs observe *Baisaki* (April). One form of entertainment that has gained popularity among Indians in Chicago and worldwide is the Bollywood movie. The term "Bollywood" combines "Hollywood" and Bombay (now known as Mumbai) and home to the world's largest movie industry. Live performances by Bollywood stars touring the United States are very well attended in large venues such as the UIC Pavilion and Rosemont Horizon. While videos and music from Bollywood have been available in Devon stores from the 1980s, theaters

The term 'Bollywood' combines Hollywood and Bombay (now Mumbai).

owned by Indians are now showing Indian movies exclusively, and mainstream theaters occasionally show them. Indian Americans have many cultural and social similarities to other South Asian Americans, including people of Pakistani, Bangladeshi, Nepali, and Sri Lankan descent.

Major issues for community:

The Sept. 11 terrorist attacks in New York City and Washington, D.C., continue to have a significant impact on the Indian American community in Chicago and nationwide. The attacks caused a backlash of hostility towards Muslims and also Sikhs, often mistaken for Muslims because of their long beards and turbans, as well as others who appear South Asian, Middle Eastern or Muslim. Indians continue to report being harassed by authorities and suspicious citizens. On a more general level, racial discrimination has a widespread personal and professional impact on Indians, as many executives encounter a "glass ceiling," small business owners face various barriers, and unskilled factory workers suffer unemployment and unequal pay. Community members also are concerned about the broken immigration system that threatens to reduce immigration from India and harm the Indian population already here. Cumbersome rules in immigration law, the backlog seeking residency and citizenship, and current and proposed anti-immigrant laws and policies are major problems for the community.

Immigrant integration also remains a constant issue. Many Indians fear their traditions will be lost unless vigorous efforts are made to preserve them. Cultural and religious activities are viewed as a viable alternative to "excessive Westernization," which is often equated with a "permissive" lifestyle. There is conflict in many Indian-American homes where teenage children, taught in school to think independently, clash with Indian parents who expect unquestioning obedience. There are also unmet social needs among the elderly, who have followed their children to America but may now live isolated, lonely lives without their traditional support system.

Foods for special occasions:

For Indian Americans, food is a part of practically every major festival and life-cycle ritual. Indians celebrate birthdays, weddings and many religious holidays by preparing rich sweets and offering them to friends and relatives. Many sweets and other special delicacies are prepared for the Hindu holiday of Diwali.

Dietary restrictions:

Some but not all Indian Americans are vegetarian and/or abstain from drinking alcohol. Many Hindus avoid beef, and many Muslims refrain from eating pork. Jainism has very strict dietary laws, and some Jains avoid eating even root vegetables because it violates their belief in non-violence against even the smallest creature on earth. Indians from various religious communities observe fasts at different times throughout the year.

Names:

There is tremendous variety in Indian names, which usually refer to the natural environment or human sentiments, such as Usha (the dawn) or Priya (beloved). Other common names are the names of gods, such as Gopal (another name for Krishna) or Lakshmi (the goddess of prosperity), Zia (light), Shaan (glory) or Habib (friend). Surnames (last names) usually reveal a person's regional origins, caste or sub-caste. Many Hindu families name children as part of a religious ceremony on the 10th day after birth.

About 17% of Indians in Chicago have no health insurance.

Political participation:

The dual residential pattern of concentration in the city and dispersal in the suburbs holds both promise and frustration for Indian Americans when it comes to political participation and civic engagement. There have been some political success stories. For example, Ald. Ameya Pawar (47th Ward) was elected the first Indian American and Asian American member of the Chicago City Council in 2011. In Skokie and Niles Township, Indian Americans have been elected to local office: Pramod Shah as Skokie Trustee, Dina Modi as Niles Township Collector, and Shajan Jose to the board of School District 69 serving Skokie and Morton Grove. Moin Khan was re-elected in 2009 as a Trustee of York Township and several judges have been elected and appointed to the Cook County Courts. But because Indians are widely dispersed in the city and suburbs, they have yet to gain the political clout that comes with redistricting of more concentrated clusters of minority communities. While Indians in Illinois may identify strongly with the Democratic Party, given the fact that the state itself is a Democratic stronghold, some in the western suburbs support the Republicans. Generally speaking, because Indians tend to vote on issues rather than party affiliation, they cannot be taken for granted as a monolithic voting bloc.

Links to homeland:

Indian Americans are concerned about the U.S. government's relations with India. India has evolved into a key global economic power and offers a labor force that is not only technically skilled but also fluent in English, which is one of the factors that led U.S. companies to outsource jobs to India. American hostility toward countries like China and now India for being competitors to U.S. businesses has had a negative impact on Indian Americans. Unlike immigrants from many other countries who have fled repression and persecution, many Indians here think fondly of their motherland, visit India often, and are sympathetic to the Indian government. According to The World Bank, overseas remittances to India are higher than to any other country.

Special health concerns:

A major concern for Indian Americans in the Chicago area is the need for culturally and linguistically appropriate health care, particularly in light of the increasing number of Indians who have limited English proficiency and the decreasing public funds available for health and social services. Indian Americans face diabetes and cardiovascular disease at elevated rates. Mental health issues, including suicide, as well as disability-related issues are also concerns for the Indian community, especially because of the associated social stigmas. About 17% of Indians in Chicago and 13% of Indians in the metro area have no health insurance.

Original by Dr. Padma Rangaswamy, Ann Kalayil and Ami Gandhi, all of South Asian American Policy & Research Institute; revised in 2012 by Ami Gandhi.

IRANIAN AMERICANS

Chicago population:
2,097

Metro population:
8,132

Foreign-born:
64% in Chicago

Demographics:

Aside from total population figures, the most recent data for Iranians was in the 2000 Census. The Iranian American community believes the Census undercounts immigrant groups, and especially the recent

Some Bahá'ís stayed after the 1893 World's Fair and set up a U.S. base for their spiritual movement.

significant wave of Iranian students enrolled in technical and scientific graduate programs here. Iranian Americans do not live in any particular part of the metro area, though significant pockets can be found in the northern and western suburbs as well as near downtown Chicago. The ethnicities of Iranians in Chicago vary, with Azari and Kurds well represented among them. The 2000 Census found that 81% in Chicago had a high school diploma and 52% a bachelor's degree. Median family income was $60,284. About two-thirds spoke a language other than English at home and 15% lived in poverty.

(Ed. note: Population figures are from the 2008-10 American Community Survey. Other data come from the 2000 Census.)

Historical background:

During the 1893 Columbian Exposition, Bahá'u'lláh, the leader of the Bahá'í religion and a delegation of his followers visited Chicago. Some of those followers stayed and created a U.S. base for their spiritual movement, which had started in Iran. This group likely represents the earliest significant migration of Iranians to the Chicago area. The Bahá'í Temple in Wilmette, with its prominent Persian architectural features, is probably their most important legacy in the Chicago area.

There are narratives of early 20th-century migration of Iranian Jews who set up a synagogue on the North Side of Chicago, the probable predecessor of the current Persian Iran Hebrew Congregation in Skokie. Otherwise, there are not many signs of Iranian migration to the Chicago before 1950s. But in the second half of the 20th century waves of Iranian students started to enroll in the Chicago-area institutions of higher education. Many of these students later created bases for their families and are probably the first group of people that we could call "Iranian Americans" in the modern dual identity that entails.

In the 1960s and '70s Chicago became a hotbed of Iranian student activism. Their numbers reached in the thousands, with the downtown YMCA being the usual first residence of a student arriving from Iran. Prominent Iranian student activists of that era, such as Mohsen Sazegara and Mohammad Amini, attended area universities and colleges. One narrative has it that the start of the global Confederacy of Iranian Students, which played a significant role in the Iranian revolution of 1979, started with a sit-in at the Iranian Consulate in 1968 at the Standard Oil building. Also some claim that during that era a few of the more radical Iranian students joined the Black Panther movement in Chicago.

There is a clear break in patterns of migration after 1979 and entire families started to arrive or become reunited with relatives in the Chicago area. Several Persian-language publications started in Chicago, along with a weekly AM radio broadcast and a television program that aired briefly in the '80s. Among these communications outlets were a women's publication called *Nimeh e Digar* (The Other Half) and the scholarly Center for Iranian Research and Analysis (CIRA), headed by Mohamad Tavakoli, then a graduate student at University of Chicago.

Current migration patterns:

It's harder to get U.S. visas now. But very elite university students at times can get them for graduate school. Sometimes they can get work visas after they have earned their degrees, which allows them to stay five more years, but that is rare.

Religion:

Most Iranian Americans here come from a Shia Muslim background, but there are also Jews, Bahá'ís, and Christians (Armenian and Assyrian as well as Chaldian). There is a Zoroastrian Temple in the western suburbs with a few of its worshipers being Iranians.

Language:

Most of the first-generation Iranians speak Persian. It is not uncommon for Azari-Turkish and Kurdish to also be spoken in some households.

Important traditions:

Birthdays, weddings and funerals are common reasons for community gatherings. Weddings and funerals have specific characteristics depending on the family's religion. Among Iranians, the women tend to be even better educated than men and have very modern roles. The clothing is usually modern and while religious Muslims might wear a head scarf for the *hijab* purposes, that is rare.

Holidays and special events:

Iranians continue their more secular holidays as public celebrations. *Nowruz,* the first day of spring (around March 21) is the start of the Iranian New Year and by far the largest of Iranian celebrations and now includes a downtown parade. *Chahar Shanbeh Soori,* (the last Tuesday night of the Persian calendar), as well as *Sizdeh Bedar* (the 13th day of the new year) are usually celebrated at public parks in the Chicago area. The ancient Iranians observed the change of every season with small celebrations that still occur in the Chicago area for the arrival of the Winter Solstice, Autumnal Equinox and the Summer Solstice.

Foods for special occasions:

On *Nowruz,* the Iranian New Year, *sabzi polo mahi* (herb rice with fish) is served. In summer, light lunch meals include dishes like *abdoukhiar,* a cold yogurt soup with cucumbers, fresh herbs and grapes, or cold melons with a salty cheese like feta with fresh hot bread. The *Yalda* celebrations in December (winter solstice) usually include *ajeel* (a dried fruits and nuts medley), as well as hearty noodle soup/stew, *aushe reshteh,* made of meat, lentils, garbanzo beans, fried mint and sour milk curd (whey). A watermelon that may have been preserved from early fall is usually a treat at this celebration, reminiscent of the good times of summers past and the ones to come.

Dietary restrictions:

Iranians of Islamic or Jewish background might be observant of halal or kosher laws.

Names:

Traditionally, Iranians either gave their children classic Persian names such as Kaveh, Dariush (Darius), Koroosh (Cyrus), Azita and Anahita; or religious names from the Islamic, biblical or the Zoroastrian traditions,

It's harder to get U.S. visas now, but elite students at times can get them for graduate school.

such as Ali, Maryam (Mary), Hassan, George, Daniel, Michael and Zahra. It is typical for an Iranian last name to end with an "i" like Tehrani or Hassani, indicating the place or the lineage that the family comes from.

Major issues for community:

Iranian Americans in Chicago are a relatively well-educated, prosperous community that tends to avoid many of the social problems of some other recent immigrants. But since Sept.11 there has been an increase in concern about ethnic profiling that has led to grassroots action in creating Iranian-American advocacy groups. Organizations such as National Iranian-American Council and Public Affair Alliance of Iranian-Americans have active Chicago chapters. Also the Iran House still publishes a periodic Khaneh, which tries to keep the community updated.

Political participation:

Iranians follow politics, but have not taken significant steps to get involved. Most Iranians here tend to liberal or progressive.

Links to homeland:

The lack of regular diplomatic relations between Iran and the U.S. causes problems. It is difficult to travel between the two countries and to obtain visas for visiting relatives. Those on student visas are often denied the required multiple entries in a timely manner, so to go back to Iran during a summer or Christmas break becomes very risky. Pasfarda Art & Cultural Exchange, whose mission is to build cultural bridges to Iran, sponsors Iranian artists' visits to Chicago and local Persian events, including musical performances by well-known Iranian pop artists. Every October, the Gene Siskel Film Center has a festival of films from Iran.

Special health concerns:

Many social and health-care services are not culturally sensitive and are not offered in the Persian language, so the elderly often end up doing without. This also applies to mental health counseling.

By Narimon Safavi, author of essay on Iran in 2011 book "What's Next?" and radio commentator on WBEZ.

IRISH AMERICANS

Chicago population:
141,087 (first ancestry)
223,007 (first, multiple ancestries)

Metro population:
727,322 (first ancestry)
1,214,150 (first, multiple ancestries)

Foreign-born:
2% in Chicago, less than 1% in metro

Demographics:

People of Irish ancestry are scattered throughout the city and suburbs, especially Cook and DuPage counties. Irish Americans are the second largest white ethnic group in the metro area after Germans. In Chicago, they are in virtually every neighborhood. The highest concentrations are in the Southwest Side neighborhoods of

Irish Americans are the 2nd largest white ethnic group in the metro area after Germans.

Beverly Hills, Mt. Greenwood and Ashburn. On the North Side significant numbers can be found in Lincoln Park, Lake View and the Near North. There also are fairly high concentrations in Edgewater, Norwood Park, Irving Park and Portage Park. Contrary to popular perceptions that Bridgeport is essentially Irish, large numbers of Italians, Poles, Latinos and others make up the majority of residents there. In the Cook County suburbs, high concentrations are in Arlington Heights, Oak Lawn, Orland Park, Palatine, Schaumburg and Tinley Park. Virtually every suburb has some Irish Americans. In DuPage, high concentrations are in Downers Grove, Elmhurst, Naperville, Lombard and Wheaton

Irish Americans here are well educated. About 95% in both Chicago and the greater metro area have a high school diploma, while 60% and 44%, respectively, have a college degree and 24% and 16% earned a graduate or professional degree. Median household income is high, $78,959 in the city and $74,009 in the metro area. In Chicago, 52% are in a management or professional job, while 43% in the greater metro area are. In Chicago 8% live in poverty, while 5% in the metro area do.

(Ed. note: Population figures for first ancestry come from the 2008-10 American Community Survey. All additional data are from the 2007-09 ACS survey.)

Historical background:

Irish Catholic immigrants came here to escape hunger, poverty, and British religious, economic and political oppression. The first Irish community appeared in Chicago in 1837. Most were attracted by the work offered on the Illinois and Michigan Canal, which connected Lake Michigan with the Mississippi River valley system, and later by the railroads. By 1843 foreign-born Irish made up 10% of the 7,580 people in the city. In the late 1840s a potato blight destroyed the major staple of the Irish peasant diet. The resulting famine led to the death of more than 1 million Irish and the emigration of as many more. The famine institutionalized emigration for Irish families, who would rather see their children leave to seek their fortunes elsewhere than remain in Ireland with no economic prospects. In 1860, the Irish were approximately 18% of the city's population. By 1870, the influx of other immigrant groups diminished the Irish-born share to 13%, and by 1890 the Irish were only 7% of the city's 1 million inhabitants.

Irish peasant immigrants started on the lowest rungs of the socioeconomic ladder. Men worked at unskilled jobs on the docks, at construction sites, on railroads, and in packing houses. Women were domestic servants. Poverty and the traumatic transition from rural Ireland to urban America created major social problems such as crime, alcohol abuse, dysfunctional families and juvenile delinquency. This, plus their Catholicism, provoked nativist hostility from Anglo-Protestants, who saw the Irish Catholics as a subversive force endangering American institutions and values. As a result, the Irish suffered discrimination in the workplace and at school. They responded by building their own communities within the Catholic parish system, with schools, hospitals, orphanages, and fraternal organizations.

In 1860, at their peak, the Irish were approximately 18% of the city's population.

The Irish played a major role in Chicago politics. Political skills had been honed in Ireland in agitating for Catholic Emancipation in 1828 and repeal of the Union with Britain in the 1840s. Since most Irish spoke English, they had a distinct advantage in negotiating Chicago's political and economic world. By the end of the 19th century, Irish Catholic men were prominent in City Hall and were employed in positions of political influence in the police and fire departments and on construction projects with city contracts. They dominated the Chicago City Council and ward committeeman posts and contributed eight mayors to Chicago.

While the Irish built their own Catholic subculture in the city to protect them from nativist hostility, their institutions also encouraged assimilation by equipping their children with an educational foundation to compete in American society. They advanced to the skilled labor ranks and, inspired by the nuns who taught them, Irish women became significant in nursing and teaching. Irish success was reflected in residential shifts from the center to the outskirts of the city and into neighboring suburbs. Starting in the 1940s, the GI Bill helped the Irish complete their journey into the middle class. When Chicago neighborhoods experienced racial change and white flight in the 1960s, many Irish joined the exodus to the suburbs.

Current migration patterns:

From 1992-94, about 2,400 Irish immigrated to the Chicago area, according to the INS. At the start of the 1990s, Congress authorized a lottery of 40,000 extra visas per year for three years to people from countries whose citizens formerly came in large numbers but no longer could do so under current regulations. Some 40% of those visas went to the Irish. Many were already in this country with temporary or expired visas. Irish immigration to the United States slowed in the 1990s and early 2000s when the "Celtic Tiger," as the Irish economy was called, boomed. However, Ireland experienced the same housing boom and bust and subsequent financial collapse after 2008 as did the U.S. It is not clear yet whether the Irish today will follow their forebears and resume emigration to the United States in search of economic opportunity.

Language:

In the 19th century some Irish (Gaelic) speakers emigrated to the United States. Most Irish immigrants, however, were English speakers, which aided in their assimilation into the mainstream.

Religion:

Roman Catholic.

Important traditions:

Much of native Irish culture was lost through centuries of British oppression, as well as American nativist hostility that pressured the Irish to become "respectable" and assimilate. Therefore, Catholicism became the primary source of tradition and culture for the Irish. Christenings, communions, confirmations, weddings and funerals are important rites of passage in their lives. But since the 1960s, a search for ethnic roots has led to renewed interest in Irish history, literature, dance, music and theater.

Holidays and special events:

Religious holidays and observances associated with the Catholic faith are important in Irish culture. St. Patrick's Day (March 17) has been the most noted Irish holiday in Chicago with two major parades – the St. Patrick's Day Parade in downtown Chicago and the South Side Irish Parade in Beverly Hills.

When Ireland's economy was weak in the '70s-'80s, many came on tourist visas and over-stayed.

Many restaurants and taverns cater to this celebration with traditional Irish folk music, various Irish brews, Irish stew, corned beef and cabbage, and soda bread. The Irish American Heritage Center at 4626 N. Knox Ave. in Chicago was founded 35 years ago to promote Irish history and culture and serves as a community center for the Chicago Irish. Chicago Gaelic Park at 6119 W. 147th St. in Oak Forest hosts an annual Irish Fest on Memorial Day weekend as well as Irish cultural and sporting events throughout the year. Notre Dame's Fighting Irish football team has a strong following among Chicago Irish who never attended the university. The Chicago White Sox were founded by Irish-American Charles Comiskey and for years were the team of working class Chicago Irish.

Foods for special occasions:

Due in part to Ireland's impoverished condition, Irish cuisine is not noted for its diversity. The foods that Irish Americans think of as traditional "comfort" foods are Irish soda bread, Irish stew, corned beef and cabbage (which is more Irish American), fish and chips (British Isles), and, of course, various forms of potatoes.

Dietary restrictions:

The only restrictions are dictated by fast days of the Catholic Church, which are far less frequent than in the days before Vatican II.

Names:

It was customary for many years for Irish Americans to give a girl a form of "Mary" in her name, after the Blessed Mother. Hence, there were many Mary Pats, Mary Janes, Mary Kays, Marions, Maras and Maries. Other popular names were Patricia or Patrick, Kevin, Joseph, Bridget, Kathleen, Colleen, Eileen, Noreen, Maureen, Michael and Daniel. More recently, traditional Irish names have become more popular, such as Sean, Brendan, Seamus, Colin, Liam and Kieran for boys and names such as Maire, Siobhan and Sinead as well as various forms of Kaitlyn for girls. In the old Celtic clan system surnames beginning with "O" (O'Brien, O'Connor) meant "grandson of" and those starting with "Mc" or "Mac" (McGuire, McCarthy) meant "son of." Names such as Burke, Joyce, and Fitzgerald trace their origins to the Normans, who invaded Ireland in the 12ᵗʰ and 13ᵗʰ centuries.

Major issues for community:

From the 1970s until the early 2000s the troubles in Northern Ireland were a concern for some Chicago Irish. With progress on peace talks, this issue has receded in importance. When Ireland's economy was weak in the 1970s and 1980s, many Irish came to Chicago on tourist visas, found jobs in construction and as nannies, over-stayed their visas, and joined the undocumented population of the city. As immigration has nearly stopped, many of the ties to Ireland have faded as well.

Political participation:

The Irish have a long tradition in political and civic affairs, as explained above. Many Irish names can still be found on the ballot for a variety of political and judicial offices. Irish Americans have tended historically to be Democrats because Republicans at one time were anti-Catholic and are seen as anti-immigrant. The Democratic party also support the collectivist values of the Irish with their support of labor unions and patronage jobs. However, since the 1980s, some Irish Americans have turned to the fiscal and social conservative values of the Republican Party .

Links to homeland:

Because the Irish began immigrating to the United States and Chicago so long ago, many of their personal ties to Ireland have been diminished. In the 19th century, Irish immigrants could not expect to "go home" but they did send a portion of their meager earnings to assist their families and to sponsor migration of other family members. Many of the more recent Irish immigrants, who came since WWII, maintain ties to family and return to visit because of accessibility of air travel. These ties diminish with the passing generations.

By Dr. Eileen McMahon, Associate Professor of History, Lewis University.

ITALIAN AMERICANS

Chicago population:
78,846 (first ancestry)
108,395 (first, multiple ancestries)

Metro population:
511,094 (first ancestry)
693,641 (first, multiple ancestries)

Foreign-born:
5% in Chicago, 4% in metro

Demographics:

Most Italian Americans here live in the suburbs. There are heavy concentrations in Chicago on the Northwest Side, with substantial numbers in Clearing, Dunning, Edison Park, Montclare, and around O'Hare, as

In the 1940s, Cabrini-Green housing project supplanted 'Little Sicily.'

well as in Armour Square, Bridgeport and areas to the southwest. In the suburbs, there are concentrations in Addison, Bloomingdale, Elmwood Park, Harwood Heights, Highwood, Hillside, Hinsdale, Melrose Park, Rosemont and Chicago Heights. Italian Americans here are well educated, with about 92% graduating from high school. In Chicago nearly half (49%) have a college degree and 20% a graduate or professional degree. In the metro area 36% graduated from college and 13% earned a graduate degree. Half in Chicago and 41% in metro are in a management or professional job. Median household income for Italian Americans in Chicago is $69,163, well above average. In the metro area it is $73,883.

(Ed. note: First-ancestry population figures for Italians are from the Census Bureau's American Community Survey 2008-2010. All other figures are from the 2007-09 ACS.)

Historical background:

A handful of Italians came to Chicago in 1850 from Northern Italy, but large numbers didn't arrive until years later. There was heavy migration from the 1890s to WWI (1914), under open immigration policy. They came for economic reasons, mainly from Southern Italy and Sicily, but several migration chains came from the Veneto and Tuscany regions of the north. Italians first settled on the near West Side (Taylor Street), and on the North and South Sides, including Bridgeport, 24th and Oakley, Grand Avenue and the Roseland/ Pullman neighborhoods. The Italian neighborhood on the Near North Side was known as "Little Sicily." About 16,000 Italians lived in Chicago in 1900. They tended to live in enclaves with others from their village or region.

The early immigrants were unskilled and often found jobs as railroad and construction laborers. Many were young men who planned to earn money and return home. Some did, but many stayed. The early immigrants had an ambivalent relationship with the Catholic Church, partly because in Italy it was identified with landowners, partly because in Chicago it was dominated by English-speaking Irish clergy. In 1903 the Scalabrini Fathers came to Chicago to minister to Italians here, eventually starting or taking over about a dozen churches. Italian immigrants in Chicago were subjected to prejudice and insult, often called dirty and lazy. Still, they were determined to assimilate into the life of the city.

By 1920, Italians made up more than 7% of the population. Some settled in the suburbs in the early decades of the century, especially Blue Island, Chicago Heights (which was half Italian in 1930), Highwood and Melrose Park. More came in the 1920s. While most were in unskilled jobs, others were small merchants, selling fruit and vegetables, shoes and clothing. There was always a significant group in small business, music and the arts. In the 1940s, Cabrini-Green housing project supplanted Little Sicily. In the late '50s and early '60s, urban renewal and industry began to encroach on other Italian neighborhoods. Taylor Street, which once held the most Italians, was carved up by the expressways and the University of Illinois. In the late '60s and early '70s, Roseland/Pullman residents were driven out by block busting.

During WWII, Italian Americans without U.S. citizenship had to register as enemy aliens.

Until war broke out between the U.S. and Italy in 1941, support in the Italian American community was strong for Benito Mussolini, dictator and founder of Italian fascism. Then second-generation Italian Americans went to war for America and that support diminished. During WWII, Italian Americans without U.S. citizenship were required to register as enemy aliens. After WWII, through the 1970s, Italians came to Chicago at a lively pace, with a mixture of economic migration and reuniting of families. In 1980, there were nearly 45,000 foreign-born Italians here.

Current migration patterns:

There has been little migration during the past few decades. However, a "brain drain" migration from Italy has netted Chicago a number of elite professionals in medicine, the sciences and the arts – including Carlo Muti, conductor of the Chicago Symphony.

Language:

Italian, with regional dialects. Fluency over the generations is weaker than many other Chicago ethnic groups, because of enemy alien status during WWII and U.S. Americanization policies. Most Italian Americans know a few words of Italian but 5% or fewer speak Italian only. But Italian language instruction at 15 Chicago area high schools and at most universities is experiencing steady growth due to Italy's popularity as a tourist destination and its prominence in fashion, cuisine and the arts.

Religion:

Italian Americans are overwhelmingly Roman Catholic. There also is a small number of Protestants and Jews.

Important traditions:

Italian Americans have big christenings, weddings, wakes, funerals and birthdays, all rooted in the expectation of strong family ties. Dozens of feast days are celebrated, some with street fairs, others by individual churches or communities. Weddings are lavish and it is traditional to give money as gifts to help defray the cost of the event. The wedding day is considered the most important day in a woman's life, and it is the marriage of families as well as individuals.

Holidays and special events:

These include the basic Christian holidays, with a big emphasis on Christmas Eve, Easter, St. Joseph's Day (March 19) and feasts of village patron saints. Festa Italiana (summer), Our Lady of Mount Carmel (mid-July) in Melrose Park, All Saints Day (Nov. 1) and Italy's National Day (June 2) and other various street festivals are observed. Columbus Day (Oct. 12) is a major event for Chicago's Italian Americans and is celebrated with a big parade.

Foods for special occasions:

Italian Americans traditionally have a Mediterranean diet, high in olive oil, fruits and vegetables. They place a high value on food and consider cooking an art and eating a celebration. There is an elaborate seafood dinner for

At the end of WWII there was a big effort to get family in Italy not to vote Communist.

Christmas Eve. The exact content depends on the region in Italy from which the family comes, but a dinner might include eels, squid, octopus, cod and smelt. On *Pasqua* (Easter), lamb and pasta dishes are served, along with special breads with whole eggs baked inside, and pies with ricotta cheese, eggs and sausage.

On St. Joseph's Day, many Italians Americans create St. Joseph's Day tables, a Sicilian tradition in which the fortunate provide buffet tables of food outside their homes for the poor. On this day, a special pasta, replacing cheese with breadcrumbs and sugar, is served. Also, *zeppole* (pastries) are eaten. Very few holidays are celebrated without an appropriate pasta dish. Specialty dishes, bread, pies and *dolci* (sweets) are produced for a variety of holidays. Italians often serve wine with their meals and some dilute their children's wine with lemon-lime soft drinks.

Major issues for community:

The negative stereotype and defamation of Italian Americans as involved in organized crime is the main issue that binds the community together. There also is concern about the negative stereotypes of the Italian government. Also, with more than 100 separate organizations, loosely united under the Joint Civic Committee of Italian Americans, the community has suffered from a lack of unity and a need to institutionalize its culture. Recent efforts to change this include: organizing parents to get Italian taught in schools; working closely with the Italian government to produce high-quality educational and cultural events here; gaining the resources to help establish programs and endow chairs at academic institutions; creating Italian and Italian American business expositions; and establishing a strong political presence. The Casa Italia, home of the Italian Cultural Center in Stone Park, has a 17-acre campus that is host to museum exhibits.

Political participation:

Italian Americans are trying to gain a statewide political presence in Illinois. They vote in large numbers and are politically active. Most were Democrats up into the Kennedy era, but many have moved up socioeconomically and may now be predominantly Republicans. Although no Italian has run for mayor of Chicago, there have been several aldermen (not so many now as formerly), county officials, a state treasurer, judges, and mayors of suburban towns. There have been about 20 suburban mayors of Italian origin. Italian Americans have begun to organize voter education, registration, informational forums and candidate support through the Italian American Political Coalition.

Links to homeland:

Italian Americans are linked to Italy by the Italian Consul General, Italian Cultural Institute, regional clubs, and lively commercial interaction via the Italian Trade Commission. At the end of WWII there was a big effort to get relatives in Italy not to vote Communist. Whenever there is an earthquake, the community lobbies for more U.S. aid. About 70% of those over the age of 50 have visited and look after relatives in Italy. Chicago's sister city is Milan. Chicago Heights, Addison and Niles also have sister cities.

Names:

Early generations named children for grandparents, using saints' names such as Anthony, Joseph, Dominic, Marco, Bruno, Primo and the feminine equivalents, like Maria. Most surnames end in vowels. Emphasis is usually on the next to last syllable.

Special health concerns:

Italians are among the Mediterraneans susceptible to Cooley's anemia, an inherited blood disease that destroys red blood cells. Italian American organizations often hold fundraisers seeking a cure for this and related blood diseases.

Update by Dr. Dominic Candeloro, Curator of the Florence Roselli Library at Casa Italia (Stone Park) and author of "The Italians in Chicago: Immigrants, Ethnics, Americans." Original chapter by Dr. Candeloro and Dr. Fred Gardaphe, now Distinguished Professor of English and Italian American Studies, Queens College. The two also edited "Reconstructing Italians in Chicago: Thirty Authors in Search of Roots and Branches" (Casa Italia, 2011).

JAPANESE AMERICANS

Chicago population:
4,347 (Japanese alone)
7,044 (Japanese alone or in combination)

Metro area population:
15,660 (Japanese alone)
24,948 (Japanese alone or in combo)

Foreign-born:
38% in metro

Demographics:

Japanese Americans are dispersed into many Chicago neighborhoods, with concentrations living in Uptown, Edgewater, Lake View and West Ridge. In the metropolitan area, Japanese Americans also tend to be dispersed, although larger concentrations live in the north and northwest suburbs such as Evanston, Morton Grove,

Incarceration of West Coast Japanese Americans during WWII stimulated migration to Chicago.

Skokie, Lincolnwood and Arlington Heights. Japanese Americans tend to be above average in educational attainment, with 57% earning a college degree in the Chicago metro area and 18% percent a graduate degree. Approximately 52% are in a management or professional job and median household income is $74,215 in the metro area. At the same time, one-quarter reported they did not speak English "very well" and 6.7% live in poverty.

(Ed note: The Chicago population numbers for are from the 2010 Census, as is the metro number for Japanese alone. All other numbers, including foreign-born, come from the 2007-2009 American Community Survey.)

Historical background:

The incarceration of the 120,000 West Coast Japanese Americans during WWII, as a result of Executive Order 9066, became a stimulus for migration to areas like Chicago. Many were given permission to leave the detention camps to find jobs away from West Coast security zones. In the early 1940s just several hundred Japanese families lived in Chicago, but during the migration from the camps, Chicago became the leading destination for those resettling to inland areas. Over 30,000 incarcerees settled here during the '40s and many found work in the manufacturing-based companies of that era. Some also worked in hotels and restaurants. The original areas of resettlement here were on the South Side in Kenwood, Hyde Park and Woodlawn, and on the North Side in Uptown. A major problem faced by Japanese Americans in Chicago was the refusal of cemeteries to sell them burial plots. The Japanese Mutual Aid Society bought a small communal plot at Montrose Cemetery and, amid considerable publicity, negotiated with other cemeteries for additional sites.

By 1950 most who had resettled to Chicago returned to the West Coast, leaving a population of about 11,000. Eventually, the majority of the Japanese American population would settle in Uptown and

Edgewater on the North Side of the city and, during the 1950s, in the suburbs of Lincolnwood, Morton Grove and Skokie.

Current migration patterns:

Today, most Japanese Americans are descendants of the immigrants who came to America during the period 1900-24, before the Asian Exclusion Act blocked immigration. Among the foreign-born nationwide, about one-third are naturalized U.S. citizens and two-thirds are not, according to the UCLA Asian American Studies Center. This may be reflective of many Japanese nationals who work temporarily in the U.S. for Japanese companies or students attending colleges and universities. Those numbers are about 20% and 80%, respectively, in the Chicago metro area.

Some of the foreign-born are Japanese nationals working here temporarily for Japanese companies.

Religion:

Although there are no precise figures, it is thought that a majority (50-60%) of Japanese Americans identify with Buddhism, the dominant religion of Japan. Most of the remainder belong to various Christian denominations.

Language:

Japanese, though most of the population is third-, fourth- or fifth-generation and therefore speaks English.

Important traditions:

Many of the traditions practiced by first-generation immigrants who came to America at the turn of the century have been altered or lost with the passage of time. Among those still maintained are Buddhist funerals where priests recite sutras to the accompaniment of bells and gongs, and the New Year's Day celebration. Third- (*Sansei*) and fourth- (*Yonsei*) generation Japanese Americans have displayed a curiosity about the culture and traditions of their ancestral homeland. This is demonstrated by their participation in ethnic festivals and pursuit of classes in Japanese language, *ikebana* (flower arranging), *judo, kendo* and musical instruments such as *taiko* drums.

Holidays and special events:

New Year's Day (Jan. 1) is celebrated with a preparation of traditional Japanese foods. Often, family and friends are invited to celebrate the New Year to offer good will. In addition, New Year's celebrations are held by prefecture associations (groups that originate from specific locales in Japan) and business organizations. The 60th birthday is celebrated as a milestone signifying that certain of life's responsibilities have been fulfilled and it is time to undertake new directions.

Food for special occasions:

The New Year's Day celebration features traditional Japanese food, including some that carry meaning, such as *kuromame* (black beans) signifying good health, and *tai* (whole fish) used to celebrate happy occasions. A popular New Year's item is *mochi,* a glutinous rice cake used as an ingredient in a traditional soup or toasted and eaten by hand with soy sauce. Until recent years the production of mochi was a community endeavor and the men, using wooden mallets, would pound the rice to the proper consistency while the women would shape or cut it. Mochi is considered a good-luck omen.

Names:

Before 1868 Japanese commoners were known by their first name and where they worked or lived (e.g. Jiro from Kobe). After the abolition of the feudal system, people chose family names that related to their environment or

Most Japanese Americans are several generations removed from their ancestral homeland.

to sentiments that appealed to them, such as Yamamoto (foot of the mountain), Yoshino (good field), or Ogawa (large river). In Japan, women's names are generally those of flowers, seasons and sentiments, such as Haruko (spring child). Men's names often refer to their numerical position in the family, like Jiro (second son) or Goro (fifth son). Japanese Americans rarely choose Japanese first names for their children, but Japanese middle names frequently are used.

Major issues for community:

In recent years, the Chicago Japanese American community has been concerned about the welfare of its aging and elderly population. This resulted in construction of Heiwa Terrace, a retirement residence, and Keiro, a long-term care facility. At a different level, Japanese Americans remain concerned about issues of defamation and discrimination. Stemming from their historical experience in America, Japanese Americans are very conscious about the emotional backlash from economic criticism that is directed toward Japan, because such criticism often leads to acts of defamation and incidents of anti-Asian sentiment and violence inflicted on Asian Americans.

Political participation:

Japanese Americans were among the first of the Asian American groups to become politically active in Chicago. Following their resettlement here during and around WWII, the Japanese American community actively sought passage of federal legislation to allow naturalization of the immigrant generation who were prevented by law from becoming citizens. Their efforts finally resulted in passage of the McCarran-Walter Act in 1952. This successful legislative effort necessitated communication with their members of Congress as well as with other public officials — a practice that has been maintained to the present time. A Japanese American has not been elected to public office at the state or local level in Illinois, although they have been involved actively in party politics. In states with sizable Japanese American populations, such as Hawaii and California, there is considerable involvement in the political process. At one time during the 1980s, five Japanese Americans served in Congress, a large number relative to their ethnic population. Among the various Asian American ethnic groups, Japanese Americans have one of the highest rates of voter registration.

Links to homeland:

Most Japanese Americans are several generations removed from their ancestral homeland, thus their linkage is not as strong as for more newly arrived ethnic groups. During and immediately following WWII, Japanese Americans distanced themselves from Japan as a means of protecting themselves from the perception of having any association with an "enemy" nation. Today, that concern has lessened and there is much less tendency by Japanese Americans to distance themselves from their ancestral homeland. They often travel to Japan for various reasons including business, tourism, and to visit relatives. As a community, however, Japanese Americans do not try to influence foreign policy issues involving Japan, except to encourage that any debate surrounding issues such as trade relations with the United States be devoid of emotional messages that may lead to acts of defamation directed at Japanese Americans. They remain sensitive to tragedies that occur in Japan. Following the earthquake and tsunami in northern Japan in 2011, they contributed generously to relief and recovery efforts.

Special health concerns:

The Japanese American population has aged since 2000, with a higher proportion of people over 65 than the general population. Fifteen percent of Japanese Americans are 65 or older nationwide. In Chicago, the Japanese American population is relatively small and dispersed as compared with some West Coast cities. Despite efforts by the community to build an assisted-living and nursing home facility, none currently exists in the Chicago area. Moreover, Japanese American elderly are more isolated or unwilling to avail themselves of the few ethnic health services offered by Japanese American community organizations. This isolation often results in their resistance to seeking adequate medical care or even, in some cases, to follow a healthy eating regimen. This form of self-abuse can also cause some elderly to tolerate discomfort and pain rather than reach out for assistance. Finally, there is a shortage of social service personnel who possess the cultural competence to administer to the needs of the Japanese American elderly.

By William Yoshino, Midwest Director of the Japanese American Citizens League.

JEWISH AMERICANS

Chicago population:
89,250

Metro (6-county) population:
291,800

Foreign-born:
14% in metro

Ed. note: The Census Bureau does not collect information on religion or give people the opportunity to check Jewish ancestry. The data here are estimates from the 2010 Chicago Jewish Population Study of the Jewish Federation of Metropolitan Chicago.

Demographics:

The Chicago metro area's Jewish population ranks fourth in the United States after New York, Los Angeles and Miami. It is about two-thirds suburban, reflecting a heavy out-migration from the city beginning in the late 1940s and early '50s. Among the native-born, most are second-, third-, or even fourth-generation Americans. The notable exception to this pattern is the approximately 23,000 Russian-speaking Jewish immigrants who came from the former Soviet Union beginning in the 1970s. A small number of Israelis and Jews from South Africa have also settled in Chicago.

In the 1880s tens of thousands came, mainly from Eastern Europe and Russia.

Since the 1950s, Jewish population and institutions have clustered on the North Side in West Rogers Park, Albany Park, Hollywood Park, Peterson Park, the North Side lakefront, and the Gold Coast. On the South Side, Hyde Park-Kenwood has several synagogues and a Jewish day school. Outside the city, most Jews reside in the North Shore suburbs of Skokie, Evanston, Wilmette, Winnetka, Glencoe, Highland Park, Northbrook, Glenview and Deerfield. Some 30,000 Jews live in the western and southern suburbs of Oak Park, River Forest, Homewood, Flossmoor and Olympia Fields. As a result of continued outward migration, northwest suburbs like Buffalo Grove, Schaumburg and Vernon Hills have seen an increase in synagogues and other Jewish institutions.

While national data suggest the Jewish community is relatively affluent and well educated compared with other ethnic and religious groups, Jews have been affected by downward national economic trends, like everyone else. In a 2010 community survey, 47 percent of respondents identified themselves as "comfortable" economically while 35 percent said they are "just making ends meet" or "cannot make ends meet" economically. Occupationally, Jews are concentrated in business and the professions, with some in education and social services.

Historical background:

Jews have lived in Chicago since the 1830s. Early immigrants came from Central Europe, especially from Germany, settling in the city center. After the 1871 fire most moved to the South Side. They were mostly in business and, to a lesser extent, the professions. The community's growth was steady but slow, probably totaling less than 6,000 after 50 years.

The 1880s saw the start of a dramatic increase in the Jewish population, as tens of thousands of immigrants came, mainly from Eastern Europe and Russia. They concentrated on the West Side particularly in the Maxwell Street area. As the community struggled to absorb increasing numbers of mostly poor immigrants, tensions arose between the older, better-educated and assimilated Reform Jews of German origin and newcomers who were often uneducated, and mostly religiously Orthodox. Moreover, the new immigrants were more likely to be peddlers or laborers whereas the earlier settlers were already several steps higher on the socioeconomic ladder. The next several decades saw the Jewish population balloon to an estimated 300,000 by 1930. This number may have increased slightly after World War II, but the population began to decline in the 1950s, as war refugees stopped coming, the birthrate declined, and migration to other parts of the country, particularly California, increased. The population had spread west to Lawndale after World War I. Almost half the Jewish population of Chicago lived in this area well into the 1940s. Synagogues and temples multiplied with the population

A low birthrate and intermarriage keep the Jewish population from increasing significantly.

increase, as did community centers, which provided welfare assistance as well as social activities. Yiddish theaters, religious schools, health-care facilities, and other communal organizations also flourished. While no longer concentrated in one geographic area, an extraordinary network of social services exists for the community and provides needed services to others as well.

Current migration patterns:

The community is now relatively stable with nearly equal numbers of children ages 0 to 17 and elderly aged 65 and above. A low birthrate and considerable intermarriage keep the Jewish population from increasing significantly. The number of Jews in Chicago increased by approximately 1 percent between 2000 and 2010 in part because significant numbers of Jews in their 20s have moved to Chicago from smaller Jewish communities. Movement to the suburbs continues, especially among those with school-age children. There is some reverse migration from suburbs to city, particularly among empty-nesters.

Language:

Chicago-area Jews, by and large, are not bilingual, though significant numbers, particularly those who are more religiously traditional, know Hebrew. Yiddish, the *lingua franca* of the immigrant generation a century ago, is now spoken only by a small number of Orthodox Jews mostly affiliated with the Vietzner Yeshiva in West Rogers Park. Russian is spoken by immigrants and many of the second-generation who came from the former Soviet Union.

Religion:

Synagogue affiliation is relatively high with an estimated 60% of the population belonging to Orthodox, Conservative, Reform or Reconstructionist synagogues. The rest do not claim membership in a specific synagogue, but may consider themselves Reform, Conservative or "just Jewish." Of the affiliated, about 15% are Orthodox; 40% Reform; 40% Conservative; and the remainder are Reconstructionist or "other."

Important traditions:

Rites of passage begin shortly after birth with a *Brit Milah* or *bris* (ritual circumcision) for boys and a naming ceremony for girls. At 13 (12 for some girls), children are welcomed into the adult religious community with a *bar-* (for boys) or *bat-* (for girls) *mitzvah*, at which the young person demonstrates knowledge of Judaism and ability to read the Torah and/or lead services. Jewish wedding ceremonies take place under a *chupah*, or wedding canopy, symbolizing the new home town the couple will build together. The ceremony includes the breaking of a glass, recalling the destruction of the ancient Temple in Jerusalem. When someone dies, burial takes place as quickly as possible, usually within 24 hours. Traditional Jews frown on autopsies and avoid embalming or cremation. Mourning, or "sitting *shiva*," for a family member who has died is an important expression of respect for both the dead and the living. Instead of flowers, donations to life-affirming causes are preferred. In varying degrees, these traditions are observed even by those unaffiliated with a synagogue.

Clothing and comportment may distinguish Orthodox Jews. In religious settings, Orthodox Jews are gender-separate. Typically, they do not shake hands. Physical contact is reserved for husbands and wives or, in some cases, family members. The most observant Orthodox Jews dress in a manner designed to separate them from secular

Traditional Jews frown on autopsies, embalming and cremation, so burial is quick.

society. Men wear black hats and suits. They do not cut their sideburns and some do not shave. Women dress modestly wearing long skirts and blouses that cover their arms. They also cover their hair with wigs, hats or scarves. While favoring modest dress, modern Orthodox Jews are more likely to blend into secular society. Men may wear hats or *kippot* (small skullcaps, sometimes called *yarmulkes*). Modern Orthodox women may cover their heads with stylish hats or scarves. Conservative Jewish men sometimes cover their heads with kippot outside of worship. Otherwise, Conservative, Reform and Reconstructionist Jews dress similarly to secular society.

Holidays and special events:

The Jewish year is based on a lunar calendar so from year to year Jewish holidays will not fall on the same day or even month in the secular calendar. Jewish holidays begin at sundown and extend until sunset the following day. *Shabbat*, the Jewish Sabbath is marked beginning 20 minutes before sundown Friday and extending to approximately 40 minutes after sunset on Saturday. The High Holy days, *Rosh Hashanah* (the Jewish New Year) and *Yom Kippur* (the Day of Atonement) are the most widely observed in synagogues. Yom Kippur is the holiest day of the year, marked by 24 hours of fasting from sundown to sundown. The Pilgrimage festivals include Passover (March or April), *Sukkoth*, the Feast of Booths (September or October), and *Shavout* (Pentacost), which commemorates the giving of the Torah on Mt. Sinai (May or June). Each of these holidays has agricultural, historical and spiritual significance. Passover celebrates the Exodus of the Jews from Egypt and includes a *Seder* meal. Sukkoth commemorates the 40 years of Jewish wandering in the desert on the way to the Promised Land. Many Jews celebrate by building a *Sukkah* (booth) where they eat during the seven days of the festival.

Minor holidays include *Chanukah*, the festival of Lights (November or December) and *Purim*, the Feast of Lots (February or March). *Chanukah* (often spelled *Hannukah*) marks the heroic battle of the Maccabees against the Syrian-Greeks in 165 B.C.E. Jews light candles (one the first night, two the second, and so on). On these nights, children play with a *dreidel* (spinning top). Because of its proximity to Christmas,

Chanukah is also celebrated with gift giving, especially in families with children. For *Purim*, the Biblical book of Esther is read in the synagogue at night and the following morning. The holiday commemorates the downfall of the wicked Haman who sought to kill the Jews of Persia. Adults and children may dress up as one of the characters from the Purim story. Families share plates of food with friends and neighbors and give money to charity as part of the holiday observance. Two other commemorations, *Yom HaShoah*, recalling those murdered in the Holocaust, and *Yom Ha'atzmaut*, celebrating the birth of modern Israel (both in April or May) are observed in public ceremonies.

Foods for special occasions:

Jewish food reflects both immigrant history and festive occasions. Virtually every holiday has a special dish associated with it, reflecting Eastern European (Ashkenazic) or Mediterranean (Sephardic) roots. In Jewish homes where Shabbat is observed, families make or buy *challah*, (special braided egg bread). At Rosh Hashanah these

The percentage of Jews who vote regularly is twice that for the general population.

breads may be round and filled with raisins. Bread has religious significance and no meal is complete without it. On Rosh Hashanah, honey cake or apple dipped in honey may be eaten to signify a sweet year. Chanukah is often celebrated with foods fried in oil to commemorate the miracle of a small amount of oil lasting eight days. For Purim, *hamantash* (a three-cornered pastry filled with poppy seeds, honey or preserves) is popular. Unleavened bread, *matzo*, is eaten during the eight days of Passover.

Dietary restrictions:

Jewish law regarding food (*kashrut*) is complex. Among other things, it requires separating meat and dairy products (and the utensils and dishes used for them), and forbids eating shellfish and meat from animals that do not have a cloven hoof and chew their cuds. Animals must be slaughtered according to specific and humane rules. Most traditionally observant Jews will "keep kosher" by following the rules of kashrut both at home and outside. Some Jews maintain a strictly kosher home but will be more flexible with what they eat outside their homes. Others avoid eating proscribed foods but don't worry about dishes or utensils and many Jews do not observe any form of kashrut at all.

Names:

In the minds of many, there are clearly identifiable names that have for hundreds of years been identified as Jewish, mostly coming from Europe. Many such names have occupational origins. Some, like Cohen (the priestly class) or Levy (guardians of the temple) have religious roots. Others, particularly first names, have clear biblical origins, like Sarah, David, Jonathan and Rachel. Because of assimilation and intermarriage, except for the most traditionally religious community, it is virtually impossible to identify someone as Jewish by first name.

Major issues for community:

The critical issues are intermarriage, Jewish continuity and the maintenance of Jewish identity in a secular society; Israel's safety and security; anti-Semitism in the United States and abroad, and the security of Jewish communities in other parts of the world. Domestically, the community is also concerned about separation of church and state, fair immigration policy, the future of quality public education in America, and prejudice and discrimination in American life generally.

Political participation:

Jews historically have been active politically, perhaps more so than any other ethnic community. The percentage of Jews who vote regularly is twice that for the general population. They have been active as volunteers and financial supporters for candidates at the local, state and national levels. Jews traditionally have voted for more Democrats than Republicans though younger Jews tend to be more independent in voting.

Links to homeland:

While Israel is not literally the homeland for America's Jews, it is the historic homeland of the Jewish people and occupies a far more central role in the life of the community than homelands do for some other ethnic groups. Religious, communal, social, political and psychological links to Israel are central to the community's definition of itself. Many Chicago Jews have family in Israel and about half of Chicago-area Jews have visited Israel, some many times. A number of Jewish organizations focus primarily on ties with Israel.

Special health concerns:

Jews of European descent are at somewhat higher risk than the general population for four genetic disorders: Tay-Sachs disease, Canavan disease, cystic fibrosis and familial dysautonomia. A genetic link to breast cancer has also been found in some Jewish women. Testing is available but a 2004 community health survey suggests less than half the local Jewish population has been tested. That survey indicated Chicago Jews are at greater health risk from hypertension and obesity than genetic diseases. Jewish rates of obesity, diabetes and hypertension mirror those of the general population in the U.S., but Jews have a lower rate for smoking and alcohol use.

By Emily D. Soloff, National Associate Director for Interreligious and Intergroup Relations, American Jewish Committee.

KOREAN AMERICANS

Chicago population:

11,422 (Korean alone)

13,418 (Korean alone and in combination)

Metro population:

54,135 (Korean alone)

Foreign-born:

About 80% in the city, 71% in metro

Demographics:

One conspicuous trend of the past 10 years has been further suburbanization from near suburbs to far suburbs. Hence while the number of Korean Americans in Cook County increased only slightly, the number of Korean Americans in Lake, DuPage, Kane, McHenry and Will counties have increased significantly since 2000.

The first Korean immigrants arrived in Honolulu in 1903, to work on sugar plantations.

Lake County, for example, has increased its Korean population by 79% to 7,334 residents from 4,089. The suburban towns and villages that have more than 1,000 Korean Americans include: Glenview, Northbrook, Evanston, Skokie, Morton Grove on the north, Mount Prospect, Arlington Heights, Hoffman Estates, Buffalo Grove, Palatine, Schaumburg, Vernon Hills and Naperville. In Chicago, Korean Americans live in such North and Northwest Side neighborhoods as West Ridge, Rogers Park, North Park, Albany Park and Uptown.

Korean Americans in the metro area are very well educated; 58% have a college degree or more and 23% have a graduate or professional degree. Just over half (51%) are in a management or professional job (compared with 37% for the overall population). Median household income is $59,595 and 14% live below the poverty line. With so many foreign-born, 45% in the metro area say they speak English "less than very well." According to community estimates, 20% of all Korean Americans families are engaged in small businesses, one-quarter of which represent dry-cleaning operations; the number of Korean American dry cleaners in the metro area peaked around 2,000 before the 2008 recession, and dominated the cleaners industry in Illinois. Many Koreans also are engaged in the selling of general merchandise, the operation of beauty supply and clothing stores, running snack shops, and the import/export business. The Korean business community is evident in Albany Park along Lawrence Avenue, and has a growing commercial presence along Milwaukee Avenue north of Dempster Street and on Dempster west of the Edens Expressway. Korean businesses within the city limits also run along Bryn Mawr, Lincoln, Foster, Clark, Peterson and Devon. Though the ambiance of the community is still first-generation, the first cohort of the second generation has come into adulthood, excelling in various professions, and has begun to play a significant leadership role in the community. The 1.5 generation – those born in Korea but raised here – still carry a responsibility to bridge between Korean Americans and the larger society. The Chicago metropolitan area is home to about 4% of the Korean American population in the United States. As the Midwest is losing its population to Sunbelt states, Illinois, which used to be the 3rd largest state in terms of Korean American population for many decades, now ranks 7th after California, New York, New Jersey, Virginia, Texas and Washington.

(Ed. note: Total population numbers for Koreans alone are from 2010. Other data are from the 2007-09 and 2008-10 ACS.)

Historical background:

Korean Americans celebrated their immigration centennial in 2003, as the first ship of Korean immigrants arrived in Honolulu in 1903 to work in Hawaiian sugar plantations. A number of U.S. states, including Illinois, have declared Jan. 13 – in commemoration of the date of the first arrival – as Korean American Day, honoring Korean Americans' contributions to their adopted country. This first phase of the Korean immigration to Hawaii ended in 1905, and the second phase of immigration to the U.S. began 60 years later with the change in U.S. immigration law in 1965 that allowed people from the Eastern Hemisphere to immigrate to this country. During the interim period few came. A small number of students came to study and settled here, as well as picture brides of the Korean laborers in Hawaii, war and GI brides during and after the Korean War of 1950-53, and Korean children adopted by American families.

In the late 1960s, many who arrived first were health professionals and of various middle-class backgrounds who came to seek better economic and educational opportunity for themselves and their children. There were also college-graduate coal miners who went to West Germany because of job scarcity in Korea, then settled in Chicago in the '60s along with their wives, many of whom were nurses. Many of these immigrants came from the generation that grew up under Japanese occupation and then lived through the Korean War. The early Koreans settled in Wrigleyville and Uptown. Some qualified for subsidized housing but most lived in cheaper rental apartments until they saved enough money to buy a modest home, usually within 5-10 years of arrival. Many worked in nursing, unskilled labor, janitorial services, and driving buses. From the early 1970s on, the Koreans who immigrated were college-educated and tended to be in their 30s, including many nurses and engineers. Eventually they invited their parents to come to the United States.

Current migration patterns:

Immigration has significantly slowed since the late 1980s because South Korea is experiencing economic prosperity and restored democracy, after the civilian candidate – not of the military regime – won the presidential election in 1992. In retrospect, the 1988 Seoul Olympics, symbolic of Korean national strength, was the turning point to halt the Korean migration to the United States. The immigrant life in America is perceived of as rough and strenuous back in Korea, hence less desirable to embrace. The Los Angeles riots in 1992 might have put some real pictures to the argument that life was hard in America. The number of direct migrations from Korea to America has steadily declined, and there have been fewer than 1,000 people annually in the recent years. In 2011, for example, only 618 Koreans reported to the Korean government their emigration to the United States.

On the other hand, the number of visa status adjusters has significantly increased. These adjusters are Koreans who had already been residing in the United States when they changed their visa status to that of permanent residence. A great majority of them were previously students, employees of American branches of Korean companies, their family members, and visitors. In fiscal year 2010, for instance, 22,227 Koreans adjusted their status in the United States, according to a U.S. Citizenship and Immigration Services statistic. It is estimated that 122 North Koreans entered to the United States since the adoption of the North Korea Human Rights Act in 2004, and a few of these refugees live in metropolitan Chicago. Although most North Korean refugees scattered in northern China prefer to settle in South Korea, some choose to take asylum or refugee status in the United States in order to seek educational opportunities and avoid discrimination in South Korea.

Language:

Korean is the only spoken and written language for all Koreans. The spoken language varies by region with different dialects. Sejong the Great created the Korean alphabet, *Hangul*, during the 15th century, which is easy to read and write and has greatly contributed to Korea's high literacy rate. Some Korean words can also be written in Chinese characters. Most second-generation children attend Saturday Korean schools to learn the language and study Korean culture and history, but their fluency level tends to be limited. As job opportunities grow in Korea in the area of international trade and English teaching, interested second-generation Korean Americans take Korean language classes in college and continue by enrolling in adult Korean language classes offered in community organizations.

Religion:

Religion has played an important role in the community by providing spiritual guidance, emotional gratification among co-ethnic Koreans, and practical support in the settlement and acculturation process. Koreans in Illinois are predominantly Protestant with about 200 congregations in metropolitan Chicago. There are also four Catholic churches/missions, and three Buddhist temples in Illinois, mostly in the Chicago metro area.

The surname Kim is held by more than 20% of all Koreans.

Independent of religious affiliation, Confucian values are deeply ingrained into everyday life of Korean Americans – respect for elders, patience and public mindedness still seem to influence the collective consciousness of Korean Americans, instilling moderation and propriety.

Important traditions:

Korean culture is hierarchical. Therefore, respect for elders is essential. When a person greets someone who is older, he or she bows and greets in a language befitting the elder. "Hi. How are you?" in the American casual way would not be acceptable. On New Year's Day, it is traditional to wear Korean dress and visit parents and grandparents and bow on one's knees (*jul*) to elders. In turn, the elders wish younger people good fortune, health and prosperity, and give them cash gifts.

Holidays and special events:

The Lunar New Year or *sul* Jan. 1 and *Chusuk* (Aug. 15 of the lunar year), the Harvest Day when the moon is brightest, are two major holidays. Although the Lunar New Year is based on the traditional lunar calendar, Korean Americans in Chicago celebrate the solar Jan. 1 as the day to celebrate the New Year. Chusuk – literally meaning Autumn Night – is celebrated based on the lunar calendar since it is the night of full moon of the 8th month, usually falling in late September. Korean Americans celebrate these two holidays by visiting the gravesites of their parents, playing games like *yut* (four-stick game), and enjoying meals with the extended family. Community organizations also coordinate special events like congregational meals and traditional games for senior citizens.

Foods for special occasions:

Korean food is very seasonal. For example, during the summer, Koreans enjoy eating *naeng myun* (a cold buckwheat noodle soup). In the winter, there are hot (both spicy and steaming) soups to go with the cold season. One traditional and special food is eaten on New Year's Day. No matter to whose house one may go, *ttuk guk* – rice cake soup in steamy beef broth – is served, often with dumplings, *mandu*, to make it *ttuk mandu guk.* During Chusuk, rice cakes with beans inside steamed with pine leaves – *songpyun* – are served. *Kimchi* – fermented salad made from Chinese cabbage, hot peppers and garlic – is a side dish at almost every meal. Korean Americans also eat a lot of hot broth like bean paste, fish or tofu soup.

Names:

Most first-generation Korean Americans transliterated their names, placing the surname last, as opposed to the traditional Korean way of having the surname before one's given name. Many Korean American immigrants name their second-generation children with English first names and Korean middle names. Most Korean first names are two syllables, one shared by all siblings and the other unique to the individual; each syllable has a distinctive meaning. Korean names reveal what hopes the family has for the newborn. The surname Kim is held by more than 20% of all Koreans. Other last names include Lee, Park, Choi and Chung.

Major issues for community:

There are four major issues that affect the Korean American community. First, it has been the steady goal of the Korean American community to achieve socioeconomic mainstreaming. Many small-business owners tend to be relegated to labor-intensive trade, often in "high risk" neighborhoods. As some of them begin to retire from their businesses and their children, entering various professional and other jobs, are not succeeding their parents, the small business is becoming a one-generation phenomenon in the community. Second, political participation has been the issue of the community with U.S. citizenship applications, voter registration, and get-out-the-vote (GOTV) campaign. The community is still looking for a workable strategy in which various efforts can be orchestrated, including fundraising for political candidates.

As children don't follow their parents, the small business is becoming a one-generation thing.

Third, a generation gap exists between parents and their children. Often second-generation youth are detached from their culture and community and unaware of their parents' background unless they take the initiative to study on their own, as only a few schools in the U.S. cover Korean and Korean American history. Fourth, the lives of Korean Americans are directly affected by U.S. policy towards Korea, both South and North. Peace and reunification of the two Koreas are very important to the Korean American community.

Political participation:

As the community achieved the initial stage of settlement and began to understand the functioning of the American system, Korean Americans enlarged their focus to pay attention to grassroots politics. U.S. citizenship applications, civics education, voter registration, candidate forums, canvassing, GOTV, and phone banking became important organizing activities of several not-for-profit community organizations, independent of party affiliations and partisan support. In the community-at-large, fundraising is often organized for political candidates, early voting among Korean Americans is coordinated, voters are mobilized in certain north suburban districts where Korean Americans constitute a significant voting bloc, and there have been several Korean American candidates in local and statewide elections. Because the community is small, Korean Americans still need to strategically align their resources – financial, votes, and professional expertise – and rigorously coalesce with people beyond the Korean community. Koreans do not seem to gravitate specifically to either political party.

Links to homeland:

There are numerous Korean-language media in the community, including two daily papers, two radio stations, and one television station. News from Korea is transmitted every day to Chicago via satellite and simultaneously available on the Internet. The second generation also acquires information about Korea – including K-pops, entertainment, dramas, and movies – through the Internet. The bifurcation of Korea and America seems to become less significant, if not irrelevant, in cyberspace. There are Korean and Internet bookstores where books, CDs and DVDs can be purchased, and these are also available in local public libraries. As the Free Trade Agreement is now ratified both in the United States and Korea, trade and visits back and forth are expected to increase significantly.

Special health concerns:

There are growing health needs by the first generation, who are often uninsured or underinsured, with a lack of services for the aging population. Because a sizeable number of Korean Americans engage in small business, if not self-employment, many cannot afford health insurance for themselves, their families and employees. If they do buy it, there is a high deductible, to keep premiums down. Also, as immigrants' diets changed

Peace and reunification of the two Koreas are very important to Korean Americans.

in America to high meat consumption, there are more health concerns about high cholesterol, triglyceride and sugar levels combined with high blood pressure. This is of particular concern to the uninsured in the pre-Medicare cohort, ages 50-64. Community organizations run low-cost screenings to help meet these needs. Special programs are targeted at women over 40, with breast and cervical cancer screenings offered at several local health facilities, as well as education programs on weight control and diabetes plus chronic disease maintenance.

Fall prevention is gaining momentum as an educational program for seniors with fragile bones who don't exercise adequately. Community organizations also are working on exercising the minds of seniors to ward off dementia, though ESL and IT classes, hobbies and leisure events that bring seniors out of isolation. Mental health needs consist of depression, anxiety, anger management and various other disorders. The idea of counseling or psychotherapy carries a stigma. The Korean culture is not a "talking culture" but rather regards silent perseverance as a virtue. As a result, conflict can be expressed in a hostile manner.

Update by Inchul Choi, Executive Director of Korean American Community Services (KACS); Jae Choi Kim, Attorney; Hyeyoung Lee, Director of Senior Services and Public Benefits, KACS. Original by Choi and Choi Kim. Portions of this were also printed at Asian American Compass, 4th edition, published by the Asian American Institute.

LITHUANIAN AMERICANS

Chicago population:
7,159 (first ancestry)

Metro population:
54,278 (first ancestry)
86,691 (first and multiple ancestries)

Foreign-born:
16% in metro

Demographics:

In the early 1900s most Lithuanians were concentrated on the near South Side in Bridgeport and Town of Lake (Stockyards). They spread to adjoining neighborhoods — Brighton Park, Gage Park and Marquette Park — and to Roseland on the far South Side. Today, small communities remain in the Marquette Park and Brighton Park neighborhoods. Over the past 25 years, significant numbers of Lithuanians have moved throughout

The Chicago area has the largest concentration of Lithuanians outside Lithuania.

the metropolitan area, to places like Lemont, Palos Hills, Oak Lawn, Downers Grove and Naperville. The establishment of the Lithuanian World Center, a 130,000-square-foot cultural, educational and religious center in suburban Lemont, was a magnet for Lithuanian Americans to move to that area. Today the number in the suburbs far outweighs those in the city. The Chicago area has the largest concentration of Lithuanians outside of Lithuania. Lithuanian Americans are well educated, with 95% in the metro area having a high school diploma, 43% a college degree or higher and 17% a graduate or professional degree. Median household income is $71,046, about $10,000 above average, and 43% are in management or professional jobs. Some 9% say they do not speak English "very well" and 5% live in poverty.

(Ed. note: First ancestry population numbers are from the 2008-10 American Community Survey. All others numbers are from the 2007-09 ACS.)

Historical background:

Chicago's Lithuanians came from two Lithuanias — Lithuania Major (Republic of Lithuania) and Lithuania Minor (East Prussia). The first Lithuanian to make a significant contribution to this nation was Alexandras Carolus, a native of the Kursas region, the first schoolteacher in New Amsterdam, NY, 1659-1661. Descendants of Lithuanians from the Kursas region maintain three Lithuanian Protestant churches here: Lithuanian Evangelical Lutheran Church in Western Springs, and Lithuanian Evangelical Reformed Church and Zion Evangelical Lutheran Church in Oak Lawn. Large-scale economic migration from predominantly Roman Catholic Lithuania Major occurred when incessant rains, followed by drought and difficulties experienced in the Lithuanian occupation by Czarist Russia, caused more than 20 percent of the population to emigrate, between 1868 and 1914. The majority came to the United States where, after 1903, they formed their largest community in Chicago.

Once here, Lithuanians were often classified as Russians because they had lived under the rule of the

Russian Empire. Further confusion resulted when Lithuanians were classified as Poles, because both were Roman Catholic, whereas Protestant Lithuanians were confused with Germans. University of Chicago researcher Carl D. Buck tried to count the number of Lithuanians in 1903 and calculated between 10,000-15,000. Arriving without any education or occupational training, they entered the lowest level of the work force. Many worked in factories. But once they learned English, sizable numbers ventured into entrepreneurial enterprises. Guided by the peasant custom of mutual assistance between neighbors, they formed self-help associations that helped them create savings and loan associations, banks and automobile dealerships. These in turn generated capital for investment in other businesses, as well as enabling the majority of Lithuanians to become homeowners. Lithuanians organized 20 banks in Illinois between 1897-1926. In 1919, the founder of the Lithuanian Chamber of Commerce, Stanley Balzekas, Sr., opened his automobile dealership which, to this day, is carried on by his son, Stanley Balzekas, Jr., founder of the Balzekas Museum of Lithuanian Culture, and his grandson, Stanley Balzekas III.

When the USSR invaded and occupied Lithuania in 1940, the Chicago Lithuanian community helped form the Lithuanian American Council, which lobbied President Franklin Roosevelt, who assured a delegation that Lithuania would one day be free again. LAC sponsored and resettled 10,000 Lithuanian refugees arriving in Chicago between 1948-52. These second-wave emigres in the post-WWII era found the first wave well-established in social, political, economic and educational spheres of urban Chicago — especially in the

In the early 1900s, many were classified as Russians because they'd been under Russian rule.

neighborhoods of Bridgeport, Brighton Park, Town of Lake and Marquette Park. There were 16 Roman Catholic parishes and schools, two hospitals, a Lithuanian press and two cemeteries, Lithuanian National Cemetery and St. Casimir's Lithuanian Cemetery. Using the established communal base, the second wave went on to create a bevy of new organizations and institutions clustered around the Lithuanian World Community, the Ateitis Federation, the multimillion-dollar philanthropic Lithuanian Foundation, and the Lithuanian Scouts Association, as well as other political, professional, cultural and academic organizations for all age groups and interests.

Current migration patterns:

The March 11, 1990, independence of Lithuania from the Soviet Union initiated a new cycle of economic immigrants. An estimated 20,000 have arrived in the Chicago area since 1990. Of these, several thousand are undocumented. This "third wave" joined established Lithuanian American organizations and have set up their own. Whereas the immigrants from 1948-52 were political refugees, the most recent ones are here primarily for a better economic life.

Language:

Lithuanian, with its archaic sound system and little-changed morphological structure, is the oldest living Indo-European language. It preserves old grammatical and lexical features found in such ancient languages as Sanskrit. Lithuanian belongs to the Baltic branch of Indo-European languages along with Latvian and Old Prussian (the latter is extinct)

Religion:

Predominantly Roman Catholic, along with Lutherans and Jews.

Important traditions:

These are primarily tied to Roman Catholic sacraments such as baptism, holy communion and marriage. Wakes and funerals are traditional Roman Catholic. Lithuania has a strong folk craft tradition, so that most Lithuanians have at least some amber, wood carvings, woven linen, and art and straw Christmas ornaments.

Holidays and special events:

The major holidays are religious: Christmas Eve and Easter. The community commemorates Independence of Feb. 16, 1918, after 130 years of Russian occupation; and the more recent Independence of March 11, 1990, after 50 years of Soviet occupation. St. Casimir's Day (March 4), for the Patron Saint of Lithuania, is celebrated

An estimated 20,000 Lithuanians have arrived in the Chicago area since 1990.

with St. Casimir's Fair, which takes place locally at the Lithuanian World Center, 14911 W. 127th Street, Lemont, on the closest Sunday. Day of Sorrow (June 15), recalls the June 15, 1940, occupation of Lithuania by the Soviet Union, and the start of killings and deportations, as well as the June 1941 massive deportations to Siberia. Other special local events include folk dance festivals and annual operas in the spring. On political holidays some participants wear folk costumes.

Foods for special occasions:

Easter eggs are decorated, with some used for games such as egg rolling and going around the traditional Easter table to exchange greetings and see whose egg will survive tapping from the others. Christmas Eve has a tradition of 12 meatless dishes. Christmas wafers are shared with others at the Christmas Eve table. Each person takes the other's wafer and kisses or shows some other sign of affection. Pancakes are the specialty on Shrove Tuesday. Other special dishes include *kugelis* (grated potatoes baked with bacon, onions and eggs), *cepelinai* (potato dumplings filled with ground beef), *virtiniai* (meat, cheese or mushroom dumplings), and *Napoleon* torts (about 20 thin layers of baked dough with butter cream and layers of fruit in between), *baravykai* (a mushroom that is a delicacy) and *saltibarsciai* (cold beet soup).

Dietary restrictions:

None, except for meatless Fridays during Lent for Roman Catholics.

Names:

Masculine names often end in *-is*, *-as*, and *-ys*. The feminine names end mostly in *-a* and *-e*. The tradition is to give a child a saint's name and a traditional Lithuanian name. For example, the co-author's first name is Alexander (a saint's name) and second name is Rimas (a traditional Lithuanian pre-Christian name).

Major issues for community:

Main concerns are preservation of the Lithuanian language and culture in face of assimilation into the broader American society; and relations between Lithuanian Americans and Lithuanians in Lithuania and worldwide.

Political participation:

Lithuanian Americans actively vote and participate in their communities. Few run for elective office, though Sen. Richard Durbin (D-IL.) is a Lithuanian American. Participation was at its maximum during Lithuania's

Sen. Richard Durbin (D-IL.) is a Lithuanian American.

struggle to regain its independence after Soviet occupation, in terms of both voting and lobbying. Lithuanian Americans are a mix of Republicans, Democrats and Independents.

Links to homeland:

Citizenship in Lithuania was not available during the Soviet occupation. Since Lithuania regained its independence, a number who were born in Lithuania have maintained dual citizenship to the extent allowed by United States law. There are strong ties among Lithuanians worldwide, with most families having relatives in Lithuania as well as in other parts of the United States, Canada and Australia. Relatives visit back and forth. Lithuanian Americans give generously to people in need in Lithuania through various charitable organizations. The Leonas Kriauceliunas Family Foundation of Lemont built and equipped the small animal clinic of the Lithuanian Veterinary Academy with a $1 million donation. The Janina Marks Foundation established an art and cultural center in Lithuania.

Original by Dr. Antanas J. Van Reenan, author of "Lithuanian Diaspora: Königsberg to Chicago," and Alexander Rimas Domanskis, Past President of the Lithuanian World Center. Updated by Domanskis.

MEXICAN AMERICANS

Chicago population:
578,100 (Mexican alone)

Metro population:
1,546,171 (alone)

Foreign-born:
47% in Chicago, 45% in metro

Demographics:

The Chicago metropolitan area has the fourth largest Mexican-origin population in the United States. Mexicans are 20% of the city's population; they are nearly 80% of the total Latino population in Chicago. Historically, the vast majority of Mexican Americans have lived in Chicago and Cook County. They continue to live throughout the city and are most heavily represented in South Lawndale, popularly

Mexicans who came during and right after WWI worked in meatpacking, steel and railroads.

known as Little Village, as well as Pilsen, Brighton Park, Belmont Cragin and Gage Park. The number of Mexican Americans in Cook County has about doubled since 1990, from 465,765, to 922,410. Mexicans have also lived in many Cook County suburbs for several decades. In recent years, they have migrated directly to the suburbs or moved there from Chicago.

Today, the vast majority of Mexican Americans live outside the city limits. Large populations live in suburban Cook County communities, including Berwyn, Cicero, Leyden and Proviso Township. Mexicans also live in Kane County, including Aurora, Elgin and Carpentersville. In Lake County, sizable Mexican American populations reside in Waukegan and Round Lake Beach. In Will County, most live in Joliet, the county's seat. In DuPage County, they are in Addison and West Chicago. Just over half of Mexican Americans graduated from high school; 51% in Chicago have a diploma and 55% in the metro area. About 9% have a bachelor's degree, and 2% a managerial or professional degree. Among those employed, about 13% are managers or professionals in Chicago. Median household income for Mexican Americans in Chicago is $41,393, while it is $46,733 in the metro area; 22% in the city and 18% in metro are living in poverty. In the city, 47% said they speak English "less than very well." In the metro area, 45% did. About 28% who were born outside the U.S. have become U.S. citizens, while 72% have not. The estimated number of undocumented Mexicans living in the Chicago metro area is 397,000 — about 65% of all undocumented in the area, according to the Institute for Latino Studies, University of Notre Dame.

(Ed. note: The total population figures are from the 2010 Census. Other numbers come from the 2007-09 ACS.)

Historical background:

Mexicans and Mexican Americans have a long history in Illinois. The 1850 Census showed 50 living in the state. Mexican immigration to Chicago has come in distinct waves. According to the 1920 Census, 1,224 Mexicans lived in Chicago, many of whom migrated from Michoacán, Jalisco, Guanajuato and Zacatecas. Mexicans first found their way here in large numbers during the Mexican Revolution (1910-20). It was possible to travel to Illinois because of the railroads (which Mexicans had helped to build). During the

United States' participation in World War I (1917-1919) and after, Mexicans migrated in larger numbers. This early generation of immigrants consisted mostly of single young men who came as contract workers recruited by *engachadores* or labor contractors in Mexico and in the American Southwest. Mexicans primarily worked in meatpacking, steel and railroad industries. They settled in the Near West Side, Back of the Yards/Packingtown and South Chicago. Women began to migrate in sizable numbers during the 1920s. Settlement houses, such as Hull House (Near West Side) and the University of Chicago Settlement House, provided a variety of services to Chicago's Mexican American as well as other immigrant communities. The settlement houses and other centers played an active role in the Americanization process, such as providing English-language classes.

By the end of the 1920s, Chicago was the fourth most popular destination of Mexicans crossing the border. Many also migrated to Chicago from Texas, and other parts of the United States. The city was home to almost 20,000 Mexican

During the Depression, many were sent back to Mexico, even if they were U.S. citizens.

Americans, who ranked first among immigrants entering the United States, according to the Annual Report of the Commissioner General of Immigration (1927). Following Texas, California and Arizona, Illinois ranked fourth (1,960) in the destination provided by Mexican border-crossers to government officials. By 1930 Chicago had become a major settlement area for Mexican Americans, with a population of 21,000-25,000. This dramatically changed, however. During the Great Depression, which began in 1929, many Mexicans were sent back to Mexico. They were forced out of the country as government officials made no distinction between citizens and non-citizens of Mexican descent. By 1940, historian Gabriela F. Arredondo notes, the number of Mexicans in Chicago was reduced by 25 percent; it had dropped to 16,000.

With WWII (1939-1945) came a second mass migration to fill vast labor shortages created by so many men being sent off to war. To address this, the U.S. government signed an agreement with Mexico to establish a temporary worker program that brought in workers, often referred to as the *Bracero* Program. It was instituted in 1942 and extended to 1964 (19 years after the war ended). The braceros worked in many types of factories including defense, on railroads, and in agribusiness. At first the program just recruited agricultural workers. But a year after its institutionalization, the U.S. government changed the Bracero Program to include industrial workers. This modification made Chicago a major site for Mexican workers; more than 15,000 braceros migrated between May 1, 1943, and Sept. 30, 1945.

During the 1950s, Mexicans, including braceros, continued to come. Many were farm workers who later found their way to Chicago, while others came directly to the city, often working in factories. Some braceros overstayed their contracts; others went home to seek legal visas to return to Chicago. These immigrants usually settled in already established Mexican American neighborhoods, often living near their workplace. However, in 1954 the Immigration and Naturalization Service instituted "Operation Wetback." The government began another sweep of Mexican American communities, with cooperation of state and local officials, in search of undocumented workers. Once again, Mexicans and Mexican Americans alike were detained, questioned, and often deported. Despite this sweep, Mexicans continued to migrate to the city.

By the early 1960s, there were more than 60,000 Mexican Americans in Chicago. This number only continued to grow. By 1970, there were 83,000. In the late 1960s and 1970s, major changes in immigration law, urban renewal, and big economic shifts all greatly affected the Mexican American community. In 1965, the law ended the racist quota system established in 1924. On the other hand, there was a severe limit of 120,000 people from the entire Western Hemisphere allowed to enter legally each year. The economic crisis in Mexico in the 1970s with the global oil crisis, the devalued Mexican currency (peso), and the U.S. and British bailout of Mexico's collapsing banking system also propelled migration to the United States. Meanwhile urban renewal expanded in Chicago; the building of the University of Illinois campus in 1963 on the near West Side, for example, destroyed a large part of one of the traditional Mexican American communities. Many of those displaced Mexican Americans moved to Pilsen, a few blocks south, and to western and southern suburbs.

During the 1970s, after the flight of many whites to the suburbs, Pilsen and Little Village were major recipients of newly arrived Mexican immigrants. De-industrialization in the U.S. also affected Chicago, shrinking the number of factories, including meatpacking and steel. Though some workers moved to suburbs, such as

The 1965 law put a limit of 120,000 on immigrants from the entire Western Hemisphere.

Aurora, for manufacturing jobs, many lost their jobs as the city relied less and less on manufacturing. New immigrants increasingly shifted to construction work and service industries, such as restaurants, hotels and landscaping. In response to these major changes, Mexicans and Mexican Americans organized to establish and protect their rights. They formed coalitions with other Latinas/os, especially Puerto Ricans, and worked together with other racial/ethnic groups, especially in the African American community. Chicago activists organized a chapter of El Centro de Acción Social Autónomo - Hermandad General de Trabajadores to fight against widespread harassment of the Mexican community by immigration agents. Mexican Americans were also active in citywide alliances against de-industrialization, police brutality and urban renewal.

Current migration patterns:

In 1986, there was a major change in immigration law. Though it allowed people here without papers to regularize their legal status, it also provided increased funding for the U.S.-Mexico Border Patrol. It intensified the separation of families. Many of those eligible to regularize their status had spouses, children and other family members in Mexico. They were prohibited from traveling to Mexico, barred from visiting family even in case of a medical emergency or death. This fueled some family members and friends to migrate without papers. This migration became a wave after 1994, with the passage of the North America Free Trade Agreement (NAFTA) – a transnational policy that lowered or eliminated tariffs when goods traveled across national borders. NAFTA had devastating economic consequences in Mexico. For instance, Mexican farmers could not compete with American agribusinesses, namely in corn production. This prompted a rural to urban migration within Mexico in search for employment, and many crossed into the United States, sometimes without papers, for basic survival of their families. This wave of undocumented immigrants continued during the 1990s.

Language:

Spanish

Religion:

The majority of Mexicans practice Roman Catholicism, but a growing number practice other religions, including Protestantism.

Important traditions:

Many of the traditional rites of passage are associated with Roman Catholicism. Children are baptized with the aid of *madrinas* (Godmothers) and *padrinos* (Godfathers). Most children receive first communion at about the age of 7, and confirmation at about 12 or 13. At 15 many girls are feted individually at a *quinceañera*, marking their entry into society as a young woman. Family is a central value to Mexican people.

Holidays and special events:

Important customs include serenading birthday wishes with a special song, the *mañanitas* (early morning). The *posada* at Christmas represents Joseph and Mary's search for shelter. Day of the Dead (Nov. 2) is a day of remembrance that melds ancient Aztec ritual with Christian sentiment; The Day of the Three Kings (12th day of Christmas) and Good Friday (re-enactment of Jesus carrying the cross) are also important. Two of the most important non-religious days of celebration are *Cinco de Mayo* (May 5), which marks the expulsion of the French from Mexico in 1867, and *El Grito de Dolores* (Cry of Dolores) or *El Grito de Independencia* (Sept. 16), when the first cry of independence against Spain was sounded in 1810.

> *Day of the Dead (Nov. 2) melds ancient Aztec ritual with Christian sentiment.*

Foods for special occasions:

Tacos and *enchiladas* in various forms reflect regional variations and tastes and are common national foods, along with *huevos rancheros* (a spicy egg dish), and various spice and chocolate combinations that make up regional *mole* sauces. *Salsas* — green and red — are relishes that use the native chiles of Mexico in combination with onions and tomatoes. Salsas have become extremely popular in the United States. Along with chile, *maize* (corn) is a staple in Mexican cooking, including *tortillas* (unleavened bread). *Tamales,* made of corn-meal mash stuffed with any combination of sweet, savory, or meat fillings, wrapped in cornhusks or banana leaves and steamed is a favorite festive dish. Tamales are often prepared communally for Christmas and other holidays

Names:

The most often-used names are Spanish variations of common Christian names: Jesús, Juan, José, Miguel, Samuel, Guillermo, Guadalupe, María, Josefina, Cristina, and Carmen. Other popular names are those with indigenous origins such as: Cuauhtemoc, Quetzali, Tenoch, Xochitl and Zitlali.

Major issues for community:

Education is highly valued in the Mexican American community. However, access to a quality education in a multi-tiered school system has raised many concerns. "Tracking" or funneling of students occurs at the district level, determining which students go to higher- and lower-quality schools, and within schools, determining which students receive better- and lesser-quality curriculum, enrichment and support services. Mexican American students are usually tracked to lower-quality programs, especially students whose home language is not English, and special-education students. The Mexican American community organized to combat and change this tracking system, historically low high-school graduation rates, severe overcrowding, lack of bilingual/bicultural education, and an often unwelcoming school atmosphere for students and their parents. They have fought for new neighborhood schools, such as Benito Juárez High School (Pilsen, 1977) and Little Village High School (Little Village, 2001). They also fight for better resources, such as a school library (Whittier Elementary School, Pilsen, 2011).

Concern about immigration, in the past and today, has led to harassment of Mexican Americans and other Latinas/os (citizens, immigrants, and the undocumented). Many who are citizens or have authorized immigration status have personal relationships or experiences with someone who faces deportation. Family separation, whether of immediate- or extended-family members, is a major concern. The emotional stress and fear of deportation runs deeply through the Mexican American community. Citizens and non-citizens share these concerns because family, neighborhood, school and work are closely intertwined. It also extends to non-Mexicans because of intimate ties with the Mexicans, as in the case of multi-racial and interethnic families where Mexicans have married with or partnered with non-Mexicans. In "mixed status" families — where some are citizens or legal residents while others are undocumented — questions of deportation raise great concern. Sometimes parents go to work and children to school not knowing if a loved one will come home.

The emotional stress and fear of deportation runs deeply through the community.

In 2005, the U.S. House of Representatives passed HR 4437, which would have made it a felony to "help" the undocumented, including providing medical services, classroom instruction and religious services, or simply giving someone a ride home. Massive opposition to the bill sparked hundreds of thousands of people to march in protest. On March 10, 2006, the first large march (estimated at 300,000) led by Latinas/os with participants of different races took place in Chicago. Due to widespread national opposition, the bill did not become law. Furthermore, national and international attention focused on the problem of the separation of families with the case of Elvira and Saul Arrellano in Chicago. Elvira, an undocumented Mexican, who worked nights cleaning at O'Hare airport, was arrested by Immigration and Customs Enforcement agents. She went public, stating that she was simply working to provide for Saul, her U.S. citizen son. In 2007 Elvira and Saul sought sanctuary at Adalberto United Methodist Church. Elvira co-founded La Familia Latina Unida (the United Latino Family) to mobilize against deportation and family separation.

Many Mexican Americans support the need for comprehensive immigration reform, particularly as it pertains to the reuniting of families. Undocumented young people in Chicago are leading and participating in the DREAM Act movement. Under the DREAM Act, those undocumented youth who came to the United States before the age of 16, have lived continuously in the United States for five years, have had no criminal offenses, and are enrolled in post-high school education or in military service, would be eligible for a lengthy process of legalization. The DREAM Act was defeated in the U.S. Senate in 2010. In June 2012, the Obama Administration offered "deferred action" to many immigrants brought here illegally as children. The Deferred Action for Childhood Arrivals policy temporarily eliminates the possibility of deportation for many young people who would qualify for relief under the DREAM Act. In 2011, Gov. Pat Quinn (D) signed the Illinois DREAM Act, creating privately funded college scholarships for documented and undocumented immigrants. Undocumented students in Illinois who meet specific criteria are eligible for in-state tuition at public post-secondary institutions. Some Mexican Americans, such as those who have lived in the U.S. for a long time, are very critical of (undocumented) immigration. For instance, Rosanna Pulido is the co-founder of the Illinois Minuteman Project, and served as its director.

Political participation:

Mexican Americans in the Chicago metro area tend to be predominantly Democrat, even in Republican counties such as Lake (Waukegan) and DuPage (Aurora). Mexican Americans have secured political representation, including William E. Rodríguez, Chicago City Council (1915), Irene Hernández, Cook County Commissioner (1974), Raymond Castro, Chicago City Council (1981), Jesus "Chuy" García, Illinois General Assembly (1992), and Sonia Silva, Illinois General Assembly (1997). In the 2000s, Susana Mendoza and Cynthia Soto served in the Illinois General Assembly. Other prominent political leaders are: Arturo Velásquez who organized the Mexican American Democratic Organization (1950s), and Rodolfo "Rudy" Lozano, who built Latino and African American coalitions in support of Harold Washington. In 1983, Lozano was killed at home; many saw him as a promising political candidate whose life was cut short.

There were 11 substantial Mexican-influential or majority wards in Chicago in 2011, which were scheduled to increase with the reconfiguration of ward boundaries. Mexican American aldermen in these wards included: Joe

In 2011, Gov. Pat Quinn (D) signed the Illinois DREAM Act.

Moreno (1st), George Cardenas (12th), Ricardo Muñoz (22nd), and Daniel Solis (25th). Mexicans outside of Mexico have been able to vote in Mexican elections since 2006.

Links to homeland:

As early as the late 20th century, hometown associations (HTAs) were formed to support fellow regional compatriots. Since the 1990s, HTAs have grown in regional representation, including Michoacán, Guanajuato, Durango and many more. The Confederation of Mexican Federations (Confemex) is an umbrella organization of hometown associations in the Midwest. Mexicans also have sent money to relatives for many years to help support them in Mexico, over $21 billion in 2010. Remittances make up an important part of the gross national product of Mexico. Furthermore, Spanish-language and bilingual media inform Mexican Americans of news, culture, politics and entertainment in the U.S., Latin American and the Caribbean.

Special health concerns:

In Chicago, Mexican Americans have poor or no access to quality health insurance. For instance, just 44 percent of residents in South Lawndale (Little Village) have health insurance. As a result, Mexican Americans often do not receive primary care or preventive screenings leading to undiagnosed conditions and higher death rates. Major health issues include: asthma, diabetes, obesity, heart disease/conditions, and cancer. Other related concerns include: the lack of accessible full-service grocery stores in Mexican American neighborhoods, the overrepresentation of alcohol advertisements targeted to Mexican American communities, the air pollution caused by presence of toxic coals plants in their neighborhoods, and the presence of lead paint in older buildings in poor communities.

Original entry by Dr. Louise Año Nuevo Kerr. Revised by Myrna García, Ruth Landes Memorial Research Fund Fellow.

MUSLIM AMERICANS

Chicago population:
105,000 (2011 estimate)

Metro population:
383,400 (2011 estimate)

Foreign-born:
About 30% in metro

Ed. note: Because the Census Bureau doesn't collect data on religion, the numbers above are a projection based on a 1990 research project entitled: "Muslims of Illinois: A Demographic Report," by Ilyas Ba-Yunus.

Demographics:

Muslim Americans are the most racially diverse and youngest community in America. They typically identify themselves as Americans rather than by their grandparents' country of origin. There are, nevertheless, seven major Muslim ethnic groups in the Chicago area: African Americans, South Asians, Arabs, Albanians, Bosnians, Africans and Turks.

Approximately 36% of Muslim Americans nationwide are young adults between 18 and 29 years of age as compared with 18% of Americans in this age group. About 40% of Muslims have a college degree or higher, compared with 29% of Americans overall, according to the Gallup Poll. Devon Avenue on the North Side of Chicago, Albany Park, 63rd and Kedzie in Chicago are areas with a relatively high concentration of Muslims.

There were about 10,000 Muslim physicians in Chicago and 3,000 Muslim cab drivers in 1990.

In the suburbs, Naperville, Bridgeview, Oak Lawn, Schaumburg and Orland Park have an increasing number of Muslims. There were about 10,000 Muslim physicians in Chicago along with 3,000 Muslim cab drivers, according to a 1990 poll. The structural designer of the Sears (now Willis) Tower and John Hancock building was a Muslim professor at IIT.

History:

The first Chicago Muslims were most likely fugitive slaves and freedmen, since historians estimate that up to 20-30% percent of all people brought from Africa as slaves were Muslims and Chicago had a good size black population by 1840s.

The World's Columbian Exposition in 1893 brought many Muslims to Chicago from Africa, the Middle East and Turkey. Jamal Effendi, a member of the Ottoman delegation opened the Columbian Exposition with *Azan*, a call to prayer. Alexander Russell Webb (1846-1916) represented Muslims at the Parliament of World Religions in 1893, held at a building that is the Art Institute today. Although a journalist, he had run a jewelry business in Chicago that was lost to the Great Fire of 1871. He then had served as U.S. Consul to the Philippines in 1887, which is where he converted to Islam.

Bosnian and Albanian Muslims arrived in the late 19th century to construct tunnels for the Chicago Transit Authority. In 1906, they established *Dzemijetul Hajrije* (The Benevolent Society), which is the oldest incorporated surviving Muslim organization in Illinois. As blacks were migrating to Illinois in the early 20th century for its relatively better non-discrimination policies, Palestinians were beginning to migrate to Chicago as well. They opened their grocery stores on the South Side and by the 1990 Census, more than 45 percent of employed Palestinians in the Chicago area worked in the retail trade. By the 1920s there were about 200 Arab Muslim families living around the industrial areas along the Gary-Hammond-Chicago axis. A similar number of the Turkish Muslim families were on the near West Side of Chicago.

By the late 1940s, the late Elijah Muhammad, the founder of the Black Muslim movement in America, had established himself in and around Hyde Park. His son, Imam W. D. Muhammad, during the 1970s made this area the largest single district of the Muslim orthodoxy when he moved to mainstream Islam by moving away from the Nation of Islam's belief in Elijah Muhammad being a prophet. Champion boxer Muhammad Ali, one of his followers, built a mosque on 47th and Woodlawn in Hyde Park that became the first mosque with minarets in the Chicago area. Pakistani and Indian Muslims from the Hyderabad *Deccan* (region) started coming to Chicago as immigration from South Asia opened up. Today Chicago has the largest concentration of Hyderabadis outside Hyderabad Deccan. They run more than half of all Friday congregations in Chicago.

> *Post-9/11, business in the Devon neighborhood was hurt by raids by security agencies.*

Current migration patterns:

The tragic events of Sept. 11, 2001, had a major impact on the Muslim community. Business in the Devon neighborhood went down because of the post 9/11 raids by security agencies and the National Security Entry-Exit Registration System. Many people simply moved back to their countries and some fled to Canada. The neighborhood never recovered. Recently, however, refugees from Iraq and Somalia have brought a small but steady flow of new immigrants to Chicago's Muslim community.

Languages:

Although English is the *lingua franca* of Muslim Americans, Muslims are language rich. Many are fluent in several languages, for example most Muslims from Mali speak Bambara, their mother tongue, Arabic, French and English. Muslims in Chicago produce about 20 weekly newspapers and radio programs in English, Arabic, Urdu and Bosnian languages. Friday sermons are mostly in English but some are in Arabic, Urdu, Somali, Bosnian, and at least one is in French.

Religion:

A Muslim is someone who believes in Islam. God has told Muslims in the Quran that Islam is the original faith revealed by God to all the prophets he sent. Muslims believe that there is only One God who created all. Allah is the Arabic word for God. Arab Christians and their Bible refer to God as Allah as well. Muslims are asked to believe in all the books revealed by God and all the prophets sent by God, angels, and the day of judgment. Muslims follow the Quran revealed by God to Muhammad, a human being and the messenger of God. The Quran asks Muslims to follow the prophetic guidance called *Sunnah*. Muslims believe that all human beings are born innocent. They are responsible for their own deeds. They will be rewarded for their good deeds in this world and in the hereafter and will suffer ill consequences if they do not repent.

A person enters Islam by witnessing that "There is no god but One God and Muhammad is the Messenger of God." Muslims take five short breaks of five to 10 minutes each every day to connect with God in worship. These five breaks occur at dawn, noon, mid-afternoon, sunset and late evening. Prayers and services are the twin tests of one's faith. Muslims fast for the whole month of Ramadan by completely abstaining from eating or drinking from dawn to sunset. Muslims pay 2.5% of their total wealth every year in charity and perform a pilgrimage to *Makkah* at least once in their lifetime. Justice, fairness, truthfulness, honesty, upholding the rights of the poor, circulation of wealth, deciding one's affairs in consultation with one another in the family and in the community are the expected behavior of a Muslim and it extends to all people, without any

There are 1.5 billion Muslims in the world, making almost every fourth person a Muslim.

differentiation between a Muslim and a non-Muslim. All the 10 Commandments of Judaism and Christianity are found in Islam as well, with the exception of the sabbath. Friday is when Muslims are asked to take time off during the afternoon prayers, although in many Muslim countries it has become a full day off.

There are 1.5 billion Muslims in the world, making almost every fourth person a Muslim. About 10 percent are Shias, who differ from Sunnis regarding who were the rightful successors to Prophet Muhammad, although they agree on all the beliefs mentioned above. The term Muslims use for mosque is *Masjid.* The first known mosque was built in 1893 at the site of the World's Columbian Exposition in what is Midway Plaisance on the South Side Chicago neighborhood. Although its photos survive, the mosque was destroyed by the fire that engulfed the exposition.

By the late 1940s there were four mosques in Chicago. Today, in the metro area, there are about 200, of which about seven are organized by Shias and the rest by Sunnis. Nevertheless, many Shias and Sunnis pray together in the mosque closest to them. Some 77% of mosques were not built as mosques but are adapted for prayer. The Council of Islamic Organizations of Greater Chicago is the representative body of Chicago-area Islamic organizations. Three mosques are affiliated with Minister Louis Farrakhan's Nation of Islam and four are established by Ahmadiyya. Their relationship with Islam is like the relationship of Mormons with Christianity. Mainstream Muslims and Ahmadiyya do not consider each other Muslims.

Important traditions:

There are many traditions Muslims follow, some universally and some from a specific culture. *Nikah* is a term for Islamic wedding, which is essentially a contract between a man and a woman in front of witnesses. A wedding sermon includes verses of the Quran reminding them of piety, good communications, and family responsibilities. *Waleema* is a feast that follows an Islamic wedding. When a child is born, he or she has an *Aqeeqa.* Someone makes a soft call to prayer, *Azan*, in the newborn's ear, charity is given and a feast is prepared. If it is a boy circumcision is done immediately after birth. *Bismillah* is the name of a feast when a child begins learning Arabic alphabets to read the Quran. An *Aameen* party celebrates the first complete Quran reading by a child.

Modest dress covering the whole body is recommended for both men and women. Head covering for women, *hijab,* is also required. Prophet Muhammad always covered his head, so many Muslim men also cover their heads, especially when praying. Muslim women are an active part of the Muslim community. Ingrid Mattson, a graduate of the University of Chicago became the first woman president of the Islamic

Society of North America, the largest Muslim organizations in the USA. Most converts to Islam in America are women. A Gallup report found that Muslim American men and women have better gender equity in terms of wealth than any other faith community in the United States. When Muslims die they are buried without delay and shrouded in unstitched white sheets. *Quran Khwani* is when people gather to offer their condolences to a grieving family and all those gathered read a portion of the Quran before offering collective supplications.

Holidays and special events:

Islamic holidays are observed based on a lunar calendar, which makes holidays move up 10 days each year. There are two Eid holidays that all Muslims observe, *Eid alFitr* and *Eid alAdha.* Eid alFitr marks the end of Ramadan, the month of fasting. Eid alAdha commemorates the struggle of Prophet Abraham and his wife

The majority of Muslim Americans have no homeland other than the U.S.

Hager. It occurs at the end of pilgrimage (*Hajj*) to Makkah. Many Muslims also celebrate the Prophet Muhammad's month of birth with *Eid Milad*. Shia Muslims mark the martyrdom and struggle of Imam Husain, the grandson of the Prophet, on the 10th day of *Muharram*, the first month of Islamic calendar, called *Ashura*. Many Muslims fast on that day, as recommended by the Prophet, to mark the liberation of Jews from the Pharaoh.

Food for special occasions:

Although Ramadan is about experiencing hunger, different ethnicities break their fast, *iftar*, with traditional dishes. Bean pie is a unique contribution of African American Muslims in Chicago and is enjoyed at community dinners. Along with American cookies and cakes, a variety of dates are eaten by Muslims at iftar. South Asian *pakora* and Palestinian *falafel* are also popular items. A special Pakistani herbal drink *Rooh Afza* and Middle Eastern *Roz bil Halib* are the special iftar drinks of Ramadan. At Eid alFitr, *sawaiyan* and *Sheer Khurma* are eaten, and kebabs on Eid alAdha are popular. All types of *baklawa*, Turkish Delight and Somali *cambaabur* are exchanged on Eid. Of course no South Asian wedding is complete without *biryani* and *zarda*. Both are rice-based dishes, biryani is cooked with meat and spices whereas zarda is a sweet dish with nuts.

Dietary restrictions:

Muslims can eat anything except a handful of items that are prohibited by God, such as pork, dead animals, blood, alcohol and meat not prepared by *halal* rules. In some ways halal is like kosher but much less complex.

Names:

All names from all countries and cultures are considered Muslim names unless there is a bad meaning to them. Names of the prophets are common among Muslims. Like Isa for Jesus and Musa for Moses. Mary is probably the most common name among Muslim women along with the name Khadija, Fatima and Ayesha from the prophet's family. God's name with the addition of Abdul, meaning slave of God, is used often, for example Abdullah or Kareem Abdul Jabbar. Muslims don't call any one just "Abdul" instead they prefer to be called by either the full name or the middle name. Muhammad is also very common name among Muslims, like Muhammad Ali.

Major issues for community:

Islamophobia is the major issue facing the Muslim community in the U.S. According to Gallup, 48% of Muslims personally experienced racial or religious discrimination in 2011. Although many Muslims died in 9/11 and they grieved with the nation, Islamophobia has emerged as the most important concern for the community. The Southern Poverty Law Center reports that there are more hate groups operating in the United States than ever before in recorded history. Many such groups target Muslims. Freedom of religion for Muslims is threatened by anti-Sharia legislation in many states. Sharia is the way Muslim practice their faith. Muslims

Muslims voted heavily for Bush in 2000, because he said he opposed secret evidence and profiling.

condemn the evil triplet of war-terrorism-Islamophobia and ask that due process of law be restored in our country by eliminating indefinite detentions without trial, secret evidence and racial profiling. Muslims are concerned about the criminalization of our inner-city youth, quality and equity in public education and health care, workers rights to bargain and a fair immigration policy to restore America's competitiveness in the world.

Political participation:

Muslims voted heavily for President Bush in 2000, because he opposed secret evidence and profiling of Muslims in the presidential debates. However, his war policies caused almost 90% Muslims to vote for President Obama. Disillusionment about politicians is high among Muslims, who tend to be independent instead of registered Democrats or Republicans.

Links to homeland:

The majority of Muslim Americans have no homeland other than the U.S. Immigrant Muslims maintain their connections with the old country mainly through service. There are dozens of charitable organizations in Chicago supporting educational, health and micro-credit projects in home countries. One such Chicago-based organization supports 730 schools in Pakistan. Chicago Muslims also have stood in support of freedom movements in Palestine and Kashmir; and they support the Arab Spring, the lawyer's movement in Pakistan, and anti-genocide movement in Gujarat, India, and Sudan. They also have opposed the wars in Iraq and Afghanistan.

By Imam Abdul Malik Mujahid, President of Sound Vision Foundation and chair of the Council for a Parliament of World Religions.

NATIVE AMERICANS

Chicago population:
13,337 (alone)
26,933 (alone or in combination)

Metro area population:
36,525 (alone)
78,288 (alone or in combination)

Ed. note: In 2010, 9,240 in Chicago identified as Hispanic, and also by race as American Indian. This increased the number of Native Americans, as many who so identified come from Latin America. This chapter is primarily about North American Indians.

Demographics:

The largest concentration of Native Americans in Chicago is in Uptown, but that is only a small portion of the city's American Indian population. The population has flowed north and west of Uptown as well as jumping to suburbs and other areas of the city. The most recent educational and economic breakdown is in the 2000 Census. More recent breakdowns are for Illinois as a whole. In 2000 in Chicago, 77% had a high school diploma, 19% were college graduates or higher and 8% had a graduate or professional degree. Nearly 29% had a management or professional job. A breakdown in Illinois in 2007-09 showed about the same percentages.

Members of more than 100 tribal backgrounds make up the Chicago Indian community.

About 16% were foreign-born. Median household income was $43,661 and 17% were in poverty.

(Ed. note: Chicago and metro population figures are from the 2010 Census. Other data come from the 2000 Census for Chicago and 2007-09 American Community Survey for Illinois.)

Historical background:

Native Americans have lived in and passed through the Chicago area for hundreds, even thousands, of years. Even after the treaties that culminated in 1833 forced American Indian nations to leave Illinois, individuals remained behind, and members of area tribes continued to travel through Chicago as in the past. In the 19th and early 20th centuries, Native Americans came to Chicago to sell fish, berries and other foods, and handicrafts; they came as entertainers, sometimes as part of Wild West shows, other times to establish encampments at major events (such as the 1893 and 1933-34 World's Fairs and the annual celebrations of American Indian Day in the 1920s); and they came as parts of delegations traveling from western reservations to meet with federal officials in Washington, D.C. A small population, numbering in the hundreds, included Dr. Carlos Montezuma, the renowned Yavapai stomach surgeon who made Chicago his home for a quarter of a century until just before his death in 1923. Indian people living in the city included professionals as well as entertainers and laborers. Women often worked as maids.

Many of Chicago's early American Indian residents had been forced to attend federal boarding schools, where they were taught manual-labor skills, but got little intellectual training. Nonetheless in the early 20th century, American Indians in Chicago developed a cadre of leaders who advocated both for Indian people and to change non-Indian perceptions of Indian people. In the early and middle 20th century, the city's Indian population was concentrated in two neighborhoods, on the South Side near Hyde Park and on the Near North Side, especially along Clark Street. Beginning around WWII, the Native American population in Chicago boomed. Because of depressed reservation economies, as well as experience serving in the armed forces, many American Indians came to the city to find work in factories. Then, in the 1950s the federal government established a policy of relocation in which the Bureau of Indian Affairs (BIA) recruited Indian people to move from reservations to cities and paid partial expenses. Chicago was one of several major cities involved in this program, which sent Indian people from all over the United States to these designated urban centers. For this reason, members of more than 100 tribal backgrounds make up the Chicago Indian community.

The BIA housed many of the new arrivals in Uptown, and others who came on their own moved there as well. Many of these new arrivals viewed the city as a temporary home and returned to their home reservation; others stayed. Jobs often were outside of Uptown, and as families became financially stable they moved to other parts of the city or the suburbs to be nearer to work. Until the early 1980s, Uptown remained the heart of the American Indian community. In 1953 the community had formed the All-Tribes American Indian Center, the first such urban center in the United States; today it is located on Wilson Avenue in Uptown. Many of the community's organizations, including health, social service, economic development and educational institutions, are still located in Uptown or on Chicago's North Side; others have followed patterns of population.

In the 1950s the U.S. recruited Indians to move from reservations to cities, including Chicago.

Current migration patterns:

Chicago's American Indian community is still considered a "fluid" community in which many families travel back and forth between Chicago and home reservations in the United States or Canada. The Chicago region's Native American population continues to grow, and there remains a constant influx and outflow of individuals and families.

Language:

Each of the more than 100 tribal groups has its own language. The most commonly used languages in Chicago are Choctaw, Ho-Chunk, Lakota, Ojibwe, Menominee, Navajo and Potawatomi.

Religion:

This is an individual choice. Some American Indian people are Christian; others practice their tribe's traditional religion. There is an active Native American Church, a religion with both Christian and Native American roots. A few individuals belong to other religions as well.

Important traditions:

Many Native American languages are considered endangered or threatened, and there is a strong attempt to maintain them. This is a difficult problem in a city with a diverse native population and relatively small numbers of people from any one tribe. Generosity has been a part of most Indian cultures, and is maintained in Chicago. Leaders are expected to help community members who are unable to manage successfully. The extended family is important. The strong American value based on property is not a primary value within the Indian community, where family and culture are much more the basis of decision-making (where to live, what to do for a living, etc.). In many American Indian cultures, it is the responsibility of aunts and uncles as much as of parents to discipline children. Extended families sometimes live all together in the same home rather than move away from one another, a condition that historically caused social workers to break up Indian families to provide children with more space.

Holidays and special events:

The fourth Friday in September is American Indian Day, as designated by Illinois State Legislature in 1919. Throughout the year, the most prominent community-wide special events are pow-wows, which occur regularly and are sponsored by community organizations. Pow-wows are social events in which people get together to dance and renew acquaintance; their meaning varies from community to community. Chicago's major contest pow-wow, in which dancers compete for prizes, is the American Indian Center Pow-wow, first held in 1954.

Chicago's American Indian community is "fluid" as many travel back and forth to home reservations.

Foods for special occasions:

These vary depending on the tribal background and affiliation. For woodland tribes, wild rice, fish or venison may be eaten on special occasions; for coastal tribes, it may be seafood or fish; for historically agricultural tribes, corn is among the foods cooked for feasting. Feasts are an important cultural base for many American Indians, and most get-togethers for any occasion include a feed-out.

Dietary restrictions:

No dietary restrictions exist community-wide; but some individuals do have restricted diets based on religion or clan affiliation. In many tribes, members of clans are restricted from eating animals of that clan, bear for example.

Names:

Most American Indian people have common English names, but many also have tribal names. Customs for giving names vary widely based on tribal differences.

The author's two children are Abaki Rebecca Faith Beck and Iko'tsimiskimaki (Ekoo) Emily Florence Beck. They are Blackfeet; their great-grandmother named them; as teenagers they both went to court to legally recognize the name she gave them. Abaki means white weasel or winter weasel woman;

Iko'tsimiskimaki means salmon-colored shell woman (a specific kind of shell used in ceremony). They are family names.

Major issues for community:

A primary issue is maintenance of culture. Many other issues overlap with concerns of other groups in Chicago's inner city: failure of the local schools to educate youth, gangs, drugs, poverty, unemployment and underemployment. The low educational levels of many adults means education at all levels is an important issue. Another problem is lack of recognition by the larger population that there are American Indians in Chicago. A Supreme Court case (Richmond v. Croson, 1989) requires cities to give minority contracts only to minorities the city can define as disadvantaged, but because Chicago's American Indian community is so small, the city did not originally think to include it in the guidelines. This led to greater community organization among Native Americans in Chicago.

Political participation:

The Native American population is too small and dispersed to create a strong voting base; however, individuals and organizations have worked on issues with the Mayor's Office for more than 100 years. The first Chicago mayor to work with American Indians was Carter Harrison, in the 1890s. Chicago's mayors have created various relationships with Chicago's American Indian community throughout the 20th century, but Mayor Harold Washington's administration was the most helpful and cooperative in its outreach. American Indians have worked on community issues with Illinois governors since the 1970s.

Links to homelands:

For many Potawatomi and Ho-Chunk people, the Chicago area is their homeland. For most Native Americans in Chicago, the connections to homeland are strong, as family members still live at home reservations; many retirees move back home to their own or their spouse's reservation; and many visit back and forth throughout the year.

Special health concerns:

American Indians are still dealing with the dietary changes wrought by colonialism and are a high-risk population for diabetes, heart disease, cancer and – for Native American youth nationwide – fatal accidents.

By David R. M. Beck, Professor and Chair, Native American Studies Department, University of Montana.

NIGERIAN AMERICANS

Chicago population:
6,007

Metro population:
10,919

Foreign-born:
67% in Chicago

Demographics:

Nigeria, on the west coast of Africa, has 30 states with more than 250 distinct ethnic groups, each with its own customs, culture, traditions, values, and language or dialect. Nigerians in Chicago come from all those states. Each ethnic group here maintains its own customs and traditions. The dominant ethnic groups in Chicago are the Yorubas from the Western region and Igbos from the East. They have accounted for an estimated 80% of

About 99% of who entered the U.S. after 1960 were students, part of an African "brain drain."

Chicago's Nigerian population, with Yorubas the more prevalent. The rest include the Hausa/Fulani, Ijaw, Benin and TIV. The most recent demographic breakdowns for Nigerians is in the 2000 Census. It showed that 95% in Chicago had a high school diploma and, because education is the main reason Nigerians came here, 53% had a college degree or more. Some 63% spoke a language other than English at home. And 17% were living in poverty. In Chicago, an estimated 80% live on the far North Side in Rogers Park, Edgewater and Uptown, with others scattered about the city, including Hyde Park, Calumet Park and the West Side.

(Ed. note: Except for population numbers, which are from the 2007-09 American Community Survey, data here come from the 2000 Census. Because the community is small, the Census numbers are extremely unreliable, especially those from the ACS.)

Historical background:

Before 1965 there were fewer than 100 Nigerians in Illinois. From 1965-79, the number in Chicago rose to several thousand, according to community estimates, and by 1990 to more than 10,000. Census numbers, however, showed a smaller number: 3,241 in Chicago in 1990 and 5,458 in 2000. About 99% of the Nigerians who entered the United States after 1960 came as students, part of a "brain drain" that has brought many of Africa's best and brightest to the United States. After graduating they found a variety of jobs, from professions such as law and medicine to small businesses, accounting and, in some cases, driving taxi cabs. A few came here for reasons other than education, such as visiting relatives or for medical care.

Current migration patterns:

Before 1980, the overwhelming majority of Nigerians returned home after graduation from college. But after 1981, through the '90s, only a small percent returned to Nigeria because of unstable and deteriorating economic and political conditions there. Immigration slowed when it became more difficult to leave Nigeria and when students had to meet requirements to pay a full year's tuition upfront. After 1999, when a civilian government was elected, there was new hope, but also some disillusionment in Nigeria. Immigration to the U.S. in general surged, with growth accelerating from about 65,000 in 2000, to 253,000 in 2010. In Chicago, however, according to the Census, there was more growth in the '90s, when the city population rose about 68%, than the 2000s, when it stayed relatively stable.

Language:

Virtually all Nigerians in Chicago speak English, because it was the official business language when Nigeria was under British rule. In addition, each ethnic group speaks its own dialect or language.

Religion:

The two dominant religions are Christianity and Islam, with roughly equal numbers in each. The Christians include Catholics and various Protestant denominations. Religion varies with ethnic group and region, with most Yorubas being Protestant and most Igbos Catholic. Those from the North are mostly Muslims. There

Virtually all Nigerians in Chicago speak English, the official business language under British rule.

are several Nigerian Christian churches and Nigerian Islamic Association places of worship, mostly on the North Side.

Important traditions:

Each ethnic group from Nigeria endeavors to transmit its customs, culture, values, traditions and language to the growing population of first-generation U.S.-born children in Chicago. Customs vary a great deal from one group to another, for example the dances and dress. Big events like weddings and graduations tend to be ethnic celebrations with guests coming from the same Nigerian ethnic group. Respect for elders in the hierarchy of authority is important across the Nigerian community.

Holidays and special events:

The public holidays observed by Nigerian Americans in Chicago are New Years Day; Nigerian Independence Day (Oct. 1), commemorating independence from the British in 1960; Christian holidays Christmas Day (Dec. 25), and Easter Day; and Muslim holidays *Maulid Eid al-Fitr* (end of Ramadan) and *Eid al-Adha* (feast of sacrifice, end of annual pilgrimage to Mecca). Nigerians also observe the American-declared public holidays such as July 4th, Labor Day and Memorial Day. Also, there is a Nigerian Festival in July at DuSable Museum.

Foods for special occasions:

Nigerian foods are made up of rice, beans, yams, cassava, assorted vegetables, fruits, meat (cow, goat, fish, chicken, etc.), prepared into delicious dishes. These foods are almost always served at special occasions, such as weddings, naming ceremonies, festive graduations, anniversaries, picnics, ethnic parties and other social and cultural events.

Dietary restrictions:

None except religion-based restrictions for Muslims.

Names:

Some are given family names; others are named according to events in the life of the family; and some names are religious. A difficult pregnancy may result in a name for the baby that shows that difficulty. Religious people may use the name for God, such as Chuku (for the Igbos), Oluwa (Yorubas) or Allah (Muslims).

Major issues for community:

Despite the fact that Nigerian Americans are tax-paying residents who make significant contributions to the city with their education, skills and expertise, the economic interests of Nigerians have not been addressed adequately.

They have not built an economic infrastructure, in part due to difficulty getting business loans.

They still have not built an economic infrastructure, in part because of difficulty getting loans for businesses.

Political participation:

Nigerians in Chicago are making a definite effort toward integrating into Chicago's political system. Although their participation is fragmented, those who are naturalized U.S. citizens tend to vote in city, state and national elections.

Links to homeland:

Most Nigerian Americans who have become U.S. citizens maintain dual citizenship. All Nigerians here have very strong ties with their families in Nigeria. Many make at least one trip home a year, visiting family and friends. Others may travel for business reasons. In recent years, some have returned to live in Nigeria.

By Dr. Sam Enyia, Professor of Communications at Lewis University.

PAKISTANI AMERICANS

Chicago population:
NA

Metro population:
20,005

Foreign-born:
74% in metro

Demographics:

The biggest pocket of Pakistani Americans in Chicago can be found on the far North Side, along Broadway and Sheridan Road and west along Lawrence and Devon avenues. Pakistanis are also concentrated in the northwest suburbs, such as Skokie and Mount Prospect, as well as west suburbs such as Schaumburg, Hoffman Estates, Lombard, Villa Park and Oak Brook. Pakistanis are generally highly educated. In the metropolitan area 91% have a high school diploma, 58% have earned a college degree and 22% hold a graduate

The Immigration Act of 1965 opened the door to those from top medical and engineering schools.

or professional degree. Median household income is $52,041 and 42% are in management or professional jobs. About 27% in the greater metro area do not speak English "very well." Some 19% in metro live in poverty.

(Ed. note: There is no breakdown for Pakistanis in the 2010 Census. The American Community Survey 2007-09 provides the most recent numbers available for the greater metro area. The latest number for Chicago itself is from the 2000 Census, when 5,920 Pakistanis were counted.)

Historical background:

A handful of Pakistanis settled in Chicago in the 1950s. This was a well-educated group that came to the U.S. with their spouses in pursuit of higher education and well-paying jobs. Strict immigration rules prevented many Pakistanis from coming here until the 1965 Immigration Reform Act, which opened the doors to skilled professionals. Then, a flood of educated Pakistanis from the best medical and engineering schools immigrated to Chicago and other large U.S. cities. Most, along with immigrants from nearby India, settled in the ethnically diverse area of Devon Avenue and soon outnumbered Jewish and Italian residents there. Quickly securing high-paying jobs, Pakistanis adjusted to life in Chicago with relative ease. Most were fluent in English and familiar with Western customs, as Pakistan had been a British colony until 1947. Almost all were Muslims and, with Muslims from India, established in the 1960s a Muslim Community Center now located at 4300 N. Elston Ave. The mosque functioned as a religious, educational and social center and continues to do so, along with many other mosques in the Chicago area, which were established later.

Pakistani students who came to Chicago in the '60s helped set up the Muslim and Pakistani student associations. The 1980s witnessed a second wave of immigrants, generally less-educated relatives of the first immigrants. Most set up their own businesses – restaurants, grocery and video stores, and clothing boutiques. Devon Avenue soon became the commercial hub of the Pakistani and Indian communities, drawing *desis* (Urdu term for people of the home country) from near and far. A portion of the street (from Western Avenue to Damon Avenue) was named Mohammed Ali Jinnah Way, after the founder of Pakistan, as an honorary designation by the City Council in 1992.

Current migration patterns:

Most Pakistanis moving to Chicago in the 1990s and 2000s have been students attracted to the dozens of colleges and universities in the area. Many attend the University of Illinois at Chicago, College of DuPage, and other big and small universities like the University of Chicago, Northwestern, Loyola and DePaul. They include both foreign and resident Pakistani students. One Pakistani American conceived and along with others established East-West University, Chicago in 1980, now included in the "U.S. News and World Report" Best Colleges guide. Since the 9/11 tragedy, all types of U.S. visas have become difficult to obtain, which has slowed the march of Pakistani students to Chicago and other large urban centers in the U.S. Still Pakistanis as foreign students keep coming in smaller numbers. The divide of Pakistani Americans between highly educated professionals with high incomes and less educated middle- and lower middle-class people working in grocery stores, restaurants or gas stations is slowly expanding. Movement to suburbia is mostly limited to the former, except for entrepreneurs who are successful in their business enterprises.

Most Pakistani Americans are Muslim because about 97% of the people in Pakistan are.

Language:

Most Pakistani immigrants are fluent in English and Urdu, the national language of Pakistan, which has roots in Arabic, Persian, Turkish and Sanskrit languages. In addition, many speak one or more of the regional languages: Punjabi, Sindhi, Balochi and Pashto.

Religion:

Most Pakistani Americans are Muslim because about 97% of the 188 million people in Pakistan are Muslim. Religion is very important to most Pakistanis, who have made an effort to pass along their religious beliefs and customs to their children. In addition to the many mosques, in the late 1990s there was a surge of full-time Islamic schools that offer both secular and religious education to their students. However, such schools have not increased in number since 2000. Only about 2% of the children go to private Islamic schools; the majority attend public schools and go to Sunday schools at the local mosques. Some children get tutored at home after school in Arabic, the language of the Quran. A small number take a year off from school to memorize the Quran.

Important traditions:

While encouraging their children to pursue the educational and economic opportunities here, most parents try to protect them from what they consider the social and moral depravity of Western culture. Pakistani culture emphasizes morality, family life and respect for elders. Much of this culture stems from Islam, such as prohibition of alcohol, drugs and premarital sex. Most Pakistani men don American clothes and keep their traditional *shalwar kameez* (loose-fitting baggy pants and long tunics) for weekend get-togethers. In Pakistan women usually do not cover their heads and hair like Arab *hijab*. They usually wear loose clothes covering their bodies well and a *dopatta*, a long scarf to partly cover their heads and upper bodies. Pakistani American women do the same, but some also wear Western-style professional suits. Education is emphasized and children are often pushed toward esteemed careers in medicine, engineering, higher education or law. Consistent with the economic status, births, graduations and weddings are celebrated with elaborate ceremonies. Pakistanis, like all Muslims, bury their dead and there are a few Muslim graveyards in the Chicago area.

Holidays and special events:

Pakistanis celebrate many religious and cultural holidays throughout the year. Aug. 14 marks Independence Day, commemorating Pakistan's independence from British rule and partition from the Hindu-majority India in 1947. It is celebrated with a parade with colorful floats and fairs. March 23 is Pakistan Day, when Muslims of the South Asian subcontinent in 1940 first agreed to create their own country, separate from British India. Pakistanis also celebrate two religious holidays: *Eid-ul-Fitr*, which keeps rotating and arriving earlier each

Aug. 14 marks independence from Britain and partition from Hindu-majority India in 1947.

year, according to the lunar calendar. It marks the end of Ramadan, a month of fasting from dawn to sunset as a means of spiritual renewal. On that day they wear traditional dress – loose-fitting pants and skirts – and go to the mosque for morning prayers, then visit friends and relatives to exchange gifts throughout the day.

About 70 days later, *Eid-ul-Adha* is celebrated in similar fashion. It is the feast of sacrifice (when Prophet Abraham sacrificed a lamb in place of his son, Ishmael) that marks the end of *Hajj*, the pilgrimage to Makkah, Saudi Arabia, that all Muslims must complete at least once in their lifetime if they can afford it financially and health-wise. Families give meat to the poor, as well as to friends and neighbors, to commemorate this occasion. They also go to the mosque for prayers. Pakistanis also celebrate, with hymns and praises, the birthday and death anniversary of Prophet Mohammad PBUH (peace be upon him) the last of the Prophetic chain that includes Adam, Noah, Abraham, Isaac, Jacob, Moses and Jesus.

Foods for special occasions:

Happy events, like births, graduations and weddings, are celebrated by preparing (or purchasing) traditional sweets, such as *laddu* and *barfi,* and offering them to friends and relatives. Some make *siwayyan*, a sweet made of milk and vermicelli or spaghetti. Pakistani Americans also distribute sweets on the birthday of Prophet Mohammad (PBUH).

Dietary restrictions:

Islam encourages its followers to eat healthy and pure foods and drinks. Muslims can eat all fruits, vegetables and grains. However, they have some restrictions on meat. Meat must be *halal* or sacrificed in the name of God. Pigs, which are considered dirty animals, are prohibited, as well as carnivores and scavengers.

Names:

Most Pakistani names are given in honor of religious figures or for the meaning of the name. They are often taken from the Urdu, Persian, Turkish or Arabic languages. Mohammad is the most common name for men. Females are often named after the mothers, wives or daughters of Prophet Mohammad, like Khadija, Maryam (or Maria), Aisha, Fatima. Last names often originate from a person's regional origins or ancestor's status. Khan and Choudhry are two of the most common last names.

Major issues for community:

U.S. relations with Pakistan concern Pakistani Americans, who oppose sanctions on Pakistan and urge the United States to help free Kashmir, the cause of three wars with India in the past 63 years. On the one hand, the two countries came close to resolving this issue under the Musharraf plan (former president Pervez Musharraf) to withdraw all armed forces on both sides from Kashmir. On the other, Pakistan is building rail and road links with China and there is some movement towards a Eurasian bloc including both Russia and China as well as Turkey, Iran, Pakistan, Afghanistan and former Soviet Republics of Central Asia. NATO occupation of Afghanistan and resulting violence continued by "freedom fighters" or "terrorists" is also causing friction between India and Pakistan. The aging Pakistani American community is also an issue. Elderly parents traditionally have been cared for by their grown children, but demanding career schedules make that more difficult. Finding suitable spouses for the young is another concern. Traditionally parents have arranged marriages – because it is considered as uniting of two families – but children today often choose their own mates, which sometimes causes dissention. While inter-racial marriages are a growing phenomenon, they are highly discouraged for fear of irreconcilable cultural differences.

> *U.S. relations with Pakistan concern Pakistani Americans, who oppose sanctions.*

Links to homeland:

Since Pakistanis mostly came to the U.S. to pursue professional and career advancement, they keep close ties to their Fatherland: frequently visiting Pakistan, sending money home to support family and clan members and also to advance charitable work in education, health care and taking care of the indigent. When disasters like earthquakes or floods happen in Pakistan, Pakistani Americans mobilize significant aid campaigns.

Political involvement:

Earlier generations of Pakistani Americans tilted toward the Republican Party because of Presidents Eisenhower, Nixon and Reagan's policies. Since the 1980s eminent Pakistani Americans are advancing their active participation in both the Republican and Democratic parties. Their voting record is growing. Very few have won election to state legislatures in the U.S. and none yet to the U.S. Congress.

Special health concerns:

Like other Americans, Pakistani Americans have health care provided through good insurance, consistent with their economic status. At the lower end of the economic scale, they lack proper health insurance. The Pakistani American community has been running a Pak-American Medical Center for the past 10 years near Devon Avenue, supported by charitable contributions. It takes care of needy members of the community and also some others. But it is run on a shoestring basis. There are no major diseases that Pakistani Americans are particularly prone to.

Revision by Dr. M. Wasiullah Khan, Chancellor of East-West University, based on original by Salina Khan, freelance journalist.

PALESTINIAN AMERICANS

Chicago population:
2,794

Metro population:
12,298

Foreign-born:
51% in Chicago, 47% in metro

Demographics:

Recent Census breakdowns are unavailable. The 2000 Census reported that 78% of Palestinians in Chicago and 75% in Cook County had a high school diploma. College degrees (or higher) were held by 19% in the city and 32% in the county as a whole. Some 84% spoke a language other than English in the city and 79% in Cook as

Most came after the creation of Israel in 1948, which led to nearly 1 million Palestinian refugees.

a whole. A significant number lived in poverty, 24% in the city and 20% in the county as a whole.

(Ed. note: Census data are very sketchy and extremely unreliable. The total population numbers are from the 2008-10 American Community Survey. All other numbers come from the 2000 Census.)

Historical background:

Immigration from Palestine began in the late 1800s. Palestinians engaged in peddling and shop keeping in cities and towns across the United States. The majority of Palestinians came here following the creation of the State of Israel in 1948, which resulted in nearly 1 million Palestinian refugees. Immigration from Palestine continued after the 1967 war, when Israel occupied the rest of Palestine, now called the West Bank and Gaza Strip. The policies of Israeli occupation, to rid the land of Palestinians to make way for Jewish immigrants, kept Palestinians coming into Chicago during the 1970s, '80s and '90s. The West Bank town of Beitunia now has more of its residents in Chicago than in the village itself. Those who came to the United States are from a variety of income levels. Like other immigrant groups, they maintained their tradition as small business owners, primarily of grocery stores.

Current migration patterns:

The Palestinians who have come to Chicago since 2000 have done so as a result of continued hardship in their home country. In addition, the Gulf War resulted in 400,000 Palestinians being expelled from Kuwait, making some of them refugees for a second or third time. Many of these refugees came to the U.S. and to Chicago. Generally, Palestinians who settle on the Southwest Side move to the southwest suburbs as soon as they have the money to do so.

Language:

Arabic.

Religion:

Muslim and Christian. Before WWII, Christian Arabs migrated to the West in larger numbers because of a perceived affinity with the West, and they tended to bring their entire families. But since 1965, Muslims have come in larger numbers, because of worsening economic and political conditions. Some Palestinian Christians are members of churches that follow Eastern (e.g. Melkite or Greek Orthodox) rites and others observe Western (e.g. Roman Catholic or Anglican) rites.

Important traditions:

The Muslim tradition of writing a marriage contract and adhering to a formal engagement process is still alive in Chicago. Some marriages are arranged, some are not; but either way, the family plays a big role in a young person's marriage. When Muslims die, they are not buried in coffins. Their bodies are washed, wrapped in a shroud and buried immediately. A person's death is followed by 40 days of mourning. On the 40th

Many settle on the Southwest Side and move to the southwest suburbs when they can afford it.

day, there is a remembrance ceremony. Palestinians encourage preservation of their language, folklore and social etiquette (hospitality, generosity and helping neighbors). There is a strong obligation to maintain close extended-family ties to cousins, aunts, uncles and grandparents. Elders are respected and cared for by family members. Nursing homes are unheard of for Palestinians. Social visits are frequent on all occasions, not just holidays. Storytelling and the oral tradition are very important.

Holidays and special events:

Muslims observe the *Eid al-Adha*, or feast of the sacrifice (when Abraham sacrificed a lamb in place of Ishmael). This feast is celebrated with prayers and an exchange of gifts. It marks the end of the *Hajj*, or pilgrimage to Mecca, Saudi Arabia, which all Muslims are encourage to make at least once in their lives. The *Eid al-Fitr* is a feast commemorating the end of Ramadan, 30 days of fasting between sunrise and sunset to renew piety as well as family ties. Ramadan and the Hajj are governed by the lunar calendar, so they do not occur at the same time each year. Christian Palestinians observe Christmas and Easter, although depending on the Christian denominations, these holidays fall on different days.

Foods for special occasions:

During Ramadan, Palestinian Muslims frequently prepare and eat special dishes like *katiyey* (a walnut-filled pancake). Special occasions often are celebrated by eating *mansaf* (lamb served over rice with a yogurt sauce). Stuffed squash and rice with almonds also are popular. Spices like allspice, cumin and cardamon are commonly used.

Dietary restrictions:

The Quran requires that Muslims refrain from eating pork and drinking alcohol. Christians do not have these restrictions.

Names:

All Arabic names have meanings. Common women's names include Sharifa (honest), Nawal (reward), Jameela (beautiful), Amal (hope) and Kareema (generous). In the Palestinian community, after the oldest child is born, the parents are referred to in terms of their relationship to that child. Thus, a father whose oldest son is named Jamal is known as Abu Jamal (father of Jamal) and the mother is called Um Jamal (mother of Jamal).

Major issues for community:

All Palestinians rally around the issue of their homeland. For decades they have been calling for an independent Palestinian state. They also have a genuine concern for the plight of all Arab peoples in the Middle East. Locally, they must combat anti-Arab stereotypes and slurs in the media, as well as a general

Most have a strong bond with their homeland, but without a state, have no citizenship or passport.

misunderstanding of who they are as a people and the story of their dispossession. Islamophobia, a fear of Muslims, has been promoted by certain personalities and social groups in the U.S., leading to a combination of discrimination and increased civic activism on the part of Palestinians.

Political participation:

Because of a strong feeling of marginalization from the American mainstream, Palestinians were not big in civic participation. But all this has changed since the mobilization of American Arabs and Muslims after the Sept. 11 attacks, for which many held them collectively responsible. Third- and fourth-generation Arab Americans have been upwardly mobile and successful.

Links to homeland:

Most Palestinians maintain a strong bond with their homeland, but because they are a stateless people, they have no citizenship and no passport. Those living in the West Bank and Gaza carry temporary residency cards. Most Arab countries won't give citizenship to Palestinians, partly because their policies are based on ancestry and partly to make a point that Israel has taken over the land that should be Palestine. Jordan, where many fled after the 1948 and 1967 wars, did give many citizenship and Jordanian passports, but that is the exception.

Many Palestinians would like to return home, but because of ongoing Israeli control of the region, this is made difficult, if not impossible. The economic situation continues to worsen. The border closures on the Gaza strip — 80% of whose population used to work as low-paid day laborers in Israel — have created an unemployment rate estimated at more than 60%. Many Palestinians came to the U.S. to make money and send it home to family members and charitable organizations that build schools and provide needed social services. Palestinians lobby the U.S. government over its unconditional support for Israeli policies, which they say violates the human and civil rights of the Palestinian population.

Original by Mary Abowd, a Chicago journalist and board member of the Arab-American Action Network, who lived and wrote on the West Bank in 1992; also contributing: Dr. Louise Cainkar. Updated by Cainkar, now Assistant Professor of Social Welfare and Justice and Sociology at Marquette University, and author of the 2009 book "Homeland Insecurity: The Arab American and Muslim American Experience after 9/11" (New York: Russell Sage Foundation).

POLISH AMERICANS

Chicago population:

139,094 (first ancestry)

187,807 (first and in combination)

Metro population:

696,809 (first ancestry)

967,233 (first and in combo)

Foreign-born:

34% in Chicago, 17% in metro

Demographics:

Poles make up more than 20% of the population in many Chicago neighborhoods: Archer Heights, Clearing, Dunning, Garfield Ridge, Hegewisch, Jefferson Park, Montclare, North Park, Norwood Park, O'Hare, Portage Park, West Elsdon. Most Polish Americans now live in the suburbs, however. Although widely

The largest wave arrived in Chicago from 1880-1932, mainly peasants and village workers.

scattered, they also are more than 20% in Bridgeview, Burbank, Elmwood Park, Forest View, Harwood Heights, Hickory Hills, Justice, Lemont, Niles, Norridge, Orland Park, Park Ridge, Posen, River Grove, Schiller Park, Willow Springs and Wood Dale. Increasing numbers are seen in Naperville. Polish Americans here are well educated, with 92% in the metro area holding a high school diploma, 35% a bachelor's degree or higher, and 13% a graduate or professional degree. Median household income is $67,492, about $7,000 higher than average, and 37% hold a management or professional job. Just 13% in metro say they do not speak English "very well" and about 5% live in poverty.

(Ed. note: First-ancestry population numbers are from the 2008-10 Census Bureau's American Community Survey. Most other data, such as foreign-born, education and economic breakdowns are from the 2007-09 ACS. The 2000 Census and an analysis by the Polish American Assn., were the sources for neighborhoods and suburbs with large numbers of Poles.)

Historical background:

Immigration to the U.S. from Poland dates back to the 1608 colonial settlement of Jamestown, Va. Later waves of Polish immigration were closely tied to the political turmoil of European history. In the 19th and early 20th century Poles were not identified as such because formally they were citizens of the neighboring empires of Austria, Prussia and Russia. As a result of the Bolshevik Revolution, defeat of Austria and Germany in World War I and the Versailles Treaty, Poland regained its independence but only for 20 years. Then Germany invaded and occupied Poland in 1939-1945, and a subsequent Soviet regime ruled till 1989.

The largest wave of Poles arrived in Chicago during 1880-1932. It consisted mainly of peasants and village workers from Galicia in Southern Poland, who migrated for economic reasons. They faced discrimination and exploitation because they were poor, uneducated Catholics who spoke no English. They found work in factories, mills and slaughterhouses here. These former agricultural workers were accompanied by numerous, and often impoverished, Polish landed gentry, who were escaping political prosecution by the occupying Russian or German authorities. Among them were members of the intelligentsia, bourgeoisie and clergy. They contributed to the building of community, churches, schools and organizations. The second wave came during and after World War II. They were refugees and displaced persons who were escaping the Holocaust, Nazi and Soviet labor and concentration camps, and had no intention of returning to Poland under the communist regime. They were citizens of a restored, independent Poland; they were more educated and had survived the war, often as slave laborers, POWs or fighters in the Allies' armed forces.

The third wave started after the 1968 political purge instigated by the ruling Communist party. There was a big surge of refugees during the Solidarity movement and imposition of Martial Law in the early 1980s until 2004, when again-independent Poland could join the European Union. This latest migration tended to be young, more urban and much better educated in the rigorous state-sponsored and free educational system in Poland. While most came as formal immigrants invited by relatives or winning the visa lottery, many entered on a temporary basis and remained after their visas expired. Immigration rules introduced after 9/11, coupled with free labor movement within the European Union and gradually improving economic conditions in

The second large wave, of better-educated Poles, came during and after World War II.

Poland, practically put an end to significant immigration to America.

Although most Poles of all three waves of immigration had not planned to stay, most did because of political complications back home and increasing satisfaction with life in this country. Chicago has long been a center of the Polish American community, known as "Polonia." In 2010, the New York City area surpassed Chicago in the distinction of having the highest concentration of Poles in the U.S., second only to Warsaw, the capital of Poland. The main Polish settlements in Chicago ran along two diagonal arteries of Milwaukee Avenue on the Northwest Side and Archer Avenue on the Southwest Side, where Poles resided in Bridgeport, Pilsen and Back of the Yards, close to the steel mills, factories and meatpacking houses. Many of the major fraternal, civic and religious organizations, some national and international in scope, were founded in the 19th century and continue to exist. Several of the long-lasting ones have an insurance base, such as the three largest fraternal organizations: the Polish Roman Catholic Union, established in 1873 with a religious focus, Polish National Alliance (1880) and Polish Women's Alliance (1898).

Chicago continues to be the center of the Polish American community and a home to the Polish Library, which opened to the public in 1915, and the Polish Museum of America, established in 1937. The archdiocese of Chicago has 55 churches built by the Polish Catholics, including the oldest parish of St. Stanislaw Kostka. There are a large number of civic and cultural institutions and many annual events such as the Polish Film Festival, Taste of Polonia, May 3rd Polish Constitution Day Parade, and the White and Red Ball organized by the Legion of Young Polish Women.

Current migration patterns:

Poles continue to come to Chicago area but in much smaller numbers and for different reasons than in the past. There was a 40% increase in immigration in the years 1990-2000, which coincided with economic boom in the U.S. and no restriction on travel abroad under the new Polish government. Many Poles came through family reunification, and the visa lottery, especially because it was possible for people already in the U.S. to change their status if chosen in the lottery. Some came because they had special employment skills. After 9/11 the strict restrictions on immigration limited the inflow of Poles. More importantly,

Poland's accession to the European Union in May 2004 practically reversed the trend. In 2012 more people are returning to Poland for retirement, family reunification or employment than are arriving in the U.S. There is also significant migration of Polish Americans from Chicago and the Rust Belt to the Southern, Southwestern and Western states, with Utah leading the charts with 66% growth in Polish population between 2000 and 2005.

Language:

Polish, with some regional dialects, such as *góralski*, which is spoken by the Highlanders who live on the South Side and in southwest suburbs. The spike of immigration in the last decade of the 20th century revitalized the Polish-speaking community in Chicago. Three daily Polish-language papers and numerous magazines are published in Chicago. The number of students from kindergarten to 12th grade in the Polish Saturday schools peaked above 20,000 in 2009. In the school year 2011-2012, there were 38 Polish Saturday schools in Chicago and the suburbs with more than 16,000 students. And close to 4,500 pupils studied the Polish

Polish immigration increased 40% from 1990-2000, coinciding with the U.S. economic boom.

language in public schools. Colleges and universities also have increased enrollment in Polish language and literature courses. Chicago hosts four major academic centers for Polish Studies at the University of Chicago, Northwestern University, the University of Illinois at Chicago and Loyola University.

Important traditions:

Polonia marks events like weddings, baptisms, first communions and funerals with Catholic ritual, enhanced by the Polish touch. Generous hospitality, as captured in the phrase "a guest in the house is like God in the house," is part of the Polish self-image often demonstrated in lavish festivities with much food, drink and an expansive guest list. Any occasion provides a good excuse for socializing, from traditional Sunday family dinner to gala lunches and dinners organized by Polonia organizations for fundraising purposes on an annual basis. More recent immigrants and the younger generation enjoy *imprezy*, various parties to mark birthdays or name days, for every person has a saint patron in a Catholic calendar. Most popular are *Andrzejki, Mikołajki* and *Barbórka*. On Easter Monday some uphold the tradition of *smingus dingus,* when people sprinkle each other with water for good luck. A newer tradition brought from Poland is the International Women's Day on March 8, when ladies receive flowers.

Holidays and special events:

Three main events in the Polish calendar have been carried over into Polonia. Christmas involves a highly decorated evergreen tree, once traditionally lit with candles, and a 13-course Christmas Eve dinner with a place set for the "hungry stranger" and hay laid under the tablecloth. Wafers, like communion wafers, are shared along with forgiveness for past offenses against one another and best wishes for the future. Gifts are opened after dinner. Even those who are not active Catholics attend Christmas Midnight Mass. Christmas Day is spent visiting relatives. Easter is the second most important religious holiday and follows 40 days of self-denial during Lent. The pious visit the decorated "graves" of Jesus at Polish churches on Good Friday. The third big holiday, Polish Constitution Day (May 3), celebrates Poland's Constitution of 1791, which was never put into practice because of the 1793 partition of Poland by Prussia, Russia and Austria. The holiday is observed with a parade. Casimir Pulaski Day (first Monday in March) is an official Illinois holiday that commemorates the Polish count who fought and died in the American Revolution. It is celebrated with a weekend parade, downtown lunch and an event at the Polish Museum.

Foods for special occasion:

While Roman Catholics are no longer forbidden by their Church to eat meat on Friday, the Christmas Eve dinner remains meatless by tradition. To mark the end of the festive carnival season a week before Ash Wednesday, Poles share *pączki* doughnuts on Fat Thursday and herring with bread and vodka on Shrove Tuesday, this tradition is called *ostatki* or *zapusty*. Easter breakfast is an important family tradition, when relatives share pieces of hard boiled eggs blessed in Church on Holy Saturday and wish each other health and happiness. This meal includes white *borsch* with fresh boiled sausage, ham, bread, butter molded in a shape of a lamb, horseradish and beets. *Pierogi*, the Polish dumplings filled with sauerkraut, mushrooms, cheese, meat or potatoes, are everyone's favorites, as are *kabanosy* (thin pork sausages), *bigos* (hunters' stew)*,* red *borsch* (beet soup), and poppy seed strudel for dessert.

> ## Another concern is the erroneous use of the phrase 'Polish concentration camps.'

Religion:

Most Poles are Roman Catholics. An interesting development in Polonia has been the creation of a Polish National Catholic Church, founded in 1873 as a revolt against Irish influence and papal control. The PNCC has local lay leaders and elected clergy who can marry. Only about 5% of Polish Americans joined the PNCC, but the religion has spread to the mother country, an unusual phenomenon. The election of the Polish Pope John Paul II and his several visits to the United States, including Chicago, has been a source of great pride for Polonia. Increased wealth of the Polish American community can be seen in the renovation of the old Polish churches such as St. Mary of the Angels, St. John Cantius and St. Hyacinth Basilica. Brand new churches are built when Poles migrated to suburbs such as Lombard. There are daily Polish-language broadcasts of religious programs, such as TV *Trwam* and controversial *Radio Maria* from Poland.

Names:

Polish is a gender-specific language. The surnames that end in "ski" change endings. Therefore sons, brothers and fathers Kowalski will have sisters, daughters and mothers Kowalska. There is a differentiation between a woman who is a professional and a woman who is married to a professional. For example, *pani doktor* is a woman doctor, while *pani doktorowa* is the wife of a doctor. *Pan* (sir) and *pani* (lady or madam) are used as titles in conversations and correspondence, progressively less among people under 30. Children are often named for the saint on whose feast day they are born, and Poles in Poland celebrate a name day rather than a birthday. In recent decades, old Slavic names such as Bartłomiej, Maciej and Radosław for boys; Alina, Bożena and Marzena for girls, became popular, next to Polish versions of traditional Christian names such as Aleksandra, with the nickname Ola and Tomasz, or its diminutive Tomek.

Major issues for community:

In 1999 Poland joined the North Atlantic Treaty Organization (NATO) as a sovereign and democratic country, and has proven to be the most supportive U.S. ally in Afghanistan and Iraq, yet Poles need to apply for, and are often denied, visas to come here, unlike citizens of 18 other NATO countries that have visa waivers. This is the number one issue in 2012. There is an ongoing effort to get Congress to pass a visa waiver program for Polish citizens who wish to visit the U.S. as tourists. The restriction is based on the fact that in the past many Poles used tourist visas to get to the U.S. and then stayed illegally to find work. That is no longer a threat, because as members of the EU they can legally work throughout Europe, and the U.S. is missing out on a large market for tourism. Another big concern is the erroneous use of the phrase "Polish concentration camps." Hitler's "final solution" of terminating the Jewish population of Europe was designed to take place mostly in Polish territory occupied by Germany. There were more Jews living in pre-war

Long gone are the days of powerful Congressmen Dan Rostenkowski and Roman Pucinski.

Poland than anywhere in the world. Jews were the second-largest minority, close to 10% of all Polish citizens, and the Jewish population in major cities was up 35%. All the labor, concentration and extermination camps were run by special German units of the Nazi Party, SA, SS, RSHA, VT and Wehrmacht.

Political participation:

Polish Americans are better educated and more affluent than ever, yet their political presence and representation have diminished on the municipal, county, state and federal levels. Chicago used to send Polish American congressmen to Washington, D.C., legislators to Springfield, and the Chicago City Council had several aldermen of Polish ancestry. Long gone are the days of powerful Congressmen Dan Rostenkowski and Roman Pucinski. Voter registration of Polish Americans in Chicago is lower than that of other ethnic groups. The late professor Helena Znaniecka Lopata attributed this phenomenon to the organizational complexity of Polonia and an internal status competition that kept community members oriented inwardly, to the exclusion of concern with mainstream political life in the United States.

This status competition makes for an unwillingness to support Polish American candidates, in part because of the common feeling that no one ought to claim higher status than any other, and in part because of the residual suspicion of one another bred into Poles by the long periods of occupation the nation suffered over most of the past 200 years. Those brought up in the communist Poland are extremely suspicious of anyone who could possibly be associated with the government. They are also antagonistic to established Polonia, feeling that it is out of touch with the changes taking place in Poland and has not sufficiently shared leadership. The Polish American Congress is the main political association of fraternal organizations and most major Polonian groups and individuals. PAC has a national network and is headquartered in Chicago. A very small percentage of Polish citizens here vote in Poland's presidential and parliamentary elections. Polonia voters tend to be overwhelmingly ultra-conservative.

Links to homeland:

Links to Poland have been strong in Polonia, because of the dynamic and often tragic history of Poland and consistent efforts of its leaders to nationalize emigrants living abroad. Immigrants and traditional Polonia have been very active in trying to influence the American government, first to help overthrow communism, later to establish ties of economic and security assistance. Individuals are often moved by a characteristic nostalgia for the imagined homeland and its tragic past.

Following the successful transition from a centrally controlled economy to a free market, corporations and

Polish Americans are eagerly investing in Poland. And the recession in the U.S., resulting from the housing bubble, prompted some young Polish Americans to launch their corporate or entrepreneurial careers in Poland. In addition there is considerable interaction between Illinois and Poland in a number of areas, which benefits both. The state and National Guard have a program to train Polish security forces for crowd control and anti-terrorism. Chicago also has police training programs with its Sister City, Warsaw. Several educational collaborations have taken root as well, one between Whitney Young and Witkiewicz High School in Warsaw, another between Northeastern Illinois University and Warsaw School of Economics.

Original by the late Dr. Helena Znaniecka Lopata, Professor of Sociology at Loyola University and author of nine books, including "Polish Americans." Update by Bożena Nowicka McLees, Director of Interdisciplinary Polish Studies, Loyola University.

PUERTO RICAN AMERICANS

Chicago population:
102,703

Metro population:
188,502

Foreign-born:
Does not apply – all are U.S. citizens

Demographics:

Puerto Ricans live primarily in the city, around West Town and Humboldt Park. In fact, in 1992 a formal "entryway" for the neighborhood was erected on Division Street. At that time, less than half were born on the Island. Puerto Ricans for the most part speak English; only 22% in the city reported they "do not speak English well."

Most Puerto Ricans here speak English. Only 22% report they do not speak it well.

In Chicago, 67% have a high school diploma, with 11% holding a bachelor's degree and 3% a graduate or professional degree. In the metro area, numbers are slightly higher: 70%, 13% and 4%. Median household income is low – $36,291 for the city and $43,231 for metro. In the metro area, 26% are in management or professional jobs. At the same time, 26% in Chicago are below the poverty line, while 21% are in the metro area.

(Ed. note: Population figures are from the 2010 Census. All other demographic data come from the 2007-2009 ACS.)

Historical background:

Puerto Ricans are relatively recent arrivals in Chicago. The 1950 Census grouped them together with Cubans, Central and South Americans, so the numbers were obscured. But we know that by 1970 about 78,000 Puerto Ricans lived in Chicago, a 125% increase from 1960. The 1980 Census reported a population of 129,000, an increase of 65% in 10 years. Now, it seems this population growth has ceased, perhaps because of the decline in manufacturing in the city. There are Puerto Ricans elsewhere in the Chicago metropolitan area (Waukegan, Aurora, Joliet), but their numbers are not very large. Puerto Rican migration into the continental U.S. has been dubbed the "airborne migration." Its most important characteristic is that this is not an immigration at all, because Puerto Rico is a territory of the United States, and Puerto Ricans have been U.S. citizens since 1917 (although ineligible to vote for President or Congress while on the Island). The population shifts are therefore just internal migrations. This characteristic precludes access to statistics on arrivals or departures.

The initial recorded arrivals of Puerto Ricans occurred around 1953, when a few families were brought to Chicago through an organized program, males as factory workers and wives for domestic service. They were settled in the Back of Yards, where there is not today a recognizable Puerto Rican neighborhood. When large groups started arriving, they settled on the Near North Side, but were displaced in the early '60s by the federal urban renewal program that erected Sandburg Village in what had been a tenement-type neighborhood with many Puerto Ricans. They moved toward Humboldt Park and West Town, where they remain. Initially, Puerto Rican migration to the Chicago area (subsequent to the major movement to New York) can be traced as a geographical westbound continuum that included Ohio and Michigan. The Commonwealth of Puerto Rico sought to protect these migrants, first farmworkers and then urban residents, by the creation of a Migration Division Office, part of Puerto Rico's Department of Labor. Puerto Ricans in Chicago created over the years a series of social and political groups. In the early '70s, para-political activism was most important in the press, with the Young Lords, a radical organization, constituting the first national movement, expanding from Chicago to New York.

Current migration patterns:

The arrival of Puerto Ricans in Chicago has slowed in the past 25 years. From data about Puerto Ricans born on the continent, it can be assumed there has been a small return movement to the Island. It is not unusual for Puerto Ricans to move several times between the Island and mainland, in a circular pattern.

Protestants, Adventists and Jehovah's Witnesses have significant Puerto Rican followings.

Language:

Spanish. The Island, after a long history of fluctuations in official policy, has declared Spanish the official language of Puerto Rico. Implications for continuing internal migration of Puerto Ricans, and for educational policies that may want to teach English and Spanish, affect not only this group but the U.S. as well.

Religion:

Accepted wisdom has it that Puerto Ricans, like other Latinos, are Roman Catholic. In the case of Puerto Ricans in Chicago, there are other very significant religious practices. Protestant denominations, Adventists and Jehovah's Witnesses have significant Puerto Rican followings. Protestant ministers, now and in the past, have taken a leading social and political role in the Puerto Rican community. *Santeria*, a religion with African roots that includes folk healing, also is practiced by many Puerto Ricans. Traditionally, Santeria's mysteries have been carefully kept among the initiated, so it is hard to ascertain the number of adherents. Santeria's practices coexist with conventional Christian observances.

Important traditions:

Baptisms and weddings are an occasion for gathering of extended families. The *quinceañera* (15th birthday) celebrates the coming out of young girls, and may include both a religious ceremony and a lavish party.

Holidays and special events:

Christmas is very important, including the Fiesta de Reyes (Epiphany) (Jan. 6), when children receive their presents from the Three Wisemen. The Feast of San Juan (June 24), honoring the Patron Saint of the Island, includes both religious and social celebrations. Constitution Day (July 25) observes the compact between the Island and the United States, and the first constitution for the Commonwealth. In Chicago, the Puerto Rican Parade, in early June, and the accompanying festival in Humboldt Park, present the largest mass gathering of Puerto Ricans in the city.

Foods for special occasions:

A delicacy in Puerto Rican cuisine is the *lechon asado* (suckling pig). *Arroz con grandules* (rice with pigeon peas) is very tasty and frequently served. *Pasteles* are made with ground green plantains, *guineos* (bananas) and other ingredients and offer a passing similarity to tamales. *Tostones* (fried slices of plantain) often accompany the meal; *alcapurrias* (a type of fritter) are not as frequently served in Chicago as they are on the Island.

Names:

The most common names are of Spanish origin, and refer to saints, such as José, Manuel, Pedro, or to the many titles of the Virgin Mary, such as María, Dolores and Socorro. Last names include Dávila, Martínez, Barceló and Rivera, names common for Spanish-speaking people.

Major issues for community:

Puerto Ricans in Chicago share concern for the future of the Island and whether its current commonwealth status will change to that of either a state or an independent country. There is a division of opinion about that here, with no overwhelming majority for any position. People who live here can vote absentee only if they are registered in Puerto Rico and have a domicile there. Education, particularly bilingual education, is particularly important both here and there.

Political participation:

Over the past 15 to 20 years, political organizations, and the community itself, have matured, and their participation in mainstream politics has increased and grown stronger. Perhaps the best symbol of this progress is the large steel flag of Puerto Rico welcoming people to Borinquen Plaza, in Humboldt Park, the heart of the Puerto Rican communities in Chicago. The growth was enhanced during the tenure of Harold Washington as Mayor of Chicago. His coalition reached out to Puerto Ricans and other Latinos. In fact, it was the election of a Puerto Rican to the City Council that marked the end of bitter opposition to Washington by a majority of the City Council. Since then, Puerto Rican communities have seen their representation in that Council and in Springfield increased substantially, as well as in the number of municipal judges and other elected offices. It is important to note that Puerto Ricans (unlike immigrants) arrive in Chicago already U.S. citizens. They consequently are more likely to register and vote than other ethnic groups, and than other Latino communities. Puerto Ricans tend to vote Democrat. They are also likely to identify with issues affecting other Latinos, such as immigration reform. In fact, the only Puerto Rican U.S. representative from Illinois, Luis Gutierrez, comes from a district that encompasses the core of both the Puerto Rican and Mexican communities in Chicago.

Links to homeland:

Puerto Ricans continue to be the "airborne migration," with relations and contacts with the Island limited only by the cost of the airfare. The status of the Island is of great political concern, and many Puerto Ricans in Chicago feel an obligation to influence Washington's decisions about Puerto Rico from here. If they live on the Island Puerto Ricans cannot vote in U.S. elections. Puerto Rico sends a representative to the U.S. House of Representatives, but his or her vote is non-binding.

Special health concerns:

In the past, Puerto Ricans had to struggle with tropical, bacterial diseases such as bhilarzia, the symptoms of which were often misinterpreted in Chicago as behavioral problems; insufficient immunizations would cause flare-ups of diphtheria, for instance. Today's health concerns are related to economic conditions: lead poisoning, high blood pressure, diabetes. Health activists have engaged in strong campaigns to prevent AIDS.

By Dr. Isidro Lucas, writer, social policy analyst.

ROMANIAN AMERICANS

Chicago population:
7,674 (first ancestry)

Metro population:
27,378 (first ancestry)
38,675 (first and multiple ancestries)

Foreign-born:
45% in metro

Demographics:

Romanians in Chicago are mainly spread across the North and Northwest Sides, bounded by Lake Michigan, Harlem Avenue, Belmont Avenue and Howard Street. Heaviest concentrations are in Albany Park, West Ridge, Rogers Park, Edgewater, Uptown, Lake View, Irving Park and Lincoln Square. A smaller number live on the South and Southwest Sides, where there are two Romanian churches, compared with 12 such churches on the North and Northwest Sides. In the greater metro area, 90% have a high school diploma, 40%

The first came in the late 1800s when the empire wanted to make them Hungarians.

a college degree or higher and 18% a graduate or professional degree. Some 37% are in a management or professional job and median household income is $62,734. A reported 8.5% live under the poverty line.

(Ed. note: First-ancestry population figures are from the Census Bureau's American Community Survey 2008-10. All other data come from the 2007-09 ACS.)

Historical background:

The first immigrants came to the U.S. at the end of the 19th century from Transylvania, because the occupying Austro-Hungarian Empire wanted to convert the Romanian population into Hungarians by changing their names and imposing the Hungarian language. In 1900 the first Romanian immigrants settled in Chicago. The majority were peasants and lived in the Devon-Clark area, where they worked for the vegetable industry "greenhouses" and Weber-Krantz. Around 1910 Romanians started to work in the construction of roads and public works for the city, so the center of the community moved to Clybourn/ Fullerton/Southport. The number of Romanians in Chicago in 1911 is said to have exceeded 5,000. The first known Romanian organization in Chicago was established on Dec. 29, 1907, under the name Speranta, and on July 15, 1911, the first Romanian Orthodox church was inaugurated. Romanians immigrated to U.S. in four phases: 1) From the end of 19th century to the end of WWI. They came mainly from Transylvania because of Hungarian oppression. More than 10,000 Romanians came to Chicago. 2) Between the two World Wars. They came mainly for economic and family reasons About 5,000 Romanians came to Chicago. 3) During communist era (1945-1989). Escaping from communism, about 20,000 Romanians settled in Chicago. 4) After 1989. A lack of confidence in the neo-communist government sent about 8,000 Romanian immigrants to Chicago in the 1990s. It is estimated that another 1,000 or so immigrated illegally.

Current migration patterns:

The '90s immigrants represent those who wanted to emigrate during communism but were not allowed to by the Romanian government. Another category is those who come to reunite with family members. Many young Romanians entered Chicago after 1990 with work, student or fiancée visas and hoped to remain here. Only a tiny percentage returned to Romania. In the mid-2000s things changed at home, with a new president and membership in NATO and the EU. Despite a recession and harsh budget cuts, immigration slowed.

About 20,000 Romanians escaped from communism and settled in Chicago 1945-89.

Language:

Descendants of Romanians speak mostly English, the second generation having abandoned the Romanian language. Newcomers speak both Romanian and English.

Religion:

In Romania, the religion is Christian Orthodox. Because of the communists' dislike of neo-Protestants, many were permitted to emigrate. Therefore, the Orthodox percentage of Romanians in Chicago dropped to about half the population here. There are two large Romanian Orthodox churches and 12 small neo-Protestant churches in the Chicago area.

Important traditions:

Romanians put great emphasis on family and maintain close contacts with extended family. Children's education is severe and rigid in order to secure a good future.

Holidays and special events:

National Day is observed Dec. 1, usually by a community gathering. Two important Christian-Orthodox holidays are traditionally observed: Christmas and Easter. Romanians also celebrate their Name Day, according to the Orthodox calendar. For example: St. Maria (Aug. 15), St. Ion (Jan. 7), and St. Gheorghe (April 23). The Children's Day (June 1) is a time for candy and gifts for the children. Women's Day (March 8), The Day of the Harvest (Oct. 1) and *Martisorul* (Spring Day, March 1) are lay holidays observed in the family. Martisorul is a typical Romanian holiday, celebrating the coming of spring. It resembles Valentine's Day. Flowers and a small token (hung from a red and white thread) are given to women and worn on blouses for about 10 days.

Foods for special occasions:

Every important holiday has a specific dish that is prepared at home. At Christmas a piglet is cooked, along with traditional *sarmale* (ground meat stuffed in cabbage rolls). New Year's Day, turkey is prepared. At Easter, lamb dishes and red eggs are served. On Harvest Day, there is pastrami and fresh-squeezed grape juice. Two typical Romanian dishes are *mamaliga* (polenta with dairy products) and *mititei* (spicy skinless sausage).

Dietary restrictions:

None, except for the periods of religious Orthodox fast, when there is no meat. But this is usually observed only by the older generation.

Names:

Family names are generally derived from villages, rivers, provinces or trades. Most can be recognized by the "escu" or "anu" termination — for example, Ionescu, Popescu, Munteanu and Olteanu. Birth names are usually biblical: Ion, Nicolaie, Vasile, Gheorghe; or old Roman: Remus, Adrian, Cornel, Claudiu, Octavian, or specific Romanian: Mircea, Calin, Bogdan, Razvan.

Major issues for community:

Romanians arriving in the U.S. are confronted with culture shock. Their expectation of America differs from the reality and most do not comprehend the freedom that exists here — a departure from their rigid past. As a result, a large number of Romanian couples who immigrate get divorced. Another concern is the low level of the education

Most Romanian family names can be recognized by the 'escu" or 'anu' ending.

that their children are subjected to in the U.S. They want the best for their children, and Chicago schools have too many problems, such as drugs and violence. For some the answer is to send their children to the Logos Christian Academy in Niles, where about 80% of the students are Romanian, and they can learn about their culture and language. For many others the solution to culture shock was a rapid integration into American society, and they do not keep close ties with the ethnic community.

Political participation:

The new generation of immigrants is not preoccupied with political or civic issues. American citizens of Romanian origin typically join the Republican Party. This is in part because of an unconscious association between the Democratic Party and the word "democracy," a term abused by the communists. Generally, the U.S. government is regarded favorably.

Links to homeland:

Almost all Romanians aspire to American citizenship. Few want to return home, though they visit frequently. Money and valuables are sent to family in Romania and many here invest in manufacturing, hotels, wineries and other ventures in the home country. In 2012 Romanian Americans in Chicago were pleased by the first visit here by their president, at the NATO Summit.

The original chapter was by the late Carol Olteanu, Founder of the Romanian Cultural Center. Information for the update was provided by Vasile Bouleanu, Founder and Past President of the Romanian Freedom Forum and spokesman for the Illinois Romanian American Community.

SERBIAN AMERICANS

Chicago population:
*5,118 (first ancestry)

Metro population:
*22,255 (first ancestry)
28,536 (alone or in combo)

Foreign-born:
35% in metro

Another 5,590 in Chicago and 14,802 in metro checked off Yugoslavian. A significant but undetermined number of these would be Serbian.

Demographics:

Generally, Serbs used to live — and some still do — in the proximity of their churches and businesses. In the past 45 years, however, many prosperous Serbs and professional young couples of the first, second and third generations have moved to the suburbs. To the north and northwest, there are Serbs in Lincolnwood, Evanston, Skokie, Glenview, Wilmette, Winnetka, Lake Forest, Barrington, Des Plaines, Mt. Prospect, Arlington Heights and Niles. To the south, besides the old settlement in South Chicago, Serbs live in Lansing, where there is a large Serbian Cultural Hall, and in the adjacent towns. There also are many Serbian homes and businesses in Bellwood, LaGrange, Downers Grove, Oak Park, Burr Ridge, Riverside, Lyons, Naperville and Joliet. In the metro area, 89% have a high school diploma, 37% a college degree or higher and 12% a graduate or professional degree. Just 19% say they speak English less than "very well." Median household income is $64,552 and 15% are in a management or professional job. A reported 5.4% live in poverty.

(Ed. note: The first-ancestry population numbers are from the 2008-10 Census Bureau's American Community Survey. All other data come from the 2007-09 ACS.)

Historical background:

Several immigration waves brought the Serbs to the U.S. They came as citizens of a variety of countries. Before 1918 they were from the Austro-Hungarian Empire, Turkey, Montenegro and Serbia; after that date they came from the Kingdom of Serbs, Croatians and Slovenians, which changed its name to Yugoslavia. The first Serbian immigration to the Midwest began in the 1880s and lasted until WWII. Most of the early immigrants (before WWI) came here to make a better living for themselves and the families they left behind. Others came to avoid serving in the Austro-Hungarian army. Most had very little education and did not speak English. They worked in the steel mills and slaughterhouses. They were considered honest, hardworking and family-oriented people who did not cause trouble and whose lives revolved around their churches and social organizations. They knew the value of education and encouraged their children to get it, sacrificing their own pleasures and standard of living for the sake of their children's advancement.

The second surge of immigrants began after WWII and lasted until around 1960. These Serbs were predominantly political immigrants and other displaced persons, who came to the U.S. in the late '40s and early '50s, and eventually were joined by their families under the War Refugee Act of 1954. These people were generally well-educated or had professional skills, but a large number did not speak English and had a hard time adjusting here to low-paying jobs. Once they learned English, they were able to compete for better-paying positions in their professional fields. When their families came, they too made sure their children got the best possible education. These post-WWII immigrants strengthened the Chicago Serbian community both numerically and financially. The third immigration of Serbs began in the early 1960s. It lasted until the end of the former Yugoslavia (around 1990) and brought relatively young, ambitious professionals who emigrated for both political and economic reasons. Among them were physicians, engineers, architects, scientists, scholars, artists and graduate students, most of whom came with a reasonably good knowledge of English. They were relatively quickly integrated into Chicago life and have been very prosperous.

Current migration patterns:

The disintegration of Yugoslavia and the wars in Croatia and Bosnia that followed in the '90s brought a new group of Serbian immigrants. Some were Serb refugees from Croatia and Bosnia; others were young people

New young immigrants are already familiar with U.S. culture, due in part to the Internet.

from Serbia and Montenegro who did not approve of the wars and did not want to be drafted and forced to fight. This immigration was at its peak during wartime, 1991-95, but it continued into the new millennium. This wave is now over, but in the past decade we have witnessed the "intellectual immigration" of many of the young population. The first years of the 21st century marked the end of the old, socialist regime in Serbia and saw the rise of new democratic tendencies, which gave hope for a better life. Yet soon Serbs became disillusioned. A bad economy and underemployment spurred many of the young, educated people to leave in pursuit of a better life in the States, many of them coming to Chicago. These young people were, and still are, in search of economic stability, job opportunities and graduate degrees. Unlike earlier generations, the new young immigrants are familiar with American culture, due in part to the Internet, and come with a good command of English.

Language:

Serbian, a South Slavic language. Serbs officially use the Serbian Cyrillic alphabet, but also know the Latin alphabet.

Religion:

Serbian Orthodox. The Serbs in America are traditionally very religious and many are active members of their churches, which also serve as the focal points of cultural and social life of the Serbian-American community. In Libertyville, St. Sava Monastery and Church house the Serbian Orthodox Theological Seminary, where future Serbian priests in the U.S. are being educated. In Third Lake, IL, the newest Serbian Orthodox Church and Monastery, Grachanitsa, was consecrated in 1984. There are Serbian Orthodox Churches in Chicago, South Chicago and Bellwood. For the latest immigrants, the church is less of a focal point, as they seek integration into the larger society.

Important traditions:

Kissing, hugging and touching are normal for Serbian Americans. Common greetings among men and women alike are to embrace and kiss on the cheek three times, first one cheek and then the other. When together, Serbs can be loud, because they are temperamental and speak all at once. In interpersonal relationships, they are open, sincere and loyal. If they are not provoked, they are very pleasant and polite, but they also are proud and strong-willed and if offended or provoked, can easily explode and be fierce opponents. Traditionally, Serbian men take off their hat or cap when entering an enclosed space. To sit in a room or classroom with a baseball cap on is considered rude and disrespectful. Serbian Americans tend to be easy-going and may be late for appointments or parties. They are very protective of their families and close-knit with their relatives. Grandparents and older relatives are respected and children are taught to help old people and be kind to them. Adult sons and daughters consider it their sacred duty to take care of their elderly parents. The ideal is for children to marry other Serbian Americans but this is getting more and more difficult to achieve. Active efforts of the Serbian American communities in the Chicago area to preserve

Adult sons and daughters consider it their sacred duty to take care of their elderly parents.

their traditions include: church schools, children's camps, sport clubs, and the establishment of the Serbian Studies program at the University of Illinois at Chicago.

Holidays and special events:

The major non-religious holidays are Serbian New Year (Jan. 13) and *Vidovdan* (June 28). The latter is a celebration commemorating heroic Serbian warriors who perished in a battle against the Ottoman Turks in the Field of Kossovo in 1389. The Kossovo battle marks the beginning of the end of Serbian Medieval prosperity. Religious holidays are Christmas, Easter, *Slava* and St. Sava Day. Christmas is celebrated Jan. 7 (which is Dec. 25 according to the old Julian Calendar).

Serbian Christmas encompasses many traditional, pre-Christian folklore elements dealing with prosperity and health for the family and fertility of the land. On Christmas Eve day, traditionally, the men of the house would go to the forest to bring the *badnjak* (Yule log) home. The cutting of the badnjak was a ritual, performed with gloves and with careful cutting, so that the tree fell to the east. The log was cleared of side branches and dragged home by oxen. At the entrance of the house, wheat and wine were poured over the log and it was welcomed as if it were a guest, because it was believed to represent the earthly abode of an ancestral soul whose visit would protect the home and bring prosperity in the year to come. After the ceremonial greeting, the log was put on the hearth, where it slowly burned until Christmas morning. In modern times, especially in the U.S., the custom is reduced to bringing home a symbolic Yule "log," a twig of the oak tree blessed in church.

Easter is called *Uskrs*. It is the most holy of holidays celebrated by the Serbs. It falls on a different date from the Protestant and Catholic Easter, because of a different way of calculating its date. Serbian custom is to color eggs for Easter. Some decorate them with wax designs and let them stand in water boiled with onion skins for reddish-brown color; others prefer to color them bright red, by boiling them in natural red dye called *varzilo*. The custom of *tucanje jajima,* an egg-breaking game, is fun for the children. Slava celebrates the Patron Saint of the Serbian Family and is lavishly celebrated in the U.S. The most frequently celebrated patron saints are: St. Archangel Michael (Nov. 21), St. Nicholas (Dec. 19), St. Steven (Jan. 9), St. John the Baptist (Jan. 20) and St. George (May 6). On this day people open their homes to guests. The custom goes back to the time the Serbs adopted Christianity (9th-10th centuries) and with it a patron saint of the family, who replaced the pagan home-protecting spirit. On the morning of the Slava, traditional food items are taken to the church to be blessed. St. Sava's Day (Jan. 27) is celebrated for the most important Serbian saint, the Patron Saint of Serbian Schools and Education. The day is celebrated the same way as family Slava, in all churches and schools.

Foods for special occasions:

The traditional Christmas roast is a very young suckling pig, roasted in the oven by city dwellers, or a bigger one cooked on a spit above a pit full of red coals. In Chicago, whole roasted suckling pigs can be ordered for holidays in several Serbian delicatessens. *Sarma od kiselog kupusa* (sour cabbage leaves stuffed with ground meat and rice and cooked with smoked pork ribs in a lightly thickened juice) is served before the roast and after the clear soup and the boiled meat and vegetables from the soup. Many Serbs, even in America, prepare their own sour cabbage for winter by putting whole heads of cabbage, well salted and covered with water, to marinate in wooden barrels for a month or two, until the cabbage becomes sour and its leaves are soft. For Christmas Eve, Lenten food is served: smoked fish, boiled beans, figs and dates, and a sweet noodle dessert

Lent is observed for six weeks before Christmas and six weeks before Easter.

with sugar and ground nuts. The traditional Easter roast is a very young whole lamb, which is difficult to buy in the U.S., or a leg of lamb as a substitute. For the Slava, Serbs prepare a sweet dish called *zito* (wheat) or *koljivo,* and a *slavski kolac* (a round, specially decorated egg-bread).

Dietary restrictions:

Lent is observed for six weeks before Christmas and six weeks before Easter. Some religious Serbs fast every Friday and some fast twice a week, on Wednesdays and Fridays.

Names:

Children are usually given the names of their grandparents, deceased or alive, but rarely their parents' names. The name is decided by the parents and the godfather. Common Serbian last names end in "ic," such as Dimitrijevic, Ilic, Jovanovic and Petrovic. In the Vojvodina region, the names also often end in "ov," such as Popov, or "in," as in Beleslin or Pupin. Common male names are Aleksàndar, Bránko, Ivan, Jovan (John), Milan, Nikola, Petar (Peter) Vladimir and Zoran. Names ending in "slav" are also common, like Branislav and Borislav. Common female names are Aleksandra, Danica, Jelisaveta (Elizabeth), Jelena (Helen), Natalija, Vera and Nada. Also popular are names ending in "slava," like Branislava, Miroslava, Stanislava.

Major issues for community:

These include preserving the traditions, religion and customs; raising children to have decent social skills; providing the best (affordable) education possible for their children; and whatever political issue is the topic of the day. For a long period in recent years, Serbian Americans were concerned about U.S. policies on Bosnian Serbs and Serbs in general, and Serbia's image abroad. But when Serbia arrested major war criminals and fugitives Ratco Mladic and Radovan Karadzic, it showed a willingness to deal with its past and thus improved its image around the world. Then in March 2012 Serbia officially became an EU candidate. Also, top tennis star Novak Djokovic has spurred more interest in Serbia and its culture, which was welcomed by Serbian Americans.

Political participation:

Most Serbian Americans consider it their duty to vote. When Rod Blagojevich was elected to Congress, Serbian Americans felt they had a voice in Washington. But when, as governor, he was found guilty of illegal actions and sent to prison, they were disappointed. They now feel they have no clout, but are generally enthusiastic about President Barack Obama's political reform and activism. Among young Serbian Americans, there are ambitious lawyers and successful business people who are genuinely interested in civic and political life in Chicago and could emerge as future candidates.

Links to homeland:

Few maintain their original citizenship or plan to return, though they visit their "old country" as often as they can. Even during the very difficult years of the embargo on Yugoslavia and the war in Bosnia, many braved difficult travel conditions to visit and help their relatives and fellow Serbs in distress. Many send money to parents and relatives regularly. In the mid-'90s almost every dollar made in charitable and fund-raising activities was used to buy medical supplies, food and clothes for Serbian refugees from Croatia and Bosnia, those who came to the U.S. as well as those who were in Yugoslavia. Since 2000, links to the home country have mainly been family visits and travel. Funds raised in the States are usually aimed at equipping Serbian hospitals with modern diagnostic technologies such as incubators, MRI and CT scan machines.

Originally written by Dr. Biljana Sljivic-Simsic, now retired Professor and Chair of the Department of Slavic and Baltic Languages and Literatures, University of Illinois at Chicago; updated in 2012 by Jasmina Savic and Marina Filipovic, both doctoral candidates at UIC in Russian Literature.

SLOVAK AMERICANS

Chicago population:
*2,549 (first ancestry)

Metro population:
*25,715 (first ancestry)
46,227 (first and multiple ancestries)

Foreign-born:
4% in metro

In addition to those reporting Slovak ancestry, an undetermined number of Slovaks were among the 2,527 in Chicago and 16,000 in the metro area listing Czechoslovakian as their first ancestry.

Demographics:

Illinois has the third largest Slovak population in the United States, the majority of whom reside in Chicago and its collar counties. The largest number live in suburban Cook County, followed by DuPage and Will.

Slovaks were in America at the time of the Civil War and some fought in it.

Most Slovak Americans are assimilated into mainstream middle-class communities, but some concentrations remain around 52nd and California and in Berwyn, Westchester, Streator and Joliet. In Chicago, there are concentrations of Slovaks in the Gage Park, Garfield Ridge and West Lawn neighborhoods. In the greater metropolitan area, 95% have a college diploma, 36% a college degree and 14% a graduate or professional degree. About 44% are in a management or professional job and median household income is $65,788. Just 3.4% live in poverty.

(Ed. note: First-ancestry numbers are from the 2008-10 American Community Survey. Other data come from the 2007-09 ACS.)

Historical background:

Some Slovaks were in America at the time of the Civil War. A Slovak American military officer, Col. Gejza Mihalotzy-Michalovsky, formed a corps known as the Lincoln Riflemen of Slavic Origin. Most Slovak immigrants came later, however.

Massive immigration to the United States began around 1880. The first settlers came prompted by the oppressive policies of Slovakia's foreign rulers and a desire for improved living conditions. The majority of the forebears of Slovaks arrived in Illinois at that time. In the late 1880s and early 1900s, vibrant Slovak settlements were established both in Chicago and in Berwyn, Blue Island, Chicago Heights, Cicero, Joliet, Riverside and Westchester. At one time, the Chicago area had 10 Slovak Roman Catholic churches. The first Lutheran church in Chicago for Slovak immigrants, Trinity Lutheran, was established in 1893 at May and Huron streets on the North Side. Five years later, the first Roman Catholic church for Slovaks, dedicated to St. Michael the Archangel, was established on the South Side at 48th and Damen. Trinity Lutheran, now at 5106 N. LaCrosse, still has a Slovak congregation. The Slovak Roman Catholic Church of St. Simon the Apostle, established in 1926 at 52nd and California, is the only remaining Roman Catholic church for Slovaks in Chicago. Many Slovaks in the area known as the Back of the Yards worked in the slaughterhouses of the Chicago Stockyards, while others labored on railroads or in steel mills. Henry Ford employed a number of Slovak *drotari* (wireworkers) in the manufacture of wire wheels for his Model A automobile, while others were employed by Pullman. American author Upton Sinclair immortalized the Slovak stockyard workers of Chicago in his novel, "The Jungle." Some additional immigrants came after WWI and again after WWII. The final surge came when the Russians invaded Czechoslovakia in 1968. Border guards unofficially opened the borders to allow people to escape.

The final surge came when Russia invaded Czechoslovakia in 1968.

Current migration patterns:

Very few Slovaks have emigrated since the start of democracy in 1993, when Czechoslovakia was peacefully divided into two independent nations: the Czech Republic and the Slovak Republic. Most Slovaks who come to the U.S. now are tourists and return to their homeland.

Language:

Slovak. Most of the 1968 immigrants and second-generation Slovak Americans (the first U.S.-born generation) are bilingual.

Religion:

Slovaks are about 75% Roman Catholic, 10% Protestant, predominantly Lutheran, 5% Greek Catholic, 5% Jewish and some Orthodox. Some espouse no religious preference.

Important traditions:

Among Catholic, Lutheran and Orthodox Slovak Christians, the most universally preserved Slovak tradition is that of the family dinner on Christmas Eve, most commonly referred to as *Stedry Vecer* (The Bountiful Evening) or *Vilia* (The Vigil). Among Catholic and Orthodox Christians, the special foods for Easter are an equally cherished custom that involves taking those foods in baskets to church to be blessed by the priest. For Slovaks of the Jewish faith, the celebration of Passover likewise decrees the preparation and serving of specifically designated foods for the Passover seder. Traditions of birth, coming of age, courtship, marriage and death are for the most part governed by religious laws and customs.

Holidays and special events:

The major Christian holidays are *Stedry Vecer* or Christmas Eve (Dec. 24), *Vianoce* or Christmas Day (Dec. 25) and *Vel'ka noc* or Easter (spring). Jewish holidays are Passover (spring), and Rosh Hashanah, the Jewish New Year (autumn). Information about a variety of Slovak events taking place in the Chicago area may be found on the website: www.slovakchicago.org.

Foods for special occasions:

Christmas Eve dinner is likely to include *oblatky* (a flat wafer spread with honey, to which garlic is sometimes added); *hribova kapustnica* (a mushroom or mushroom/sauerkraut soup); farina with honey and cinnamon; fried fish; peas; mashed potatoes or *pirohy* (a potato-filled dough, boiled or fried and served with butter and onions); and a dish called *opekance* or *bobalky* made of small yeast dough balls, scalded milk, sugar or honey and fresh-ground poppy seeds. The meal is usually followed by servings of unshelled mixed nuts and various fruits such as apples, oranges, dates and figs, as well as servings of horn- or crescent-shaped pastries called *rozky* filled with a walnut, prune or other fruit filling, and walnut and poppy seed-filled pastries rolled up like jelly rolls and called *orechovy kolac* and *makovnik*. Also served are a braided, sweet Christmas bread called *vianocka* and wine. On Easter, there are hard-boiled eggs, smoked *sunka* (ham), *klobasy* (smoked sausage), *slanina* (smoked bacon), *cvikla s krenom* (a mixture of grated beets, horseradish root, salt and vinegar), rye bread, *syrek* (a custard-like cheese made of eggs milk, salt, sugar and vanilla) and a baked stuffing called *plnka* or *nadievka*, made from white bread rolls, diced ham, eggs, onions, broth and various seasonings. Easter breads called *paska* and *babka,* as well as *vel'konocny baranok* (a special Easter cake in the shape of a lamb), also are served. As on Christmas Eve, *rozky,* and wine round out the meal.

Names:

In former days, when large families were the norm and infant mortality high, newborn Christian children often were given the first name of the same-gender sibling whose death had preceded their birth. Today, common first names for boys include Jan, Jozef, Pavol, Peter and Juraj. For girls, popular names are Maria, Anna, Katarina, Magdalena and Helena, although westernized first names are becoming more popular. Male surnames are likely to end in "ek," "ik," "ak," "ka," "ko," "ec" or "sky." Surnames for females contain the suffix "ova," except for those with a "sky" ending, which changes to "ska."

Political participation:

American Slovaks are strong believers in the power of the ballot box. They are estimated to be evenly distributed between the Republican and Democratic parties.

Major issues for community:

U.S. government support for the Slovak Republic joining NATO was the main issue for Slovaks in the U.S. in the 1990s. Slovakia achieved both NATO membership and European Union membership in 2004. In 2009 Slovakia adopted the Euro as its national currency.

Links to homeland:

There is considerable travel back and forth for immigrants and the first two generations born here, especially since Slovakia became a free and democratic country. The Slovak World Youth Congress draws from all over the world to the Slovak Republic. Slovaks come to Chicago to visit relatives. In August 1995, then President Michal Kovac of the Slovak Republic was in Chicago to accept the American Bar Association's prestigious 1995 CEELI Award for his efforts to establish democracy in the Slovak Republic. While here, he visited St. Simon the Apostle Church. In 2012, President Ivan Gasparovic and a Slovak government delegation visited Chicago to participate in the NATO Summit.

The original chapter was written by Thomas Klimek Ward, then Honorary Consul of the Slovak Republic and Founder and Chairman of the Slovak American Cultural Society of the Midwest. The update is by Ward and Rosemary Macko Wisnosky, new Honorary Consul of the Slovak Republic.

SWEDISH AMERICANS

Chicago population:
15,879 (first ancestry)
28,193 (first and multiple ancestries)

Metro population:
113,943 (first ancestry)
167,567 (first and multiple ancestries)

Foreign-born:
1.6% in Chicago, less than 1% in metro

Demographics:

The overwhelming majority of the Swedish population in the metro area is suburban, widely scattered but living primarily in the north and west suburbs. Cook, DuPage and Lake counties have the highest numbers of people with Swedish ancestry. In the city, Swedes are mostly on the North Side, with Andersonville and North Park remaining the predominant enclaves. Swedish Americans have a high level of education. Some 98% in Chicago and 96% in the greater metro area have a high school diploma. About 32% in the city and 44% in metro have a bachelor's degree, with 23% in Chicago and 16% in metro holding a graduate degree. Median household income is $66,097 for the city and $71,801 in metro. In Chicago 45% hold management or professional jobs, while 57% in the metro area do. Just 7% in Chicago and 4% in metro live in poverty.

About 1.3 million Swedes came to North America between 1850 and 1930.

(Ed. note: First ancestry population figures are from the American Community Survey 2008-10. Multiple ancestry and all other demographic data come from 2007-09).

Historical background:

Approximately 1.3 million Swedes came to North America between 1850 and 1930. Most came between 1870-90. In 1880, Chicago had 12,982 Swedish residents born in Sweden, and another 5,112 Swedish Americans born in the U.S., totaling 3.6% of the city's population at the time. The original Swedish enclave, "Swede Town," was bordered by Erie Street, Wells Street and the Chicago River. Emigration was heaviest from southern Sweden. In 1880, 64% of the Chicago Swedes were working in handicrafts and industry, 17% in trade and communications and 17% in domestic work. At that time, 66% of Swedish workers were male, 24% female. The majority of the Swedish population in Chicago was under the age of 35. In the trades there was an emphasis on carpentry and bricklaying. Swedes and other Scandinavians did much of the work to rebuild after the Great Chicago Fire.

In 1900, a reported 48,836 Chicagoans born in Sweden and 157,236 claiming some Swedish ancestry lived in the city of Chicago. Only the Swedish capital, Stockholm, had more Swedish residents. Economic crises, notably in timber, iron and agriculture, as well as labor, temperance and religious upheavals, brought many of the Swedes to Chicago. The immigrant community was complex, often dividing along religious and secular lines, as well as by class. Older immigrants had a rural background. New arrivals after 1900 tended to come from urban and industrial situations. Swedish movement to the suburbs occurred between 1880 and 1920. By 1920 Swedes were the largest single ethnic group in city neighborhoods of Albany Park, North Park, Andersonville, Belmont-Cragin, Lake View, Englewood, West Englewood, Austin, Armour Square, Hyde Park, Woodlawn, South Shore, Greater Grand Crossing, East Side, Morgan Park and Roseland. Swedes related most closely socially and occupationally with Danes, Norwegians and Germans. Intermarriage in 1900 was most common with Norwegians, followed by Danes, Germans, English, Irish, English, Canadians and Scots. Swedish Americans numbered about 140,000 in 1930, as some residents moved out from the city.

Swedes and other Scandinavians did much of the work to rebuild after the Chicago Fire.

Current migration patterns:

Current immigration is minuscule. Most visits by Swedes to the United States are short-term and temporary, primarily for business or education.

Language:

Third- and fourth-generation descendants are more likely to speak English than Swedish in the home. Those remaining from the first and second generations speak either language, depending on the setting. Swedish is spoken in the home primarily by recent arrivals, most likely those here for business or education.

Religion:

Formerly the State Church of Sweden, Lutheran is the predominant religion. Those not from a Lutheran tradition are most likely from another Protestant free church tradition, including: Evangelical Covenant, Free Church, Methodist, Baptist, Pentecostal or Salvation Army.

Important traditions:

These revolve around the major religious and secular holidays of Advent, Christmas, Easter, Midsummer, Walpurgis Night, Flag Day and St. Lucia Day. Swedish Americans value education and public service. They believe good citizenship means being loyal, honest and industrious.

Holidays and special events:

St. Lucia Day (Dec. 13) and Midsummer (June 23) are related as celebrations of light. St. Lucia, the Catholic Saint who represents light, comes in the darkest of winter to bring light as a reminder of longer days and more light to come; Midsummer celebrates the longest days of the year with a big festival in Chicago's parks that includes cultural events such as the Maypole dance, folk music and food. A Lucia Fest has been held at the Daley Center for a number of years. Midsummer is celebrated in the Andersonville neighborhood and at several parks along the Fox River Valley near Geneva and Elgin. *Julotta* is an early morning Christmas service, held in a number of area churches, with at least part of the service often conducted in Swedish. Flag Day (June 6) is like Swedish National Day and celebrates Sweden and the

Swedish people. Activities, including a parade and speeches by community leaders, are coordinated by the Central Swedish Committee, an umbrella organization for Swedish groups in Chicago. Swedish flags are hung from homes.

Foods for special occasions:

St. Lucia Day is celebrated with the eating of *lussekatter* (saffron buns) and drinking coffee, most often in bed during the early morning. Other foods that are part of traditional celebrations include *glogg, pepparkakor* (ginger cookies), *risgrynsgrot* (rice pudding), hardtack, herring, salmon, ham, and *semlor* (round, unsugared buns).

Names:

Common last names include Johnson, Peterson, Olson, Nelson and Carlson, all ending in "son." That is because traditionally each generation was given the father's first name with "son" added. The last name kept changing until the late 19th century, when surnames started to be carried from generation to generation. At that time,

> *Common last names include Johnson, Peterson, Olson and Nelson, all ending in 'son.'*

those in the military often were given names referring to places and nature, ending in "strom" (stream) or "dahl" (valley) for example, because there were too many Johnsons and Petersons in the military to keep them all straight.

Major issues for community:

Preservation of ethnic heritage is a major concern of the community and is carried out by the Swedish American Museum Center, the Central Swedish Committee and its member organizations, the Swedish-American Historical Society (an international organization headquartered in Chicago) and by the Center for Scandinavian Studies at North Park College through programs, concerts, exhibits, classes, conferences, workshops and other activities.

Political participation:

Swedish Americans traditionally have identified more with the Republican Party, though the trend may be reversed for those living in the city. This is a reflection, somewhat, of the rural/urban dichotomy of Swedish settlement in the U.S. There is a history of active and conscientious involvement in voting and community activity, often through churches, fraternal lodges and other organizations. While they do not necessarily have "clout," Swedish Americans have influenced reform movements to root out corruption in political and labor organizations.

Links to homeland:

Most links to Sweden are through business, travel and education. A major split occurred between Sweden and the United States during the Vietnam War, when Sweden was critical of U.S. involvement. Sweden became a refuge for those avoiding the draft. That rift healed, however, and contacts between the two countries are positive. A very active Swedish-American Chamber of Commerce promotes business between the two countries. The community lost a major link with the dissolution of the consular office (there are now honorary consulates). All major Swedish government functions are now funneled through New York and Washington.

By Tim Johnson, Curator of Rare Books and Special Collections at University of Minnesota Libraries.

UKRAINIAN AMERICANS

Chicago population:
10,187 (first ancestry)

Metro population:
35,565 (first ancestry)
49,439 (first and in combination)

Foreign-born:
41% in metro

Demographics:

Ukrainian Americans are well educated. In the greater metro area, 94% have a high school diploma, 52% a college degree and 22% a graduate or professional degree. Nearly 45% are in a management or professional job and median household income is $63,626. Some 25% say they do not speak English "very well." Less than 8% live

Forced to leave Ukraine by the Soviet onslaught, the 3rd immigration was largely political.

below the poverty line. Ukrainians in Chicago are known to be concentrated in Ukrainian Village, bounded by Division, Mozart, Huron and Damen. Those living in the suburbs are scattered.

(Ed. note: First ancestry population figures come from the 2008-10 American Community Survey. All other numbers are from 2007-09 ACS.)

Historical background:

The United States has had three mass immigrations from what is today Ukraine: The first began in the 1880s and ended in 1914, at the start of WWI. Dominated for centuries by foreign powers, Ukraine did not exist as a separate nation-state at the time of the first mass immigration. Most early immigrants from Ukraine were poor, illiterate and unskilled peasants, seeking a better life in America. Many were unaware of their ethno-national heritage, calling themselves by their ancient name, *"Rusyns."* Few early emigres returned to Ukraine. It was during these early times that the community established its churches and fraternal benefit societies. Most were from the Transcarpathian region. With financial help from the Czarist government, they built the Holy Trinity Russian Orthodox-Greek Catholic Church at Leavitt and Haddon in 1903. A second group built St. Mary's Greek Catholic Church at 50th and Seeley in 1905. Immigrants from the Galician region also were arriving during this period, settling in an area bounded by Division, Racine, Orleans and what is now Roosevelt Road, where a parish was established in 1905. They bought a church and renamed it St. Nicholas Greek Catholic Church. Land later was purchased at Rice and Oakley and a new St. Nicholas was completed in 1913. A Byzantine-Slavonic masterpiece, it is now a cathedral. Another community of Ukrainian immigrants settled in the Burnside area, where Sts. Peter and Paul was completed in 1909. At about the same time, a group of Ukrainians moved into the Back of the Yards, where a church was completed in 1912.

Ukraine declared its independence in 1918, only to be divided among its neighbors at the end of WWI. Most members of the second immigration (1920-39) were ethno-nationally conscious, literate and semi-skilled. They came looking for work and committed themselves to Ukraine's resurrection as a nation-state. Their reasons for emigrating were both economic and political. They gave new life to the existing community here. The third mass immigration (1948-55) was composed largely of skilled and professional people, permitted to enter the U.S. following passage of the Displaced Persons Act of 1948. They too were committed to Ukraine's freedom crusade. Forced to leave Ukraine on the eve of the Soviet onslaught, this immigration was largely political.

Current migration patterns:

After Ukraine became an independent nation-state in 1991, a new immigration to Chicago began. An estimated 2,000 Ukrainians arrived legally in the '90s, and another 500-1,000 probably arrived legally but remained illegally, overstaying their visas. The INS, which did not separate out Ukrainians, counted nearly 12,000 legal immigrants from the former Soviet Union from 1990-94. Many were from Ukraine. Recent immigration from Ukraine has slowed.

Language:

Ukrainian. Most immigrants from western Ukraine also speak Polish, while those arriving in the 1990s speak Russian. Saturday schools are used to preserve the Ukrainian language. There are two in Chicago and one in Palatine.

Religion:

Most Ukrainians (about 65%) in the metro area belong to the Eastern-rite (Byzantine) Catholic Church; some 30% are Ukrainian Orthodox; 5% are Baptist. Many of the more recent immigrants from Ukraine are Jews.

Holidays and special events:

The most important religious holidays are Easter and Christmas. Easter traditions begin in Lent, when many families begin making elaborate *pysanky* (Easter eggs) The process includes a lighted candle, beeswax, a *kistka* (funnel-like tool for writing designs on the eggs with melted beeswax), and various dyes into which the eggs are alternately dipped as more designs are added. The colors and designs symbolize love, happiness, church, spring, etc. *Verbovyi Tsyhden* (Holy Week) begins with Willow Sunday (Palm Sunday in the Latin rite), when pussy willows are distributed in Ukrainian churches throughout the Chicago area. Many Ukrainian Americans abstain from meat during the week. Holy Thursday services include the washing of the feet of priests by the bishop. On Good Friday Christ's "burial shroud" is laid out on the alter. On Saturday the faithful take decorated baskets containing Easter breakfast food and pysanky to be blessed by a priest. The severe fast is broken after liturgy Sunday. On Epiphany, another religious holiday (the baptism of Jesus in the Jordan River), the faithful gather in church (or outdoors) for the blessing of water, samples of which are taken home. In the weeks following, priests visit families to bless their home. Other important holidays are Independence Day (Aug. 24), proclaimed in 1991; and the birthday of Taras Shevchenko (March), Ukraine's poet laureate.

Foods for special occasions:

On Christmas Eve, a 12-course meatless, dairyless family dinner is served. Traditional dishes include *prosphora*, a specially baked bread that the head of the family gives each member with honey and wishes for the New Year; borscht (clear beet soup) with *vooshka,* a triangle of dough filled with mushrooms; *varennyky* (dough filled with potato and sauerkraut); *holoptsi* (cabbage rolls made with rice and mushrooms or buckwheat); and *uzvar* or compote (dried fruit cooked together in a juice). *Kutia* (a very sweet dessert make from baked wheat, poppy seeds, honey, raisins and nuts) traditionally is thrown against the ceiling and if it sticks it is a favorable omen for a good agricultural year. On Easter the essential meal includes: *paska* (Easter bread); *babka,* a delicate egg-rich yeast bread; *kovbasa* (fresh pork sausage); hard-boiled eggs; mayonnaise made from hard-boiled egg yolks, mustard and horseradish; and cheesecake and other pastries.

Important traditions:

Language maintenance, church attendance and organizational membership are important traditions for Ukrainian Americans. Assimilation is eroding these customs, however. Marriage to non-Ukrainians is running extremely high. Church and organizational membership are dwindling. The more recent immigration is either indifferent to organized Ukrainian life or still too unsettled to consider membership. While some have recently opted to join churches, many are still reticent to join voluntary organizations. This is

Now that Ukraine is independent once again, travel is far more frequent.

probably a carryover from the Soviet days when "voluntarism" was mandatory. Ukrainians are thrifty. The Ukrainian Self Reliance Credit Union is one of the largest federal credit unions in the United States. The two Chicago institutions that have grown in membership and prospered in recent years are the Ukrainian National Museum and Ukrainian Museum of Modern Art. Both host regular exhibits, seminars, music recitals and films. They have full-time staffs and volunteers who are either recently arrived immigrants or the children of third-wave immigrants.

Names:

Common names are Michael, Stephen, Nicholas, Volodymyr (Walter), Gregory, Oksana, Alexandra (Lesia), Laryssa, Martha and Mariana. Many Ukrainian surnames end in "ko," "sky" or "wycz."

Major issues for community:

Issues of concern are assimilation and its effect upon Ukrainian American institutions, Western media defamation, and the future of Ukraine as an independent nation-state.

Political participation:

Although Ukrainians could once boast of having a state senator, participation in American political and civic affairs is minimal. The major political focus was and remains on Ukraine. Most Ukrainian Americans do vote, however. In Chicago, in local politics, most are Democrats. In national elections they tend to vote Republican because they view the GOP as more aware of the Russian threat. This has been the case since President Franklin D. Roosevelt recognized the Soviet Union. The recent "re-set with Russia initiative of the Obama Administration has only confirmed this view.

Links to homeland:

Ties are very strong. Now that Ukraine is independent once again, travel is far more frequent. Money is constantly being sent to relatives in Ukraine. Attendance is high at events featuring cultural, political and intellectual groups and individuals from Ukraine. Donations to institutions in Ukraine are extraordinarily generous. These include the Children of Chernobyl Fund, the National University of Kyiv-Mohyla Academy, and the Ukraine University in Lviv. Ukrainians remain informed about events in Ukraine by reading *Svoboda*, a Ukrainian-language daily, and The Ukrainian Weekly, an English-language publication, both of which have reporters in Ukraine, and a number of local newspapers recently established by fourth-wave immigrants that are distributed free of charge.

By Dr. Myron Kuropas, Retired Adjunct Professor at Northern Illinois University, National Co-chairman of the Ukrainian American Justice Committee, and author of two monographs on the Ukrainian community in the U.S.

VIETNAMESE AMERICANS

Chicago population:
8,930 (Vietnamese alone)
10,118 (alone and in combo)

Metro population:
21,363 (Vietnamese alone)

Foreign-born:
79% in Chicago, 67% in metro

Demographics::

The majority of Vietnamese in Chicago live in Uptown, Edgewater, Rogers Park, Albany Park and West Ridge. Clusters also can be found in northwest and western suburbs, such as Wheaton, Lombard and Skokie.

The fall of Saigon in 1975 resulted in an unprecedented exodus, mostly of leaders.

Median household income for Vietnamese is $60,572 (very close to the overall population average) in the metro area, yet 15% in the metro area live below the poverty line. In terms of education, 28% of Vietnamese adults have a college degree, with almost 9% holding a graduate degree. About 26% are in management or a profession. Just over 48% said they do not speak English very well.

(Ed. note: Population numbers are from the 2010 Census. All other data come from the 2007-09 ACS.)

Historical background:

The presence of the Chicago Vietnamese community is a relatively recent phenomenon. Only about a dozen Vietnamese families were here prior to 1975. The fall of Saigon in April 1975 resulted in an unprecedented exodus of Vietnamese fleeing South Vietnam for fear of persecution by the new communist government. Under the Indochina Refugee Assistance Program, in 1975 alone 128,250 Vietnamese were admitted to the U.S. as refugees. A large percentage of those arriving in the first wave of refugees in 1975 were former South Vietnamese government officials, religious leaders, writers, journalists, businessmen and military commanders.

The Refugee Act of 1980 for the first time allowed the U.S. to establish a framework for federal refugee assistance. Many Vietnamese escaped by boat across the South China Sea or walked through Cambodia into Thailand to seek political asylum in several countries. A number of special programs were instituted to assist Vietnamese seeking resettlement in the U.S. The Vietnamese population in the U.S. represents widely diverse socioeconomic strata. Among the later arrivals were fishermen, farmers and urban dwellers. Amerasians (children of American men and Vietnamese women) and former political prisoners were included in the later wave of arrivals in the early 1990s. The majority of Vietnamese now living in the Chicago area survived many traumas. Prolonged armed conflicts and the perilous escapes from Vietnam left many without intact families. Former political prisoners were isolated from their families and tortured. Many require extensive counseling and assistance to rebuild their lives. Amerasians abandoned by their fathers and discriminated against in their homeland are still looking for their place in the U.S.

The flow of Vietnamese refugees came to trickle in the early 1990s when the U.S. and the United Nation established an "orderly departure program" and slowly transitioned the refugee resettlement program to an immigrant program where individuals from Vietnam apply to come to the U.S. through family reunification or other legal immigration categories open to all countries. The U.S. and Vietnam established normalization of diplomatic relations in 1995. As the result, there are now Vietnamese coming to the U.S. as diplomats, foreign students, tourists and business people.

The first group of Vietnamese arrivals in the Chicago area was resettled in Uptown because of a few key voluntary agencies working there and the availability of affordable housing. This first group established a social and economic foundation on the North Side, through the creation of religious and community-based organizations and the development of a vibrant small-business strip on and around Argyle Street, between Broadway and Sheridan Road. The area then became a magnet for later arrivals, who spread farther north and west to

The majority of Vietnamese now living in the Chicago area survived many traumas.

Edgewater, Rogers Park and Albany Park. These neighborhoods all had affordable housing and an ethnically diverse population, where Vietnamese found themselves more welcome. Vietnamese community leaders have worked closely with leaders of other refugee communities, such as Cambodians, Chinese, Laotians and Ethiopians, on joint projects to find jobs for new arrivals and to provide necessary adjustment services. Joint efforts also have resulted in an economic development program, helping to create and expand small businesses and build new homes. Over the past two decades, some Vietnamese moved or resettled in the suburbs where there are job opportunities, more affordable housing and access to quality education.

Current migration patterns:

Immigration has slowed. Based on data from the Department of Homeland Security, approximately 30,000 Vietnamese immigrants and refugees came to the U.S. annually in recent years. Within this number, those with refugee status account for less than 1,500 on average. These numbers represent a significant reduction from the 1990s, when approximately 55,000 Vietnamese came to the U.S. annually.

Language:

Vietnamese. There are minimal differences in vocabularies and intonations among people who are from the North, Central and South Vietnam.

Religion:

The majority of Vietnamese practice what could be considered a combination of Buddhism, Confucianism and Taoism. Catholicism also claims a significant following. There is also a growth of Vietnamese Protestants, partially due to the active participation and assistance provided to Vietnamese refugees by many churches. A smaller number practice Cao Daism. There are two major Vietnamese Buddhist temples located on the North Side of Chicago (Quang Minh Temple and Truc Lam Temple). Two Catholic churches have significant Vietnamese congregations (St. Henry Parish on the far Northwest Side of Chicago and Queenship of Mary Parish in Glen Ellyn). For Vietnamese protestants, there are The Uptown Baptist Church and First Vietnamese Methodist Church in Chicago as well as Wheaton Vietnamese Christian Missionary Alliance Church and Vietnamese New Hope Christian for those living in the western suburbs.

Important traditions:

Vietnamese culture has adapted to many other cultures as the result of colonization and survival needs. Traditional values, heavily influenced by Confucian teaching include: reverence for education and learned individuals, respect for the elderly and people in positions of authority, and pursuit of harmony rather than confrontation. Men are assumed to hold a superior social position. A traditional family expects the woman to defer to the wishes of her father, husband and sons. Among the younger generation, many no longer practice these traditional values because they conflict with the common values in the U.S. Many younger people have had to play the role of decision-maker in the household because of their fluency in English and understanding of U.S. customs and practices. This reversal of the leadership role, normally held by the parents or the elders, has created much social displacement and tension in some households. Many women also are working, which presents new challenges in traditional households.

Other traditions: For the newborn child, there are special celebrations the first full month after birth and the first full year. For marriage, contrary to U.S. practices, Vietnamese tradition dictates that the groom's family assume the cost of both the engagement and wedding ceremonies. The wedding usually includes a ceremony at

Close to three-quarters of Vietnamese immigrants have become U.S. citizens.

the home of the bride, where the groom's family pays respect to the bride's family and formally asks to take her away to become a member of their family. Another ceremony is held at the home of the groom to formally welcome the bride to her new family. At death, for a Buddhist, a monk often prays for the soul of the departed to reach Nirvana. Vietnamese Catholics observe what is practiced by Catholics worldwide. White is the color of mourning.

Holidays and special events:

Most holidays and special events are based on the lunar calendar. TET/Lunar New Year (first day of the first month, in late January or February) is the biggest Vietnamese holiday of the year and is celebrated, traditionally, for at least three days. It is seen as an opportunity for renewal and the beginning of all good things and is usually a time for family reunion and a welcoming of spring (Vietnam is a tropical country and spring usually arrives in January or February). The Trung Sisters' Anniversary (sixth day of the second month, from late February to late March) is observed as a national holiday to pay respect to these heroines, who in 39 A.D. succeeded in driving the Chinese out of Vietnam after 247 years of domination. This is a day to pay respect for the talents and contributions made by Vietnamese women in history and culture. Ancestor Day (March or April) observes the anniversary of the death of King Hung Vuong, founder of the Vietnamese nation. The elderly organize this observation each year. Mid-Autumn Festival (September) is primarily a children's festival, normally held in the evening when the full moon can be seen. The children have special lanterns made in beautiful images of flowers, birds, stars and other shapes that are candle-lit for processions through the streets. These traditional holidays have been modified to adjust to the conditions in the U.S. The celebrations are usually held on weekends, when the majority of Vietnamese are not working, instead of on the actual holidays. Celebrations that traditionally were observed in a family setting are now community-wide events.

Foods for special occasions:

Banh chung (sticky rice "cake") is made for the Lunar New Year, usually in the shape of a square or cylinder, with sweet rice on the outside and meat with mung bean in the center. The "cake" is wrapped in banana leaves and steamed. Sometimes the meat is replaced with banana when the cake is served as dessert. *Banh trung thu* or moon cake (made of mung bean and flour with berries, nuts, fruits and egg yolk inside) is made for Mid-Autumn Festival and is usually consumed with tea. Vietnamese cuisine uses extensive fresh and raw vegetables, including many types of fresh herbs – such as mint, cilantro and basil.

Dietary restrictions:

Vietnamese Buddhists avoid eating meat on special Buddhist holidays. Many faithful followers are vegetarians year 'round.

Names:

There are only about 100 family names for the whole population of some 70 million Vietnamese. Most common are Nguyen, Le, Tran, Pham, Phan, Vo and Huynh. People with the same family name are not always related to one another, and Vietnamese rarely address each other by the family name. Contrary to the U.S.

Some new arrivals suffered prolonged stays in prison camps.

practice, in Vietnam, the family name comes first and the given name comes last. Living in the U.S., many reverse the order. Some have chosen not to do so. Vietnamese women do not change their last name when they marry. In formal settings women may be addressed by their husband's name, but their legal name is never changed. Given names generally have a meaning selected with great care by the parents to reflect their aspirations. Names normally express a quality or virtue. For men, Hung (courage), Liem (integrity) and Trung (fidelity) are examples. Women's names can also be of beautiful things; for example Hong (rose), Lan (orchid) or Van (cloud).

Major issues for community:

Newly arrived immigrants and refugees need assistance to learn English, acquire skills so they become employable, and make appropriate social adjustments to be fully integrated with the local community. Some individuals suffering the trauma of a prolonged stay in the prison camp, also know as the re-education camp established by the communist regime, also experience mental health problems. Youth delinquency is an issue in for some families. Most of the Vietnamese population is foreign-born, which means there is a varying degree of social and cultural adjustment, based on the length of residence in the U.S. Those who were born in the U.S. tend to be fully integrated and have no English language problem. Some generational conflicts between the first and second generation exist, but in general the community is relatively cohesive. A growing number of seniors need assistance to avoid social isolation. The Chicago Vietnamese community, has built a strong support network for its seniors. There is even a Vietnamese cemetery located within the Rosehill Cemetery on the North Side of Chicago, a sign that the community has established strong roots here.

Political participation:

Being political refugees, many Vietnamese understand the need to comprehend and participate in the civic and political life of their new country. Close to three-quarters of Vietnamese immigrants have become U.S. citizens, demonstrating a high interest in civic integration. This rate of naturalization is fairly high in comparison with other immigrant groups. Over the past three decades, Vietnamese have built community institutions through which they can more effectively be politically active. A small number of Vietnamese in the Chicago area have been appointed to serve on various public bodies. At the national level, especially in states and cities where Vietnamese make up a large percentage of the local population – such as Houston, Texas, and San Jose, Calif. – Vietnamese have run successfully for elected offices or been appointed to important public positions. The older generation of Vietnamese tends to be more conservative, whereas the younger generation tends to be more progressive.

Links to homeland:

Many Vietnamese refugees, especially the older generation and former political prisoners, think of themselves as exiles awaiting the opportunity to return to the homeland (if the communist regime should fall). This sentiment has changed over the years as the Vietnamese, particularly the second generation, builds a stronger attachment to the United States. Furthermore, Vietnam has become more open after the normalization of diplomatic relations with the U.S. in 1995. Many Vietnamese in the U.S. have returned to visit and explore opportunities to build links with Vietnam for business or humanitarian assistance reasons. A few older Vietnamese living in the U.S. are also exploring retirement in Vietnam.

A number of Vietnamese Americans in leadership positions continue to believe that until the government of Vietnam is changed from communist to democratic, the Vietnamese community in the U.S. needs to serve as the voice for change inside Vietnam. This position was once a major source of community tension, but the Vietnamese community here has moderated its position over the years. The younger generation, which has little or no knowledge of Vietnam, wants to explore and learn more about its roots. Those who have succeeded want to help alleviate poverty and the multiple problems in Vietnam that prevent the country from moving forward. Businessmen want to participate in the emerging Vietnamese market. The Internet and ease of international travel have helped Vietnamese people on opposite sides of the globe keep in close contact and share information much more openly than ever before.

Special health concerns:

Vietnamese suffer from higher rates of cancer, tuberculosis and heart disease than most other racial and ethnic groups, studies on Vietnamese communities across the U.S. have found. A Santa Clara County (Calif.) Department of Public Health study, released in December 2011, reported that cancer was the leading cause of death among the county's Vietnamese residents – accounting for a larger percentage of total Vietnamese deaths in 2011 than for the county as a whole. The report found Vietnamese adults more likely than other racial and ethnic groups to suffer and die from liver, lung and cervical cancer. The rates for heart disease, diabetes and high blood pressure were also disproportionately high. Because more than 134,500 Vietnamese live in Santa Clara, this study is significant since it is based on a large sample. The study also cited the fact that "40% of survey respondents reported having suffered from a mental health problem last year." Vietnamese women have the highest incidence of invasive cervical cancer in age groups 30-54 and 55-59, according to the National Cancer Institute (2001). And University of California/San Francisco researchers also found that, "in California (2000), 35% of Vietnamese men smoke, a rate 1.5 times higher than the proportion among all men. Cultural acceptance of smoking is traced back to life in Vietnam, where the proportion of men who smoke is 73%."

By Ngoan Le, formerly Executive Director of the Vietnamese Association of Illinois, now Vice President of Program at the Chicago Community Trust.